with Life-changing Philosophies

DEEP TRIVEDI

Author of the Bestsellers 'I am The Mind' & 'I am Krishna'

Also available in Hindi, Marathi and Gujarati

CONTENTS

From the Author's Desk....1

01. Wow, Mullah! You are Amazing!....2
02. The Magic of Surrender....5
03. In Search of Reality....8
04. Who Can Outwit a Sannyasi?....11
05. Vincent's Immortal Painting....14
06. When God Walks with You....15
07. A Sannyasi Defeats Alexander The Great!....17
08. The Human Mind – A Pandora's Box....19
09. The Marvellous Mother....21
10. Smile Away Your Worries....23
11. The Elephant and the Mouse....25
12. The Jewel in the Crown....26
13. The 'Greedy' Pot....28
14. Anger Management....31
15. Wisdom of the 'illiterate' Businessman....32
16. The Forty-eight-legged Animal....33
17. Think Like Tolstoy....36
18. The Right Time to Discuss God....37
19. Are You a Puppet?....39
20. Lao Tzu Imparts Wisdom and How!....41
21. What Sort of a Lesson Is This?....43
22. The Ticket to Heaven....45
23. The Gurudakshina....47
24. It's All in the Mind!....50
25. The Story of Vishnu and Narada....51
26. Kabir and the Dead Cow....54
27. In Search of God....56
28. The Poor Woodcutter and the Lord of Death....58
29. Who Is the Fool?....59
30. The Farmer, the Mouse and the Snake!....61
31. When Prayer Flows from Within....63
32. The Boy Who Made His Dream Come True....65
33. The World's First Robot....68
34. The Turning Point in Steve Jobs' Life....70
35. The Bell and the Bone Experiment....71
36. The King Mosquito and the Elephant....72
37. Pandemonium at Sea....74
38. The Disciple's Awakening....76
39. The Ascetic and the Scorpion....78
40. You Are Fooling Yourself, Not Me – Christ....79
41. The Right Treatment....81
42. Practice What You Preach....82
43. The Truth of the Matter....85
44. When Size Does Matter....86
45. Can Anger Be Suppressed?....88
46. Is Man Really Free?....89
47. Pride Has its Fall....90
48. The Three 'Brilliant' Magicians....93

DEEP TRIVEDI

Deep Trivedi is a renowned author, speaker and pioneer in spiritual psychodynamics. He writes and conducts workshops with an all-pervasive perspective, guiding individuals towards the achievement of their full potential. To date, he has led millions of people onto the path of success and happiness through his works.

In his voluminous works, Deep Trivedi has extensively explained Nature, its laws, its behaviour, its psychology and the effect it has on human life. No aspect of life and human psychology has been left untouched by him. He states that lack of psychological knowledge and understanding is the sole reason for all the sorrows and failures that pervade human life.

He has authored the bestsellers 'I am The Mind', 'I am Krishna', 'The Black Book of Soul', '3 Easy Steps To Win At Life' and many more. His bestseller 'I am The Mind' has been published in several national and international languages. He has been awarded the Times Power Men Award 2018 for his Immense contribution to society.

His command over the biggest psychologies of life can be gauged by the fact that he holds the record for 'Maximum Workshops on Human Life', 'Maximum Workshops on Psychological Aspects of Tao Te Ching', 'Maximum Workshops on Ashtavakra Gita' and 'Maximum Workshops on Bhagavad Gita', spanning 168 hours, 28 minutes, 50 seconds in 58 days in different National and International record books. He also holds the record for 'Maximum Number of Quotations on Human Life' (about 12038) on subjects such as Soul, Human Life, Psychology, Laws of Nature, Destiny and many more. He has also been awarded an Honorary Doctorate for his works on the psychology of Bhagavad Gita. His interactive workshops have brought about a revolutionary transformation in people's lives by addressing their day-to-day concerns. These workshops have been conducted in front of live audiences across India.

He is known for his special ability to touch upon the deepest aspects of life and explain them by using lucid language, leaving no scope for ambiguity. The distinct spiritual-psychological language and expression in his writings and workshops begin to have an instant effect on the mind of the reader or listener, which makes Deep Trivedi a pioneer in this field.

To know more about Deep Trivedi, visit www.deeptrivedi.com

DEEP TRIVEDI The Speaker

Deep Trivedi uses a unique combination of psycho-spiritual content, voice, language and expression, which effectuates an instantaneous transformation in his viewers and listeners. Millions of lives have been transformed just by listening to him.

His interactive workshops have brought about a revolutionary transformation in people's lives by addressing their day-to-day concerns. Deep Trivedi sheds light on every aspect of human life and mind. He has extensively spoken on The Bhagavad Gita, Tao Te Ching, Ashtavakra Gita, Secrets of Nature, Mind, Soul, Time, Destiny, and numerous other topics such as:

- **Ego**
- **God**
- **Guilt**
- **Love**
- **Anger**
- **Future**
- **Wealth**
- **Phobias**
- **Religion**
- **Complex**
- **Marriage**
- **Freedom**
- **Partiality**
- **Day-Sleep**
- **DNA-Genes**
- **Path of Life**
- **Personality**
- **Expectation**
- **Acceptance**
- **Hypocrisy**
- **Creativity**
- **Confusion**
- **Good-Bad**
- **Involvement**
- **Concentration**
- **Laws of Nature**
- **Time and Space**
- **Mind and Brain**
- **Self-Confidence**
- **Joy and Happiness**
- **Natural Intelligence**
- **Power of Transformation**

49. Where God Resides 95
50. A Father's Love 97
51. Who Is the Stingiest of Them All? 100
52. The Lion Cub's Complex 103
53. The Demon Who Tricked God 105
54. Be 'Aware' of Your Desires 107
55. The Magician Tricks the King 108
56. The Prayer of an Innocent Child 111
57. The Secret of Buddha's Effulgence 112
58. Who is the Real Master? 114
59. The Friend Who Did Not Change 116
60. King Janaka and the Wise Disciple 119
61. The 'Honest' Villagers 123
62. When Kabir Turned into a Thief 124
63. An Unforgettable Lesson in Happiness 127
64. The Disciple with a Difference 131
65. The Lost Chance 133
66. The Magic of Acceptance 135
67. When Imagination Runs Wild 138
68. The Donkey's Shrine 140
69. Was Krishna Really a Deserter? 143
70. The Washerman and His Donkey 144
71. When Socrates Defied Death 146
72. A 'Quiet' Message 149
73. Helen Keller – The Angel of Fortitude 150
74. Dayanand Saraswati's Moment of Truth 154
75. Turning the Tables! 155
76. It's All a Matter of Time 157
77. When Bhima Mocked Yudhishthira 161
78. What a Waste of Time and Energy! 163
79. The Fickle-minded Youngster 165
80. Be the Light unto Yourself 167
81. The Midnight Hymn 168
82. The Joy of Living 170
83. The 'Stiff' Measure 172
84. The Jain Monk and His Muslim Disciple 174
85. The 'Leap' of Faith 176
86. When Galileo Faced the Gallows 178
87. Light Up Your Life! 180
88. False Valour 181
89. Appearances Are Deceptive 184
90. Ghalib – The King of Poetry 185
91. The Witness and You 186
92. Only Time Will Tell 188
93. When Christ Appeared on Facebook 189
94. Kabir, God's Own Man 192
95. The Double-edged Sword 193
96. More to it than 'Meats' the Eye 193
97. From Sinner to Saint 196
98. A Heart of Gold 197
99. When Porus Lost the Battle but Won the War 198
100. Alms with a Difference 299
101. They Beg to Differ 201

Third Edition: 2022
Price: Rs 299/-

Printed in India

Concept, Illustration and Design:

www.aatmaninnovations.com

Publisher: Aatman Innovations Pvt. Ltd.
Place of Publication: Mumbai

ISBN 978-93-84850-66-1

From the Author's Desk

In my experience, I have realised that narrating stories interlaced with humorous anecdotes is the best way to explain psychological perspectives in a manner that people can grasp them instantly. They are easy to remember, and when it comes to instilling an idea into the innermost recesses of the mind, they are a matchless tool.

At the same time, it is a harsh reality of life that man is bogged down with innumerable problems. Be it physical ailments or psychological disturbances, matters of the world, family or his work life, man today is struggling to keep himself from falling apart. It is an unspoken truth, that everyone wishes to be free of troubles and unhappiness. Several psychological guidelines, in various forms, have been enumerated by great men of wisdom to help man break free from the struggles of life. But it is not easy for everyone to acquire an in-depth understanding of these pearls of wisdom and use them to their benefit. In this context, taking a leaf from the book of my vast experience, the efficacy of these psychological learnings when explained through the medium of stories and humorous anecdotes, leave a far greater imprint on the mind of the reader.

With this objective in mind, I have endeavoured to highlight the psychological aspects of several popular stories and humorous anecdotes in an engaging manner. My aim, in doing so, is to not only rivet the attention of the reader, but also make him delve deeper into the profundity of the message. Additionally, I have penned many of the stories and humorous anecdotes myself. All in all, I am sure this interesting book, 101 All Time Great Stories with Life-changing Philosophies, will not only make for an enjoyable read, but also bring about the necessary transformation in your life. It is with this hope that I present to you this treasure trove of short stories.

DEEP TRIVEDI

1 Wow, Mullah! You Are Amazing!

Mullah Nasruddin needs no introduction. He is perhaps the most compelling character of the folklore of the Middle East. An inhabitant of Turkey, who probably lived around the thirteenth century, Mullah Nasruddin is the star of a mind-boggling array of stories transcending time, nationality and culture. These stories range from simple jokes that elicit a quick laugh, to those with behavioural and spiritual undertones, having a specific moral attached to them. The rib-tickling manner in which he would impart profound knowledge is unparalleled in the world.

Now that I have introduced you to Mullah Nasruddin, let me also reveal another aspect of his maverick personality. Interestingly, neither did Mullah visit a mosque, nor did he ever offer any prayers. The people in his neighbourhood were so distressed by his unconventional behaviour, that they called Mullah an atheist and an infidel.

One day, they convened a meeting in which it was decided that they would meet Mullah and collectively persuade him to visit a mosque and offer prayers. In the evening, they set off to Mullah's house and tried every trick in the book to convince him to visit the mosque and pray. Now, Mullah was a smart man with a razor-sharp intellect. He patiently listened to them, and then calmly spoke, "Look brothers, please do not expect me to visit the mosque. But since you all insist, I will certainly pray to Allah at least once a day. However, let me make this very clear; I will pray to Allah at my own convenience and in my own way."

Pleased that their efforts had finally paid off, the neighbours immediately nodded in consent. They were happy that Mullah had at least agreed to pray, even if it was just once a day. It was so much better than not praying at all! Satisfied with their success, the neighbours left for their homes for a good night's sleep. But little did they know what Mullah had in store for them!

At the stroke of midnight, a booming voice suddenly broke the stillness of the hour, waking up the entire neighbourhood with a jolt. Sitting up on their beds and rubbing their eyes in bewilderment, people wondered who this lunatic could be, shouting at this unearthly hour. They could clearly hear a man's voice invoking God. "O Allah!" cried the man. "Please send me a hundred dinars; I will not let you off the hook until you do so! Until you send me a hundred dinars, I will continue to offer my prayers to you in this manner every single night! And please remember! I will take a hundred dinars only, not a single dinar less!" Saying this, the man abruptly ended his prayer and the eerie sounds of the night had once again descended on the neighbourhood. Hearing this strange prayer, people soon realised that the man was none other than the eccentric Mullah, who had chosen the hour to supplicate before Allah. Much to the dismay of the neighbours, this became a daily ritual. Every day, at the stroke of midnight, Mullah would step on to his terrace and, with hands outstretched towards the sky, he would invoke Allah to grant him a hundred dinars and not a single dinar less! He also made it a point to pray at the top of his voice.

Mullah's strange prayer at that unearthly hour began to give the entire neighbourhood sleepless nights. The neighbours now felt that an atheistic Mullah was better than a lunatic one ranting in the middle of the night! Everyone now regretted having convinced him to pray. So, once again, they went to Mullah's house and requested him to stop his prayers. But Mullah was in no mood to relent and stubbornly said, "My brothers, now that I have begun praying, no one can stop me from continuing to do so. Only Allah can stop my prayers by granting me a hundred dinars."

Now, why on earth would Allah grant Mullah a hundred dinars? So, the onus fell on the local residents themselves to find a solution to the problem. A meeting of all the local residents was held to deal with the issue of 'The Screaming Mullah'. Several suggestions were offered during the meeting, but only one out of them seemed practical. The idea was that the neighbours would first collect ninety-nine dinars, with each local resident contributing according to his capacity. One man would hide near the Mullah's house at night with the pouch containing the dinars in his hand. The moment Mullah finished his prayers, this man would toss the pouch of dinars over to his terrace. The neighbours were sure that on seeing only ninety-nine dinars in the pouch, Mullah would reject the money and throw the pouch back. After all, he had repeatedly declared that he would accept only hundred dinars and not a single dinar less. In this way, the locals would not only get their ninety-nine dinars back, but they would also be free of Mullah's loud prayers for good. Mullah too would resign himself to Allah's will, assuming that He was not yet ready to grant him a hundred dinars.

The proposed plan was approved unanimously, and they all commended themselves for having devised a marvellous plan that would outwit the astute Mullah Nasruddin. At the stroke of midnight, Mullah went to the terrace and began praying loudly, as was his routine. The moment the prayer ended, the pouch, filled with ninety-nine dinars was thrown on the terrace. Mullah was ecstatic on seeing the pouch. He instantly opened it and began counting the dinars. But to his disappointment, there were only ninety-nine dinars in the pouch. He could not understand how Allah had sent him a dinar less, when he had been extremely specific in his demand while praying! Thinking that he had probably erred, he counted the dinars again. But no, there were only ninety-nine dinars. Mullah thought that since it was late in the night and he was feeling sleepy, he had probably made a mistake while counting. He shook his head vigorously, rubbed his eyes, focussed intently on the dinars, and began counting them again, and again. But even after counting them thrice, there were only ninety-nine dinars! Meanwhile, the local residents hiding in the darkness near Mullah's house heaved a huge sigh of relief. Everything was happening exactly in accordance with their plan. They were certain that the eccentric Mullah would reject the money as the pouch contained a dinar less. Waiting expectantly in the shadows for the Mullah to throw the pouch back, the residents were, however, in for a rude shock. After counting the dinars thrice, Mullah suddenly smiled. Putting the dinars back in the pouch and lifting it high in the air, he shouted, "Oh Allah! You are such a professional! I just realised that you have charged me a dinar for the pouch!" Still looking at the sky, he shook his head and smiled in mock disbelief. Then, with the pouch in one hand, he went inside, kept it in his cupboard and went off to sleep.

The local residents were aghast at this totally unexpected turn of events. Their meticulous plan had fallen apart. Their hard-earned money had been lost! And even though Mullah had stopped praying, the residents were forced to spend another sleepless night, this time worrying about their money. The next morning, as soon as the sun rose, all of them gathered at Mullah's house. They wanted to know why Mullah had pocketed the ninety-nine dinars, when he had specifically asked for a hundred.

Guffawing, Mullah replied, "Why worry over such a trivial matter? Really, this is not something new for you, is it? Tell me, do your offerings ever reach Allah? Don't the *maulvis* take your offerings and mislead you, saying that Allah has not accepted your offerings since they were not made with a pure heart? You do not utter a word against the *maulvis.* So, none of you should protest against me either. I too have decided to keep your dinars for myself, using the excuse that Allah has become professional and has charged me a dinar for the pouch."

MORAL: Now, no one knows whether the local residents understood the logic behind Mullah's action. But you should understand that none of your offerings at temples, mosques or churches have ever reached God, and they never will. In fact, God is what He is precisely because all that He accepts are your pure and sincere emotions and nothing else. So, why are you mindlessly squandering your hard-earned wealth in temples, mosques and churches? Instead, donate this wealth to the poor and needy. Then you can be certain that your offerings shall reach Allah!

2 The Magic of Surrender

Tansen, the most revered vocalist of the Mughal era was one of the nine gems (Navratnas) of Emperor Akbar's court. Akbar was deeply enamoured and captivated by Tansen's voice and music. One evening, the two were enjoying some moments of leisure and the conversation veered towards music. Akbar looked at Tansen with a smile and said, "Tansen, I don't think that a vocalist of your calibre was ever born before, or will ever be born in the future!"

Hearing the lavish praise from the emperor, Tansen laughed and replied, "Why are you speaking about the past and future, Your Majesty? A vocalist of a much higher calibre than mine is present among us today! And he does not live too far away either." Akbar was startled by Tansen's words. "What? Who is he?" the emperor asked, with a puzzled look on his face. Tansen smiled proudly and said, "He is my guru, Swami Haridas. And please believe me when I say that my music is of no consequence compared to his musical prowess." Akbar emphatically retorted, "That is not possible! Perhaps, it is your reverence for your guru that compels you to say so."

"Absolutely not, Your Majesty! Every word of what I have said about my guru is absolutely true. And I am not saying this merely out of deference to him. My guru, Swami Haridas is far more talented than I am," Tansen replied in a reverential tone.

Still unconvinced, Akbar knit his brows and said, "Alright, if what you are saying is indeed true, then ask him to come to my court and sing for me. I want to hear him sing and judge for myself."

Tansen smiled and replied with his head bowed, "My guru will not come to your court, Your Majesty. If you want to hear his music, we will have to go to him instead."

Akbar was a great connoisseur of art, so he immediately left with Tansen for Swami Haridas' house. However, just when they were approaching the house, Tansen suddenly asked Akbar to stop near a bush. In a hushed tone, he said, "Let us hide behind these bushes, Your Majesty, and wait for my guru to begin singing."

Irked at such an unusual request from Tansen, Akbar protested, "Why should we hide here? Go and tell your guru that the king himself has come to listen to his singing."

In a placatory tone, Tansen replied, "It is not possible, Your Majesty. Your arrival or departure makes no difference to my guru. He will sing only when he is in the mood to sing." Akbar was a little irritated by now, as this was a very unusual experience for him. No one had ever dared to make the emperor wait for anything before this, and that too behind a bush! But then, he realised that it was futile to pressurise Tansen or his guru. Akbar was a true aficionado of art, and after all that Tansen had told him about his guru, he was even more curious to listen to Swami Haridas' singing.

So, both of them quietly hid behind the bush and waited patiently for Swami Haridas to begin singing. Finally, around midnight, the enchanting notes of a night-time *raga* (traditional pattern of musical notes in Indian music) wafted across the starlit sky, leaving Akbar absolutely spellbound. Swami Haridas had begun singing. Tears rolled down Akbar's cheeks as he listened to the mellifluous notes emanating from the divine voice. Swami Haridas' virtuosity was indeed unparalleled! Akbar realised that Tansen had been absolutely right. Indubitably, Swami Haridas was a far greater vocalist than Tansen, whom he had earlier considered to be the world's best!

When Swami Haridas concluded his singing, Akbar and Tansen quietly moved out from behind the bushes and began their journey back to the palace. On the way back, Akbar asked Tansen, "Why can't you sing like your guru? Give it a try. Nothing is impossible in this world."

Tansen smiled slowly in response and said, "It is not possible, Your Majesty."

Stunned at Tansen's brusque reply, Akbar enquired, "Why would you say so?"

In a solemn tone, Tansen replied, "Your Majesty, it is not a matter of talent or practice. I sing to please and entertain you, on your orders. So, I can never sing the way my guru does. An act becomes extraordinary and reaches a divine level only when a person performs of his own volition, and for his own joy."

MORAL: It has often been observed that despite being talented and putting in a lot of efforts, many people are unable to achieve positive results. Why is it so? That is because they often use their talent to impress others, or they suppress their own talent and become puppets, dancing to someone else's tune. Even the efforts they put in, are for the purpose of acquiring respect and wealth, but they forget that, in the bargain, their real talent becomes dormant. You must bear in mind, that all those who have achieved phenomenal success in life, have achieved it, because they used their talent for their own joy. As a consequence, their talent blossomed to a level that has enthralled the entire world. So, if you possess a unique talent, become passionate and immerse yourself in it, derive enjoyment from it and revel in it! Stop thinking about acquiring wealth and status, for, both will follow automatically the moment you surrender yourself completely to your talent.

3 In Search of Reality

In ancient India, there were many kings fabled for their prowess in battle, their military might or their integrity. But there were very few known to have attained the sublime heights of spirituality. One such exceptional king was Janaka, the ruler of Mithila. He was the father of Sita – a woman of many virtues and Lord Rama's wife in the epic Ramayana, a much-revered Indian scripture.

A fervent seeker of truth from a young age, King Janaka was fond of hosting lengthy discussions on spirituality and religion in his court, which would continue throughout the day. These discussions were attended by a number of famed religious scholars of the kingdom and wandering ascetics who held the king in high regard. These discussions were generally followed by dinner, after which, the king would retire to his chamber for a peaceful sleep, feeling contented at having learnt something new about religion and spirituality during the day.

However, one night, Janaka's sleep was disturbed by a very strange dream. He saw that a powerful emperor had invaded his kingdom, causing widespread devastation.

To escape certain death in battle, Janaka had to retreat deep into the forest. He was lonely and exhausted after the battle, and the consequent escape to save his life had only added to his fatigue. Standing in the middle of the dense forest, he was now gasping for breath. Soon, he found himself sinking into an abyss of depression at having lost the gruesome battle. As if that was not enough, the pangs of hunger further aggravated his misery. For several days, Janaka continued to roam aimlessly in the dense forest. Finding nothing to eat in all these days, he was on the verge of dying of starvation. Fortunately, one day, a man passing through the forest saw Janaka lying under a tree in a pitiable condition with his spine curved and legs folded, touching his chin. The man had no clue that this wretched man in front of him was the famed King Janaka. He took pity on him and offered him a piece of bread. For Janaka, it was nothing short of a blessing. He immediately sat up and hungrily grabbed the bread, thanking the man profusely with folded hands. He was just about to eat the bread, when suddenly a large crow appeared out of nowhere, snatched the bread from his hands and flew away. It was the only morsel of food that he had received after all these days, and it had been snatched away from his hands! That was the last straw for Janaka. He lost his composure and let out an ear-splitting scream. And the moment he screamed, Janaka woke up with a start, drenched in sweat, only to find himself in his royal bed in his own palace.

Momentarily numbed by the dream, Janaka, who was spiritually inclined, had developed the habit of analysing all his experiences and learning his lessons from them. Reflecting upon his strange dream, he thought, 'While dreaming, I was actually fast asleep in bed, but my mind was totally lost in the forest. While escaping into the forest, I was certainly running to save my life. The crow had definitely swooped down on me and snatched my bread away. And there is no doubt that I had screamed out aloud and was drenched in sweat. So, what was I really doing at that moment? Was I fast asleep on my bed? Or was I wandering in the forest after being defeated in battle? Which of the two situations was the reality?'

Indubitably, his query was genuine, but the answer eluded him! Janaka, from that very moment, became obsessed with finding the answer to this question. He forgot his responsibilities towards his kingdom, family and everything else. In his quest to discover the truth, Janaka convened numerous assemblies and also invited scholars from far and wide to provide an answer, but to no avail. His restlessness and anxiety became a matter of serious concern for everyone around him, including his family and council of ministers. Several physicians were called to cure his condition, but their efforts were rendered futile. Highly distinguished religious scholars of that time too, could not provide a satisfactory answer to Janaka's query. As the news of Janaka's quest spread far and wide, it soon reached the wisest sage of that time, Ashtavakra, who immediately set out to meet Janaka. As soon as the sage presented himself in the court, the king immediately posed his query. Ashtavakra smiled and replied in a gentle, calm tone, "Your Majesty! Your defeat in battle and wandering in the forest in your dream was not the reality. And your presence in your royal chamber was not real either."

Janaka was bewildered on hearing such a strange reply, for, some scholars whom he had consulted earlier had declared that the first state was the reality, while others had opined that the second state was the real one. But here was sage Ashtavakra, asserting that none of the two states were real! However, considering that Janaka had been in such a confused and listless state for so many days, his bewilderment at Ashtavakra's reply was at least indicative of his alertness and his intellect functioning as sharply as ever. Truly, that was an achievement in itself! Even as the king tried to comprehend what the sage had said, Ashtavakra elaborated upon his earlier remark, "When you were dreaming of wandering in the forest, you were physically present in your palace, which means, your wanderings in the forest were not real. Similarly, though you were physically present in your palace, your mind was wandering in the forest. Therefore, your presence in the chamber was not real either."

Convinced by Ashtavakra's explanation, Janaka's curiosity was fuelled even further. He asked the sage, "If none of the two states were real, then what is real?"

Ashtavakra looked deep into Janaka's eyes and replied, "What is real is the witness within you, who was watching both these states unfold. He was watching when you were in your bed and dreaming. And he was also watching when you were wandering in the forest in your dream. But this witness was totally detached from both the states."

Ashtavakra's enlightening reply hit Janaka like a thunderbolt. He felt he had found a new direction in life, and made it his life's mission to realise the witness within him at any cost.

Eventually, Janaka became Ashtavakra's student and under the sage's guidance, realised the witness within himself. The series of enlightening discussions between Ashtavakra and Janaka, which led to this realisation, is famously known today as the *Ashtavakra Gita*.

MORAL: We too will have to stoke the fire of curiosity within ourselves in order to elevate our minds to the highest level. Gradually, we will have to awaken our sense of being the witness; if not completely, then at least partially. We will have to understand that not only happiness, sorrow, the vicissitudes of life, material objects, relatives, friends and foes, but even our ever-changing emotions are not our own. We are only a witness to all of them. None of them belong to us. Therefore, the fact is, no event or incident on the outside, or within us, can ever influence us.

4 Who Can Outwit a Sannyasi?

Long ago, in a village in central India, there once lived a great sannyasi. Wise and compassionate by nature, he led an extremely simple and austere life, never accepting alms that he did not require. He lived in a small, one-room hut and his only worldly possessions were a few utensils and two blankets. These blankets served the dual purpose of clothing him and keeping him warm.

One night, during winter, the temperature outside had dipped drastically. However, unperturbed by the bitter cold, the sannyasi, as was his routine, was sleeping on one blanket which he had spread on the floor, and used the other blanket to cover himself. Now, genuine sannyasis rely only upon themselves for everything, and this sannyasi too, did not feel the need to lock the door of his house to protect him from burglars and wild animals. So, the door of his hut always remained unlocked whenever he slept.

Meanwhile, a hungry thief had stealthily entered the village, and was on the prowl for a place to burgle. He attempted to break into several houses, but to no avail. However, just when he was about to give up, he chanced upon the unlocked door of the sannyasi's hut. Wasting no time, he quietly entered the hut and groped in the dark, in the hope of laying his hands on something valuable. Several minutes ticked by, but to his dismay, all that the thief could find was a small cylindrical vessel and a broken cup. The thief found it hard to believe that there was nothing of value in the hut. So, he searched again, and unable to find anything of value to steal, he felt disappointed. He had certainly not ventured out on such a chilly night just to steal a couple of broken utensils! He stood still in the darkness, wondering what to do, unaware that he was being watched.

The sannyasi was a light sleeper. He had woken up the moment he had heard the door of his hut creak open. Pretending to be asleep, he had been quietly watching the thief rummaging through his hut, enjoying the thief's bewilderment and dilemma. In the meanwhile, the thief's desperation and irritation too were on the rise as seconds ticked by. After enduring so much trouble, he had to steal something; he just could not go empty-handed, else it would mean that he had failed. And even a thief hates failure! So, he pulled away the blanket covering the sannyasi, and also picked up the utensils. Satisfied that he had finally managed to steal something, he opened the door of the hut to scamper away.

Just as the thief was about to take flight, the sannyasi decided to act. "Stop!" he commanded in a loud voice piercing the stillness of the night, immediately halting the thief in his tracks. The sannyasi stood up and in a stern voice, ordered the thief to step back inside the house. Despite the chill in the air, beads of perspiration broke out on the thief's brow as he meekly re-entered the hut.

Seeing the thief quivering with fright, the sannyasi lowered his voice and said in a soft, gentle tone, "Please forgive me, brother. You came here on such a cold night and I could not help you at all. I do not possess anything that will bring you satisfaction. So, the next time you plan to visit me, do inform me in advance. I shall collect enough alms from people to give you so that you don't have to leave disappointed."

The thief was already quite frightened on hearing the sannyasi's stern voice. And now, the sannyasi's compassionate tone and his incredible invitation to visit again, left him totally flabbergasted. His hands became numb and the blanket and utensils slipped and fell on the floor. Disoriented, he was about to flee without taking anything, when the sannyasi once again ordered him in a stern voice, "You will have to leave with whatever you have stolen! And before leaving, shut the door so that I don't freeze because of the cold!" The poor thief! The commanding voice of the sannyasi had cast a hypnotic spell over him, compelling him to follow his instructions like a robot. He grabbed the blanket and utensils again, and darted out of the hut, closing the door behind him.

Unfortunately, by dawn, the thief was caught by some villagers who had recognised the sannyasi's blanket that the thief was carrying.

Enraged that the thief had burgled the innocent sannyasi's house, they bound him and dragged him before the village council to punish him for his deed. The village council too, was irked after hearing the thief's misdemeanour. After all, the sannyasi was a highly revered figure in the entire village. Everyone felt that he should be severely punished. While the villagers were deliberating upon the kind of punishment to be meted out, news of the thief's arrest and impending punishment reached the sannyasi. Without wasting time, he rushed to the village council and pointing towards the thief said, "This man is no thief! You are making a mistake, my brothers. Who said he stole the utensils and blankets from me? The truth is, when he had come to visit me last night, it was I who had gifted them to him with great affection. He is, in fact, such a kind man that he even shut the door of my hut on his way out to protect me against the cold. So, please release him at once!"

Now that the sannyasi had endorsed the thief's innocence, the village council was left with no alternative but to release him. So, though the thief had escaped punishment and was set free, the sannyasi's compassion had captured his heart. The moment the village council dispersed, he fell at the sannyasi's feet, sobbing bitterly. With hands folded in reverence, he pleaded, "Forgive me, O wise one! And take me as your humble servant." The sannyasi refused him outright, but the thief persisted with his pleas. Moved by his change of heart, the sannyasi finally relented and accepted the servitude of the thief, and both started heading towards the sannyasi's hut. Needless to say, the stolen utensils and blankets also found their way back to the sannyasi, along with the thief. Once they had reached the hut, the sannyasi suddenly burst into laughter. The thief, totally bewildered by the sannyasi's laughter, stared at him with his mouth agape. Controlling himself with great difficulty, the sannyasi said to the thief, "Did you understand my ploy? Not only have my stolen belongings returned to me, but they have also brought along with them a servant! Always remember, a sannyasi never makes an unfavourable deal."

MORAL: This is what is called self-confidence. And such self-confidence is a virtue of one's own mind, which cannot be attained by being dependent on others, whether the dependence is on a highly capable person, a great principle, abundant wealth or power. Always bear in mind whether it is wealth, a person, an object, a thought, a religion or any kind of power, they cannot infuse a person with self-confidence. It is only on the strength of one's own talent that a man can soar to greater heights of self-confidence, just like the ascetic who had complete confidence in his asceticism.

5 Vincent's Immortal Painting

All of you must have surely heard of the legendary Dutch post-Impressionist painter, Vincent Van Gogh, who is one of the most influential figures in the history of Western art. Vincent's sole passion in life was painting. A mere stroke of his brush would infuse life on a stark white canvas. And the sheer joy he derived from the myriad colours that took shape under his deft fingers lent an inimitable quality to his paintings. He had never painted with the intention of acquiring wealth, status and fame through his art. He painted for the sheer love and joy of painting, so it was hardly surprising that his paintings turned out to be incomparable.

Vincent, therefore, spent all his waking hours doing what he knew best – painting. After the completion of a painting, he would put it aside and begin a new one. And when his little studio could no longer hold his finished canvases, he would give them away to his friends; in fact, he would take the paintings himself and hang them in their drawing room! However, his friends were philistines, and could not empathise with the passion that drove Vincent. So, no sooner would he leave their house after hanging his painting, than his friends would immediately remove them and put them away in some dark and dusty corner of their house! 'Why ruin the beauty of the drawing room?' they would think. But Vincent's fervour for painting never waned and he continued to pursue his passion with single-minded devotion. And when his paintings piled up, he would once again head to a friend's home and gift it to him. The friend would hang it on his wall to please Vincent, and later, dump it in a corner of his house the moment he left. Vincent never realised that he had hung his paintings on those same walls on earlier occasions.

One day, Vincent happened to trek up a hill and came upon a sight that took his breath away. It was evening and the sun was about to set. Bathed in the iridescent glow of the setting sun, the green hills were enveloped in a golden hue. What a grand spectacle it was, indeed! Enraptured by the breathtakingly beautiful landscape, Vincent decided to immortalise this splendour of Nature in a painting. And thus, for months, Vincent trekked up the hill every single day to capture the ethereal beauty of the setting sun on his canvas. Such passion was bound to yield amazing results. And sure enough, Vincent's painting of the sunset turned out to be a masterpiece. It caught the attention of the world, propelling him towards international fame and success. Soon enough, there was a huge demand for his old paintings too, and in no time, they too began selling for a huge price. For Vincent's friends too it was a windfall, as the paintings, which they had looked down upon with disdain, were now proudly displayed in their living rooms. Some of them even made a fortune by selling those paintings at incredibly high prices!

MORAL: Success is achieved only when one works, and the extent of success is directly dependent on the quality of one's work. Needless to say, a superlative quality in one's work is possible only with intense concentration. Apart from this, there is no other formula or rule for success. If one focusses totally on the task instead of its result, then success is only a matter of time; sooner or later, one is bound to achieve it. Therefore, always bear in mind that Krishna's exhortation to Arjuna in the Bhagavad Gita to, "Perform your deeds diligently without worrying about their fruit," is the greatest formula for success.

6 When God Walks with You

Once upon a time, there lived a devout man who observed rigorous penance for several years to please God. Pleased with his devotion, God appeared before the man to grant him a boon. Overwhelmed by God's sudden appearance, the man did not feel the desire to ask Him for anything. Finally, when God insisted, the man requested God to be with him at all times and in all situations. And lo and behold! His wish was immediately granted. Wherever the man went, he noticed an extra pair of footprints walking beside him. Now, this was truly a miracle! The man could hardly believe his eyes as he looked down at the footprints with wonder and amazement. He realised that it was indeed God, who was walking along with him!

Feeling extremely happy, the man walked with a spring in his step, his faith and confidence soaring to the sky. God had decided to stay with him permanently! What more could he have asked for in life? However, there was also a nagging anxiety at the back of his mind – 'What if God leaves me?' And so, he was always alert. To allay his doubts, the man would sometimes deliberately walk through a jungle or on a mud path to confirm God's presence beside him. And the moment he sighted the extra pair of footprints beside his own, he would not only feel reassured, but also say a quick prayer in gratitude.

Financially well off, the man led a happy family life, enjoying all the worldly comforts with his wife and two sons. Lacking in nothing, the man was not only a true devotee of God, but also led a well-settled and prosperous life. And the icing on the cake was, that God was now his constant companion.

However, as it is said, change is the only constant in life. There came a time in the man's life when the tide turned. Suddenly, one day, both his sons passed away in an accident. Unable to bear the shock of losing both their young children, his wife lost her mental equilibrium. Naturally, the man too, was deeply shocked by the sudden and tragic turn of events. He could not concentrate on his work and consequently, suffered heavy losses in his business. He was completely overwhelmed by difficulties and his life turned into a series of misfortunes. He even began to think to himself, 'Life has nothing more to offer me, so why not devote the rest of my life in worshipping God?' As soon as this thought crossed his mind, he renounced the world and went into the forest to live the life of a sannyasi. Walking in a despondent frame of mind, suddenly, his eyes fell on the ground and he noticed that there was only one pair of footprints. The man was stunned. 'So, even God has forsaken me now!' he thought. His grief and dejection turned into fury, which he began unleashing on God. 'You too have abandoned me in my darkest hour! Oh! You are so callous! In fact, you are worse than a human being! You are not worthy of my devotion! I have realised, that it is useless to renounce the world for you! I will return to the world and lead a normal life right now! I am better off living my worldly life!'

As soon as the words were out of his mouth, God, who was present within him, appeared instantly and spoke in a reassuring tone, "My son, you are needlessly becoming disillusioned just because you saw only one pair of footprints. Compose yourself for a moment and think. Both your sons died, your wife lost her mental equilibrium..... did you think you had the strength to endure such grief? No! I am the one who has been bearing the brunt of all the adversities that have besieged you. Look carefully, the two footprints that you see are not yours. They are mine. I have been carrying you in my arms ever since your children died, to prevent you from slipping into an abyss of sorrow and from committing an irrational act."

MORAL: Indeed, this is the only truth of life! Whenever a person is besieged by trouble, his soul directly bears the brunt of it. The soul knows that the person's ego is incapable of bearing the trauma. You too must have experienced this many a time. You may also have realised that just the thought of enduring difficulties or tragedies makes it appear impossible to bear them. But when they actually occur, one does muster the capability and strength to bear them. You acquire that strength precisely because the brunt of that difficulty or tragedy is borne by your soul, and your soul is your God, which remains stable in every situation because of His very nature. His stability softens the impact of the blow, which you are then able to bear easily. Now, what more can God do for you apart from this?

7 A Sannyasi Defeats Alexander The Great!

In 326 BC, Alexander the Great set foot on the Indian subcontinent, and within a very short span of time, had conquered the North Western provinces of India. However, he was unable to advance further into the subcontinent because of a mutiny in his army, and was preparing to return to Greece with the enormous wealth he had plundered. Suddenly, an idea struck him. He thought, 'Since I am taking so much wealth from India, why not take an Indian sannyasi too as a token of this vast country?' After all, the sannyasis of India also enjoyed a great reputation across the ancient world. He immediately ordered his soldiers to capture a sannyasi, and within no time, they presented a sannyasi named Dandyayana before Alexander. Standing before Alexander, Dandyayana questioned the reason for being brought there in such an unceremonious manner.

Alexander replied, "Do not be afraid, O sage! You have been brought here, because I want to take you to Greece with me. I want to show my people what an Indian sannyasi looks like. Do not worry, I will treat you with great honour."

Dandyayana replied solemnly, "I appreciate your sentiment, O king! But I do not wish to go to Greece!"

Alexander immediately replied, "Perhaps you are not aware, but I have the greatest regard for sannyasis and *fakirs*. Come with me and I promise you that not only will you be felicitated in my kingdom, but I shall also have a magnificent *ashram* built in your name." Smiling in response, Dandyayana said, "O king, do not waste your time trying to tempt me, for sannyasis can never be won over with temptation. I will not travel to Greece with you under any circumstance."

Slightly taken aback on hearing the sannyasi's words and seeing his resolute demeanour, Alexander laughed and mocked at him, "Listen to me! I have conquered the entire world. No one can stop me from doing what I wish to. So, when I have decided to take you to Greece with me, you will just have to come. And since you have no choice but to come, I suggest you do so willingly and come with me!"

Unperturbed by Alexander's arrogance and veiled threats, Dandyayana replied gently, "It is one thing to conquer and plunder a kingdom, but to forcibly take a sannyasi against his will is a different matter altogether. So, dear king, there is no way you can forcefully take me to Greece without my consent."

Intoxicated with pride and ego after his numerous conquests, Alexander guffawed and said, "What nonsense! Who will stop me? I will teach you a lesson right now!" Saying this, he ordered his soldiers to tie the sannyasi with a rope and put him aboard a chariot. His command was obeyed instantly, and Dandyayana soon found himself on a chariot, bound by a rope. Alexander then came close to the wise sannyasi and hissed arrogantly, "Do you still think I cannot take you with me?"

"Yes," said Dandyayana even more emphatically.

Stunned by Dandyayana's reply and his calm demeanour, Alexander demanded, "What makes you think so?"

Looking straight into the king's eyes, Dandyayana spoke evenly, "You have merely bound my body. You certainly have the power to do that. But tell me, do you want my body or my ascetic consciousness? If you want my ascetic consciousness, I assure you that it will certainly turn silent upon reaching Greece, because it is within my control. So, all that you will be left with, will be my body. And what will you do with that?"

Listening to these words laden with profound wisdom from the sannyasi, Alexander was astounded. He had finally realised that indeed, it was easy to conquer and plunder kingdoms, but conquering a sannyasi's heart and taking him against his will was a different matter altogether. Expressing regret, Alexander apologised to Dandyayana for his rude behaviour and immediately set him free.

MORAL: In Nature's scheme of things, not just the sannyasi's, each and every person's consciousness is absolutely free. And no one can ever compel a person to do anything against his own will. It is the shackles of greed and fear that bind a man mentally, making him a slave to other people. Therefore, if a human being, no matter where he is or what kind of a person he is, banishes greed and fear from his mind, then he too is a sannyasi. Because, then, no one will have the power to enslave him even for a moment. You must clearly understand that the very word 'sannyasi' is actually a proclamation of one's absolute independence.

8 The Human Mind – A Pandora's Box

Friendship, as we all know, is the most beautiful relationship. And its beauty lies in the fact that it is unconditional. True friends are unconcerned by each other's financial or social status.

They are friends because they like each other just the way they are. Let me narrate a story of two close friends. One hailed from an affluent family, while the other came from a modest background. In spite of this disparity in their backgrounds, the bond of friendship remained as strong as ever.

One day, it so happened that the friend who was poor was in urgent need of a scooter to purchase goods for guests arriving at his home that afternoon. Since his rich friend owned a scooter, he decided to borrow it from him for a day, and so, he quickly set out for his house. He had barely walked a few steps when he suddenly halted in his tracks as a doubt assailed him, 'What if my friend refuses to lend me the scooter?' But then another thought popped up immediately in his mind, 'No, he will not refuse me. After all, in all these years of our friendship, I have never even once asked him for anything. So, why will he refuse to lend me his scooter for a day?' But no sooner had he dismissed this thought, than his mind was assailed by yet another doubt. 'He will definitely refuse to lend the scooter to me! He is not as guileless as he seems! I am sure he will have plenty of excuses to avoid giving it to me. For instance, he could say that there is no petrol in the scooter! But if he does say that, I can always counter him by telling him to give me the keys and I will get the petrol filled.'

Reassuring himself thus, he confidently resumed his steps towards his friend's house. Alas! It was not long before his mind was back to playing mischief. He began to think, 'I am sure he will come up with numerous excuses to avoid lending me his scooter. His friendship is just a pretence, and nothing more. He will not even hesitate to say that the tyre of his scooter is punctured! Or he could say that he is expecting guests today, so lending me the scooter will not be possible!'

Agitated by the thoughts running amok in his mind, he was fuming by the time he reached his rich friend's house and angrily rang the doorbell. Coincidentally, it was his rich friend himself who opened the door. By this time, the poor friend's rage was at its peak, and he instantly vented it on his rich friend. "You and your useless scooter may go to hell for all I care! I have had enough of you rich people! You can never be true friends with anyone! And I don't want to be friends with you anymore! Do you hear me? Our friendship ends right here, right now!" Saying so, the poor friend stomped off. Flabbergasted by his dear friend's unexpected appearance at his house and his sudden outburst, the rich friend stood at the door, scratching his head, wondering which scooter and which rich people he was ranting about. Meanwhile, his friend had already left in a huff after having vented his anger.

MORAL: This is precisely how the human mind works. It runs amok on its own, and makes even non-existent things appear real! A person's mind often holds him accountable for matters that do not concern him at all. And when it comes to relationships, it does not allow them to sustain at all. Hence, if you want to experience the joy of good relationships and acquire a better understanding of people, then, instead of finding faults with them, you must first learn to clearly recognise and thoroughly understand the shenanigans of your own mind.

9 The Marvellous Mother

The legendary scientist Thomas Edison's name is synonymous with numerous path-breaking scientific inventions that have now become an inseparable part of human existence. However, not many people are aware that the person who guided him towards his illustrious career, and also laid its foundation, was none other than his extraordinary mother, Nancy.

Thomas was Nancy's seventh child. At the age of seven, he was sent to school, like other children of his age. However, he was extremely inquisitive by nature, and this curiosity created a problem for him at school. He always had a barrage of questions for his teachers, who were soon fed up of answering him. Finally, they could not take it anymore and called his mother to school one day. They informed her that her son was a very dull boy, and also badgered them with inane questions. Nancy was surprised by the teachers' opinion about her son. She knew that Thomas was certainly not a dull boy. As for his habit of asking questions, well, Nancy felt that it indicated a thirst for knowledge. Nancy realised that the teachers' complaint against

Thomas was absolutely baseless and they were, in fact, suppressing his natural curiosity. She was so furious at the teachers that she immediately pulled him out of the school.

The following year, Thomas was enrolled in another school, but here too, his inquisitive nature attracted the ire of his teachers. So, the subsequent year, he was enrolled in a third school. But neither did Thomas' habit of asking questions change, nor did the attitude of the teachers. Only the schools he attended, kept changing. Needless to say, Nancy was traumatised and saddened by this instability in her son's early academic life. She could not tolerate anyone calling her son dull or insulting him. One day, she decided that she had had enough. She dashed off to Thomas' school and told the teachers in an icy tone, "My boy is not dull! It is your observations and assessments that are poor! You are unable to see the innate talent and great potential in my boy!" Nancy immediately had Thomas' name removed from the rolls of that school too and took him home with her.

Nancy had been a teacher herself, and was aware that once a child's self-confidence is shaken, it is difficult for him to regain it. Therefore, she decided that she would not send Thomas to school anymore, but would teach her child at home instead. As for Thomas, he was deeply touched by his mother's love and faith in him.

Under the tutelage of his mother, little Thomas put his heart and soul into his lessons and studied diligently at home. Soon, he evinced a special interest in science and technology, and was specifically inclined towards conducting scientific experiments. His mother stood by him, encouraging him all the time. Holding on to the love and support of his mother, the day finally dawned, when he was hailed as a great scientist with a world record of 1093 patents registered in his name. The list also includes his most important invention – the electric bulb that dispelled darkness and has lit up the entire world by its luminosity. Edison always remained grateful to his mother, Nancy, for standing by him like a rock and being the prime motivator, instrumental to his success. Expressing his deep gratitude to her, Edison had once said, "I was deeply moved by my mother's decision not to send me to school anymore. It was on that very day, I promised myself that no matter what happened, I would never break my mother's trust in me and would never ever let her down. The teachers labelled me a dull student and what did my mother do? She refused to believe them and pulled me out of school instead! Now, what more could I want from such a loving, wise and devoted mother?"

MORAL: This is a lesson that every mother should learn from Nancy. It is the mother who gives birth to a child, and it is the mother alone whom the child is closest to. And, it is only a mother's trust and affection that a child craves during childhood. However, these days, as soon as a child is two or three years old, most mothers send their toddlers off to nursery school. It would seem as if they want to quickly become free of this 'burden' of having to raise their child. Can children raised by strangers, ever become Thomas Edison? To achieve greatness in life, a child does not need formal education. Ask yourself this question: "Did Thomas Edison feel the need to acquire a formal education?" What a child really needs to achieve fame and success is his mother's love and trust. All the mothers of the world must bear in mind that it was only because of his mother's love for him, and her trust in him, that Edison went on to become a legendary scientist. And you too, have to endeavour to achieve that stature of motherhood.

10 Smile Away Your Worries

It was a dark and cold night. In spite of the late hour, the light in one room of the house across the street still burnt bright. A man was pacing in his bedroom in an anxious and distressed state. His wife, who had woken up on hearing the noise in the room, was surprised to see her husband pacing the floor. Still lying on the bed, she continued to watch him quietly. His body language clearly indicated that he was under stress. The woman had never seen him in this condition before, so was naturally worried, wondering what was troubling her husband. Finally, unable to keep quiet, she asked her husband why he was so restless and tense.

In a woeful tone, her husband replied, "Actually, two months ago, I had borrowed two hundred thousand rupees on interest from our neighbour, Mr. Banerjee. I have to return the amount tomorrow morning. But I have not been able to arrange for it. I know Mr. Banerjee is a stickler for schedule, and he will be at our doorstep first thing in the morning. I am at my wits' end; I cannot think of a way to extricate myself from this situation."

For a moment, even the wife became anxious, on seeing her husband's predicament. But she was blessed with a cheerful disposition, and could not be bogged down by anxiety for long. She looked at her husband and said calmly, "Well, ideally, this should not have happened. But are you sure you cannot arrange for the money by tomorrow?"

"Yes, I am! That is why I am so worried. Otherwise, you know me; I don't like being in such a situation myself," said the husband, sounding more tense than ever.

"Of course, I know that," consoled the wife. "But still, take a little more time to think. Perhaps you could find a solution."

The husband immediately replied, "I have tried everything, my dear. Nothing more can be done now."

"Well, if you cannot, then so be it," said the wife as she got up from the bed and walked towards the main door of their house. The husband was puzzled, wondering where she was going at this late hour. Just then, the wife turned to him and said, "I will be back in a moment." And before the husband realised what she was doing, she had left the house and was ringing the doorbell of Mr. Banerjee's house. The late hour made no difference to her. The intrepid wife had decided to solve her husband's problem immediately. She put her ear to the door to listen if someone was approaching to answer the door. Soon, the door was opened slowly by Mr. Banerjee himself. He was surprised to see his neighbour's wife standing at his doorstep at this late hour. But before he could ask her, what the matter was, the wife immediately greeted him and came straight to the point, "Mr. Banerjee, did my husband borrow two hundred thousand rupees from you?"

With a puzzled look on his face, Mr. Banerjee instantly replied, "Yes."

"Is tomorrow the date when he has to return the money?" she questioned further.

Mr. Banerjee replied in the affirmative again, wondering why the woman was interrogating him at that late hour, in such a manner.

"Sorry, Mr. Banerjee," the wife said, "But my husband has not been able to arrange the money. So, you will have to wait for a couple of months more for it." Saying this, she made her way back home, leaving Mr. Banerjee at the door, scratching his head in bewilderment, trying to understand why his friend's wife had come in the middle of the night to tell him this.

Meanwhile, perturbed by the fact that his wife had gone out of the house in the middle of the night, the husband became even more restless. 'Where has she gone at this hour?' he wondered. 'Has she gone somewhere to arrange for the money?' The calm and reassuring attitude that his wife had displayed earlier surprised him, but before his mind could come up with any more conjectures, his wife returned. And before he could say anything, she told him, "I met Mr. Banerjee and told him that you could not arrange the money, and that he will have to wait for a couple of months to get his money back. So, now, you go off to sleep and let Mr. Banerjee worry instead!"

MORAL: Ideally, you must never hold on to any worries. But if you cannot help it, then you must understand that it is futile to expend your energy in worrying over a problem that has no solution. Being concerned about finding a solution is alright. But worrying endlessly with no solution in sight, is pointless.

11 The Elephant and the Mouse

Sometimes, a meeting of two contrasting personalities becomes so amusing that people continue to recount it with great delight even after aeons. Take, for instance, the story of the elephant and the mouse. In terms of size, both are poles apart. Interestingly, the two rarely cross each other's paths, but no one has barred them from coming together, have they? At times, the elephant does encounter the mouse and vice versa. And when they do, their meeting invariably becomes the talk of the town. One day, an elephant was ambling along on a road, when his eyes suddenly fell on a small mouse. Generally, an elephant never notices a mouse. But this elephant did. And he was extremely surprised to see such a small creature scurrying around.

Using his trunk, the huge mammal gently stopped the mouse in its tracks and exclaimed, "Oh gosh! You are so tiny!"

Visibly rattled by the elephant's remark, the mouse's pride was pricked. His inferiority complex lying dormant, came to the fore, and defending himself, he said, "Actually, of late, I have not been keeping well; else, I was also as big and strong as you!"

MORAL: If we observe ourselves closely, it is our complex of superiority or inferiority which drives us to respond to people in a manner similar to that of the mouse. But no matter who or what kind of people we are – whether big or small, short or ordinary-looking, wealthy or poor, successful or struggling – why are we reluctant to accept ourselves the way we are? What is important is our existence; why don't we understand this simple fact?

12 The Jewel in the Crown

One day, during Emperor Akbar's reign in India, a soldier from his royal court was sentenced to eat half a kilo of slaked lime. Clearly, he must have committed a grave crime, for, it is a known fact that no one can possibly stay alive after eating such a huge amount of slaked lime. Now that the sentence had been announced, the soldier had to procure the slaked lime the next day and eat it in the presence of everyone in Akbar's court. So, obeying the emperor's command, the soldier went to purchase the slaked lime from a shop nearby.

Sounding dejected and bereft of hope, the soldier requested the shopkeeper for half a kilo of slaked lime. Surprised at such an odd request, the shopkeeper wondered, 'Why would a person ask for half a kilo of slaked lime?' Suspecting that something was amiss, the shopkeeper insisted on knowing the reason behind the soldier's demand for such a large quantity of slaked lime. Mournfully, the soldier replied, "As part of my punishment, I have to eat half a kilo of slaked lime in the royal court tomorrow."

Feeling sorry for him, the shopkeeper mulled over the problem for a while, and then said, "Don't worry, my friend. Perhaps, I may be able to help you. Follow my instructions and no harm will come to you. First, go and buy half a kilo of clarified butter."

The shopkeeper's words instilled a ray of hope in the soldier and he dashed off to buy the clarified butter. After he returned with it, the shopkeeper gave him his half a kilo of slaked lime and said, "Tomorrow, just before you set out for the royal court, eat half a kilo of clarified butter at home, and then eat half a kilo of slaked lime in the court. However, remember my advice: once you have finished eating the slaked lime in court, you must return home immediately. Do not linger around, and your life might just be saved."

The soldier could not believe his ears! The shopkeeper's advice was like the proverbial straw for a drowning man. Relieved, the soldier took the clarified butter and lime, thanked the shopkeeper profusely for his help and made his way back home.

Following the shopkeeper's instructions, the next morning, the soldier ate half a kilo of clarified butter just before leaving from home. When he reached the court, he ate the half kilo of slaked lime in the emperor's presence. Now that he had duly served his sentence by eating the lime, the royal court granted him permission to go home so that he could spend his final hours with his loved ones.

Without wasting a moment, the soldier, as instructed by the shopkeeper, hurried back home and immediately vomited the lime along with the clarified butter.

Although his health did suffer and he felt weak, by the next morning, he was as fit as a fiddle. Brimming with energy, the soldier decided to report on duty the next day. The first man who saw the soldier approaching the palace, screamed and fled from the spot, thinking he had perhaps seen a ghost. Within minutes, news of his return spread like wildfire among the palace staff. Unable to believe what they had heard, they hurried to the soldier's regular post to see him. Indeed, the soldier was standing nonchalantly at his post, obviously in the pink of health. Everyone knew he had consumed half a kilo of slaked lime the day before and were amazed to see that no harm had come to him.

News of the soldier's survival eventually reached the emperor. Akbar heard the news in disbelief, and immediately summoning the soldier, asked him how he had managed to stay alive.

Kneeling on the floor with his head bowed before the emperor, the soldier honestly recounted his conversation with the shopkeeper, who had advised him to consume half a kilo of clarified butter, which had saved him from certain death. On hearing the soldier's story, Akbar forgot the crime of the soldier and the fact that he had actually escaped punishment. Instead, he was thinking about the shopkeeper who had saved him. Impressed by his intelligence and foresight, the emperor immediately summoned the shopkeeper to the court and appointed him as his Prime Minister. In due course of time, the shopkeeper rose to become one of the nine gems of Emperor Akbar's court. Do you know who the shopkeeper was? Well, his name was Mahesh Das. Later, the emperor changed his name to Birbal - the man with a razor-sharp mind. Years later, Birbal was honoured with the title of 'King' by Akbar.

MORAL: It is this quality of Emperor Akbar which is worth emulating. Friends and family have their own place, but talent should never be discriminated against, in favour of any kind of relationship. Talent should be rewarded and honoured without bias. Like Akbar, everyone is an emperor of their own world, and to progress in life, it is one's own responsibility to surround oneself with talented people without harbouring prejudice of any kind. Bear in mind, almost everyone has a close circle of friends and relatives; but the person who progresses in life is the one who has a close circle of talented people around him. You must also remember another universal truth of life: no one in this world is perfect or complete. Therefore, if you want to progress in life, then you too will have to develop that insight which can recognise talent, as well as a large heart like Akbar's, which respects such talent.

13 The 'Greedy' Pot

In a small village in India, there once lived a wealthy man whose affluence was the envy of the entire village. In spite of having amassed so much wealth, his fervour to expand his business and accumulate more wealth did not abate. He was also blessed with a happy family. However, despite possessing everything that a person could wish for, he was far from being content. He was distressed at the morose state of his life, devoid of fun and cheer.

One day, a sannyasi happened to visit his house. After meeting the wealthy man, the sannyasi was quick to gauge that in spite of possessing everything, the man was dissatisfied with life. The rich man, seeing this as the perfect opportunity to get his woes redressed, fell at the sannyasi's feet and lamented, "O wise one! I have everything in life except happiness. Please use your great powers to infuse my life with happiness!"

The sannyasi replied with a benign smile, "It will take me only a moment to make you happy again, provided you fulfil a condition!" He then arched his eyebrows and said, "But I doubt your ability to do so."

Sensing scepticism in the sannyasi's voice, the wealthy man immediately stood up and in a decisive tone proclaimed, "What are you saying, O wise one? I am ready to do anything to attain happiness in my life." With just a trace of a smile lifting the corner of his lips, the sannyasi took out a small pot, and handing it over to the man, said, "Alright then, fill this pot with gold coins and jewels and bring it back to me."

Calculating quickly in his mind, the rich man felt that this was an excellent deal; all he had to do was part with some of his wealth to attain everlasting happiness. Rushing immediately to his treasure vault, he brought out a handful of gold coins and jewels and poured them into the pot. But the small pot remained empty.

'Never mind, I have more than enough gold and jewels to fill this pot,' he thought and once again filled the pot with valuables and gold coins. However, even after repeatedly filling the pot four-five times, it remained empty. Gradually, the pot had almost consumed his entire wealth, but still showed no sign of filling up! The magic trick that his pot was playing and the look of bewilderment on the man's face had brought a slight smile on the sannyasi's rugged countenance. It was beyond the man's comprehension. But since he had promised the sannyasi that he would fill the pot, he had to keep his word. So, he continued walking to his treasure vault, bringing fistfuls of valuables and pouring them into the pot. But the little pot devoured all his wealth and still remained empty. Finally, the man, who had turned into a bundle of nerves, fell at the sannyasi's feet and with hands folded in deep reverence, said woefully, "O wise one! Pray, tell me, what is the pot made of? It has swallowed my entire wealth, but still remains empty!"

Laughing heartily, the sannyasi replied, "My dear man, this pot is made of ambition and aspiration. Let alone your wealth, even if you fill this pot with all the wealth in the world, it will still remain empty! You too are like this pot, insatiable and always greedy to acquire more wealth. The ambitions of your mind and brain have surpassed all limits, so, no matter how much wealth you earn, you remain dissatisfied. You already have far more wealth than you will ever need in a lifetime. The day you are able to break free from this vicious circle of ambition and aspiration, you will stop chasing wealth. And only then will you be able to utilise your wealth to do something worthwhile for yourself and for others. And my dear man, only then will you find both, happiness and contentment."

Hearing such pearls of wisdom from the sannyasi, tears welled up in the rich man's eyes and in a voice filled with emotion, he said, "I have finally understood, O wise one! But what should I do now? Your pot has devoured all my wealth!"

Laughing at the rich man's hapless state, the sannyasi turned the pot upside down. And lo and behold! Out tumbled all the rich man's gold coins and jewels! The rich man was elated upon getting his wealth back. His life had been transformed forever. Promising himself to heed the sannyasi's advice, from that day onwards, he became resolute. He made drastic decisions to reduce his business activities and instead spent time with his family. Whenever possible, he also began donating a significant amount of his wealth to charities. Finally, his efforts bore fruit and within no time, his life underwent a phenomenal change, bringing him everlasting happiness and contentment.

MORAL: Have you understood this important lesson of life? Introspect carefully: are you too being driven by ambitions and aspirations? Has your greed for wealth blinded you to the extent that neither do you have time, nor can you enjoy your hard-earned wealth? If that is the case, then beware! Money is a primary necessity in life. But you must earn only as much as you can enjoy during your lifetime. There is absolutely nothing wrong in earning wealth if you are generous enough to also use it for charitable purposes. Blindly running after wealth not only puts you in trouble while earning it, but also leads to a multitude of business problems. And even after struggling hard to earn it, this wealth does not give you happiness at all, because you are not large-hearted or generous enough to spend it or give it in charity. So, pause for a moment, apply your intelligence and think: can there be a form of foolishness in this world greater than this?

14 Anger Management

This is the tale of a businessman, who owned a large garment manufacturing company. One day, he left home in a huff after a heated argument with his wife over a petty domestic issue. As he had to attend an urgent meeting, he abandoned the argument midway. However, he carried this belligerent mood with him to work. Since his wife was no longer with him, he could not vent his anger on anyone. Suppressing his anger, he reached his office in a foul state of mind. But because of his anger, he was unable to focus on the meeting. Later, still simmering with rage, he was pacing up and down in his cabin, mulling over the fight with his wife. Just then, there was a knock on his cabin door and the office manager walked in to submit the weekly report, clueless about what was in store for him. Deliberately finding some mistakes in the report, the boss scolded his manager. Puzzled at the boss' behaviour, the poor manager maintained a stoical silence, trying to understand what his mistake was. Suppressing his anger with great difficulty, he walked out of his boss' cabin.

When the manager reached his cabin, he summoned the accountant with the books of accounts. After flipping over a few pages, the manager, finding some minor faults, admonished the accountant. Scolded for no apparent reason, the accountant too became angry. He returned to his desk, and immediately called his office assistant and vented his anger on him. Obviously, the hapless assistant could do nothing, but swallow his pride before his senior and bear the insults. But, once the office assistant reached home, he could not control his anger anymore and vented it on his wife. And how do you think the wife reacted? She instantly went out of the house and without any valid reason yelled at her children who were playing in the courtyard. Naturally, the children could not understand the reason behind their mother's ire. They suppressed their rage against her and continued playing. But the moment they got an opportunity, they picked a fight with a few other children in their neighbourhood. Thus, the unresolved fight between the owner of the company and his wife had finally culminated in an unnecessary fight between the children.

MORAL: Observe your life carefully. You vent your anger either on those who are close to you, or on those whom you consider weaker than you. And since it is a law, that anger cannot be suppressed, everyone keeps venting their suppressed anger against powerful people on those who are close to them or are perceived as weaker than them. Hence, if someone is venting his ire on you for no reason, then instead of feeling hurt or thinking that he has lost his mental balance, it is psychologically prudent to perceive it as a sign that the person considers you close to him. In times of distress, who will the poor fellow turn to, if not his loved ones?

15 Wisdom of the 'illiterate' Businessman

There once lived a businessman in Mumbai who had had no formal education. He lived with his wife in a large mansion. One day, he had to travel to Kolkata to attend an urgent meeting. Since the meeting was important, the man had made the necessary preparations for his travel a day in advance. However, on the night before he was due to travel, his old, loyal watchman had a disturbing dream. He dreamt that the plane his boss was travelling in, from Mumbai to Kolkata had crashed, killing all the passengers. Early the next morning, the watchman rushed to the businessman's house and told his wife about his dream. He requested her to stop the businessman from travelling to Kolkata. Scared out of her wits on hearing the watchman's dream, the wife panicked and immediately called her husband pleading with him to cancel his trip. Irritated and annoyed with his wife's repeated pleas, the businessman, albeit a bit reluctantly, had to bow to his wife's wishes.

The next day, just as the watchman had dreamt, the scheduled flight that had taken off from Mumbai to Kolkata did crash, and all the passengers were reported dead. Hearing the news, the wife not only thanked her stars but immediately called the watchman to express her gratitude and gave him a handsome reward. He certainly deserved it. However, to everyone's astonishment, his boss, whose life the watchman had saved, immediately dismissed him from service! Shocked, his wife asked him to explain the reason for such a harsh decision. Now, although the man was uneducated, he was wise and intelligent. Replying in a monotone, he said, "The watchman's dream and the crash were a mere coincidence. But the important question is, how could the watchman sleep while on duty? What will happen if a thief tries to rob our house while the watchman is fast asleep, lost in his dreams?" Unable to refute the logic behind her husband's argument, the wife could do nothing but sympathise with the watchman.

MORAL: Happiness, sorrow and problems are all intricate parts of our lives. It is important to remember that whether a person is besieged by adversities or whether his life is flooded with happiness, he must never become overwhelmed or lose his composure. He should never lose sight of reality. Although the businessman had evaded death because of the watchman's dream, he had maintained his composure. His attention remained focussed on the actual duty and responsibility of the watchman. Otherwise, it is commonplace for ordinary people to lose their composure when faced with success, failure, sadness or happiness to the extent that they lose sight of the larger picture. And this, in fact, is the prime reason why human beings get repeatedly embroiled in grave problems.

16 The Forty-eight-legged animal

Once upon a time, in a forest, there lived a strange animal with forty-eight legs! It would wander around the forest all day with a swaying, whimsical gait, lost in its own world. At times, it walked as if it was marching to its own unique rhythm with a sense of abandon, like that of a joyous elephant. But it was certainly not a slow animal. In spite of its numerous legs, it could run at an astonishing speed when circumstances warranted. These unique characteristics of the animal had made it extremely popular amongst the other animals in the forest. But, alas! Its happiness was short-lived.

One day, to its misfortune, it met a sannyasi who was passing through the forest. Now, since aeons, sannyasis have been considered to be erudite. But can a sannyasi ever refrain from delivering a totally unsolicited sermon, without rhyme or reason? And how can a sannyasi qualify to be called a knowledgeable person if he does not find fault in you? This sannyasi too, was no different from his ilk.

Awestruck by the unique sight of the forty-eight-legged animal, the sannyasi stood admiring it for a moment. He had never seen such a creature before, and was impressed. But, as mentioned earlier, how can a sannyasi be considered worth his salt unless he finds fault with even the most perfect of beings? In fact, the very reverence that sannyasis receive from their followers, depends on this trait of finding fault in others. Their businesses run on the very premise that their words are the gospel truth, while everything that others say is false. So, compelled by habit, the sannyasi keenly observed the animal for a while and then commanded it to stop. Halting immediately in its tracks, the animal bowed reverentially at the sannyasi's feet just like human beings. The sannyasi was pleased at the animal's gesture and blessed it. And then he launched into a sermon! He told the animal, "You walk as if you are unconscious." The poor animal was startled to hear this. The sannyasi continued, "It is extremely important to always be aware of your actions. While walking, you should pay close attention to which foot you lift first and which one touches the ground. Bring this process of walking under control; otherwise, this unconsciousness will destroy you one day."

The poor, naive animal! It instantly looked down at its forty-eight legs and felt the sannyasi was right. It thought, 'I am really unaware of which foot I lift first and when. I should stop behaving impetuously before it is too late.'

So, the animal immediately began controlling and monitoring the movement of its feet to be able to walk with precise control. When it did finally manage to control its movement, alas, to its dismay, it could not move even an inch forward despite several attempts! Flustered, the poor animal, now became totally engrossed in the task of moving forward. It persisted in its efforts for several hours, but to no avail. Meanwhile, the sannyasi stood there with a smile, taking immense pleasure in the poor animal's struggle.

Having toiled for several hours in this manner, the animal finally realised the futility of its actions. It thought, 'Oh, just forget this awareness! When I have been automatically walking perfectly all my life, why should I put in so much effort now? Let me just walk naturally, the way I always did.' But the poor animal was in for a nasty surprise! It had already put in too much effort in trying to be aware of the movement of its legs. As a consequence, its legs had forgotten their natural, rhythmic gait. It had already failed to walk with 'awareness'. And now, because it had forgotten its natural gait, it could not move at all and stood transfixed in one spot.

The poor animal was petrified, and seeing no solution in sight, called out to the sannyasi in desperation, "Help! I cannot walk! What do I do now?" But, what could the sannyasi do? His job was to preach, and he had already accomplished that. Assuming a grave expression, the sannyasi told the animal, "There is nothing I can do to help you. It is the karma of your past life that has robbed you of your ability to walk." The animal was stunned to hear this, but before it could say anything else, the sannyasi nonchalantly walked away, leaving the poor animal to its fate. Time passed by, but the poor animal remained immobilised, and after years of suffering, breathed its last in the same spot.

MORAL: This is exactly what is happening to all our acquired knowledge and endeavours in life. Fortunately for humans, so far, no knowledgeable person has taught us how to breathe, or extract oxygen from air. And no scriptures have been written on these natural actions either; otherwise, man would have lost his life in his attempt to extract oxygen from air. And then these knowledgeable people, quoting the scriptures, would have said, "People died because they paid the price for their karma!"

Unfortunately, the problem is, many people claim to possess knowledge, but most of them do not understand Nature's automation. The truth is, that the ability to understand automation is the supreme, irrefutable and most practical knowledge of all. Whether the actions are of Nature, humans or flora and fauna, they are all absolutely automatic and natural; it is only a human being's externally acquired knowledge which hampers their natural way of being. Everyone is vying with each other to exchange knowledge even where it is unnecessary. And this is what has robbed humans of happiness. This is the sole reason why both, happiness and success have been eluding human beings. Otherwise, happiness and success are the birthright of every person.

17 Think Like Tolstoy

One day, a man approached the famous writer Leo Tolstoy, and in a dramatic manner, informed him that a close friend of his had said something about him. The man expected Tolstoy to become curious and eagerly ask what was being said about him. However, he was the enlightened scholar, Leo Tolstoy; how could he have scaled such great heights of wisdom were he to be influenced so easily? Contrary to the man's expectation, Tolstoy responded in a simple manner and said, "If what you have to say to me is important for me to know in terms of my work, then say it; if it suggests a new and a better path for me in life, then say it immediately; and if it helps someone, then say it instantly. But if it does not serve any of these three purposes, then I have no interest in hearing what you have to say."

Tolstoy was absolutely right, because any kind of information or knowledge becomes worthwhile only if it serves at least one of the three purposes mentioned above. However, you keep garnering a lot of unnecessary information either to satiate your curiosity, or because of your habit of meddling in affairs that do not concern you at all. And it is these attempts to cross the boundary of Nature's three-dimensional theory, for which you are compelled to pay the price on a daily basis.

MORAL: Have you ever thought why only a handful of the teeming multitudes achieve tremendous success and are also remembered for centuries? And why are the rest easily forgotten by everyone, including their own relatives, within just a few days of their death? A simple explanation would be, because human life is a play of Time and Energy. Everyone has 80-100 years to live; successful and legendary people do not misuse their Time and Energy, while the rest of us never utilise our Time and Energy efficiently. Instead, we remain immersed in useless thoughts and actions all our lives. I hope you have understood what I am trying to explain. Indeed, for those who are intelligent, a mere hint is enough.

18 The Right Time to Discuss God

Over two thousand five hundred years ago, when I travelled from place to place to guide people towards the right path to the Truth, there was one thing that I had strictly forbidden them – asking me about God and religion. How could I, Gautama Buddha, talk about God when I did not even believe in his existence? But people failed to understand this simple truth and no matter where I went, they would badger me with questions about God and religion. And whenever they did so, I would narrate a story to them. So, today, let me narrate the same story to you.

Once upon a time, a scholar managed to learn the language of the lions. Now that he had made the effort to learn their language, he naturally wanted to put his newly-acquired skills to use. So, off he went into the forest looking for a lion to converse with. Soon, he saw a lion passing by. The man stopped it and asked, "Hello, dear friend, what is your religion? Which God do you believe in?" The lion stared at him with a blank expression and walked away. Concepts like God and religion were alien to the lion, so what could it say? The man was disappointed by the lion's silence. He had learnt the language of the lions so that he could understand their mind and their way of life. But he had failed in his very first attempt to do so. He thought that this lion was probably an introvert. So, he went in search of another lion who could answer his questions. After a few hours, he came across another lion and repeated his questions. But he received a similar response from this lion too–a silent stare. Disappointed once again, the man walked deeper into the forest to search for other lions. In the next few days, he met several lions in the forest. But he was still unable to elicit a response from any of them. They would all stare at him and silently walk away, ignoring him as if he did not exist! Losing patience, the man finally asked one of the lions, "Is there no one amongst you intelligent enough to tell me about your religion and the God you believe in?" The lion replied, "None of us will be able to answer your questions. But why don't you go to our king? He is the most knowledgeable of us all, perhaps he will be able to answer them."

Feeling hopeful, the man immediately went to meet the king of the lions. Standing before the king, he posed his query right away, "O mighty king of lions! Please tell me: who is your God, and what is your religion? I had asked this question to many of your subjects, but to my astonishment, no one seemed to know anything about their own God and religion! I find this very strange."

The king of the lions was truly wise. On hearing the man's questions and seeing his bewildered expression, the king guffawed and said, "The lions could not answer your questions because they have been strongly advised against making unnecessary use of their intelligence. We have been taught to use our intelligence in a prudent manner, only where and when required. In fact, under normal circumstances, we do not need to use our intelligence at all. We are absolutely content with the way Mother Nature has created us; we lead a spontaneous and simple life, and are happy. Therefore, we never feel the need for any God or religion. In fact, we have heard that all of Nature's other creatures, except for human beings, are also content with the way they have been created. Our wise ancestors have told us that humans have brought God and religion into existence because they are not content with their existence. No other creature has ever felt the need for either God or religion."

The king of the lions continued, "To tell you the truth, you humans make unnecessary and excessive use of your intelligence. That is why, you are compelled to lead a contrived, complicated and superficial life. And when you become distressed as a consequence of it, you begin to run helter-skelter looking for refuge. You devise religions and invent God. And because of this, you create more trouble for yourself. One fails to understand why you humans cannot spontaneously lead the kind of life that Nature has granted you. Life itself is the greatest blessing of God. Life itself is religion! If you have been gifted a certain kind of life, why don't you live it as it is? Why do you needlessly make such excessive use of your intelligence to seek religion and God? Religion and God automatically become an integral part of a life that is lived properly. So, dear human, we the lions, who lead our life joyously, do not understand your ways. That is why we have scant interest in you humans, who are such complex creatures. Think deeply. Have we ever come to your city to study you humans? On the other hand, you take great interest in us. You lock us up in cages in the zoo, and enjoy looking at us. You come to the forest to study our behaviour and mannerisms. As for us, we don't even prey on humans, unless it is a matter of life and death! We are actually afraid of eating human meat! Because who knows, after eating it, even our minds may become corrupt and we too may become affected by your warped thinking and begin seeking God and religion, thus complicating our simple, natural lives! Oh no! Even thinking of it makes me shudder! So, I am sorry, brother, but please leave us alone!"

MORAL: For your benefit, my dear readers, I am repeating the lion's advice to the brilliant scholar. Discuss any subject under the sun, except God or religion; you see, your time is precious and so is mine. There are countless other things in this life that we need to know and understand. Let us conquer those frontiers first. Always remember, only those who have overcome life's difficulties may feel the need to understand God and religion.

19 Are You a Puppet?

One day, a little child expectantly looked at his father and asked, "Father, may I go out to play?"

"Why do you ask, my son? I have never forbidden you from playing before," replied his father. "Playing makes children strong. So, you certainly have my permission to play, but your mother may not allow," he said with a grave expression.

The child, who was excited at the prospect of playing with friends, suddenly felt dejected on hearing his father's prediction. He began thinking of ways to convince his mother to allow him to play. Watching the myriad emotions flitting across his child's face, the father began thinking of a way to convince his wife to permit their son to play outside. Suddenly, he remembered a kink in his wife's personality; she suffered from an inferiority complex. He instantly knew what had to be done, and a mischievous smile lit up his face. Eager to quickly put his plan into action, he told his son, "Go to your mother right away and tell her that you want to go out and play, but I have forbidden you from doing so. Your wish will be granted instantly."

The child could not fathom the wisdom behind his father's words, but decided to follow his instructions. Besides, he thought that his mother would not permit him to go out to play, so what was the harm in testing if his father's plan worked or not? So, off he went to his mother and told her in a sad voice, "Mother! Mother, I want to go out and play, but father has refused." The moment she heard this, the mother's inferiority complex came to the fore. She haughtily told her son, "You can definitely go out and play, my child. Let me see, how your father tries to stop you!"

MORAL: In psychological terms, if a person suffers from an inferiority complex, it means he feels that something is lacking within him. You must also understand that a person always pretends to be an expert in those areas where he feels incompetent or useless; or he takes desperate measures; for instance, being assertive and aggressive to compensate for his feeling of inferiority. But this, in worldly parlance, is termed as a superiority complex. There are two important lessons we need to understand from this story. One is, that every manifestation of superiority on the outside, actually indicates an underlying feeling of inferiority. And the second is that, whether a person's internal complex manifests as superiority or inferiority, ultimately, both make him a puppet in the hands of others.

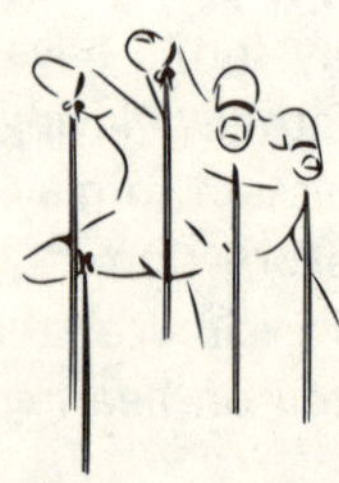

Lao Tzu Imparts Wisdom and How!

This is an anecdote from the life of the eminent Chinese philosopher Lao Tzu, who had a remarkable understanding of matters pertaining to human life. Word of his teachings soon spread far and wide and people began travelling from afar to gain wisdom from him. Lao Tzu, however, had a peculiar way of imparting knowledge. Some would be able to easily understand Lao Tzu's methods, while others would feel even more confused than they were before meeting him! Nevertheless, his fame spread far and wide.

One day, when the king heard of Lao Tzu's teachings, he wondered, "If this mystic is as great as I hear, and the entire kingdom is benefitting from his wisdom, then why should I miss out on this opportunity to receive his wisdom?"

The next day, the king set off for Lao Tzu's house with his entourage. When he reached the mystic's house, the king found him engrossed in digging a pit in his garden. The king ordered his soldiers to inform Lao Tzu of his arrival. He expected Lao Tzu to become ecstatic on learning of his arrival and come rushing to meet him. However, much to the king's chagrin, nothing of that sort happened! The soldier had returned after informing Lao Tzu, but to everyone's surprise, the mystic still continued to dig the pit. Taken aback, the king felt embarrassed at being snubbed before his entourage, but waited patiently for some time. But, even after waiting for a considerable time, there was still no sign of Lao Tzu. The king became furious and began pacing the ground behind Lao Tzu's garden, to attract the mystic's attention. But Lao Tzu was engrossed in digging and seemed oblivious of the king's presence. Some more time elapsed, but there was still no sign of Lao Tzu. Irritated with this behaviour, the king thought, 'Is he a *fakir* or an insane man? I would have understood the wait if Lao Tzu had been doing something important or had been praying. But here, he is merely digging a pit and has kept me waiting all this while!' In the heat of the moment, the king felt that he should leave. However, good sense prevailed and he thought that since he had travelled so far, it would be better to meet the mystic, and resumed pacing even more furiously outside the garden.

Lao Tzu was a true *fakir*. He continued digging with absolute concentration. By now, the king's patience was wearing thin, with every passing moment. He wanted to return to his palace, but curiosity prevented him from doing so. He definitely did not want to leave without finding the reason behind the mystic's strange behaviour. He had come here to gain knowledge, but the *fakir* seemed insane to him, and the king was no longer interested in acquiring knowledge from him. All he wanted to know was why the *fakir* was behaving in this manner. While the king was lost in these thoughts, Lao Tzu had finished digging and immediately came over to receive the king. "My apologies, Your Majesty," he said humbly. "I have made you wait for a long time, so please come inside and rest for a while."

The king, who was now beside himself with rage, ignored Lao Tzu's gentle words and fumed, "I had come here to gain knowledge from you, but now I am not interested. I only want to know why did you keep me waiting for so long, when you were merely involved in the menial task of digging a pit?"

Looking into the eyes of the king for a moment, Lao Tzu smiled and replied, "Your Majesty, please understand that no task is ordinary or extraordinary. And as far as knowledge is concerned, I have already imparted it to you; whether you want to receive and imbibe it or not, is up to you."

Stunned at the reply, several thoughts raced through the king's mind. 'What knowledge is he talking about? And when did he impart it to me, when we had not even met? This man is certainly insane!' However, Lao Tzu's words had fuelled his curiosity further. The king began wondering whether Lao Tzu was really insane or if it was just a pretence. Then another thought crossed his mind. 'Well, if the entire village believes that he is an enlightened mystic, then all of them cannot be insane! Or, perhaps they are? Human beings are unpredictable, after all. Hence, I cannot leave this place today without finding out if it is Lao Tzu who is insane, or is it the villagers; or is it that both are insane... or perhaps none of them are insane!' The king was confused. In order to clear his doubts and prevent them from spinning out of control, he politely asked Lao Tzu, "Tell me, O *Fakir*! What knowledge have you imparted to me? For I have only seen you dig a pit since the time I arrived."

A smile spread across Lao Tzu's calm countenance and in a compassionate tone, he replied, "This is where you have gone wrong, my dear king. You did not observe carefully; actually, I was not digging the pit, but I had become the action of digging. So, had you paid close attention to my absolute concentration at work while digging, then you would have learnt everything; for, nothing in life is worth learning apart from such unwavering concentration and intense passion."

MORAL: If you too want to achieve great success in life, then you must thoroughly understand the relationship between task and action. During the performance of a task, two things come into play – the doer, and the deed being done. In most cases, the doer is present, but he does not concentrate on the deed. Most people fall in this category, and this is the reason why none of their actions ever yield the desired result. The second category includes people who consider the doer and the deed as separate, and they perform their deed accordingly. The number of successful people in this category is quite high. And then, there are those extremely rare people who become so engrossed in the deed, that only the deed remains, and the doer disappears. These are the ones who achieve phenomenal success in life and attain legendary status in their chosen field. These are the three categories of people divided on the basis of the three-dimensional theory. Always remember that a dance performance becomes extraordinary only when the dance exists and the dancer merges in the action. So, all you need to do is to learn this art, and I assure you that you too, will definitely attain phenomenal success in life.

21 What Sort of a Lesson Is This?

There was a strict, disciplinarian mother who lived in a city with her nine-year-old son. Nurturing the sole desire to see her son grow up to become a great man, she watched him like a hawk, pulling him up even for the slightest of mistakes. One day, the son returned home half an hour late from school. Without waiting for an explanation for the delay, the mother seized the opportunity to scold him severely and slapped him hard. In a stern voice, she then told him, "Take this as a lesson. No matter what happens, you must always return home from school on time."

The boy had learnt this lesson well. Blessed with a special quality, if he was reprimanded for a mistake, he made sure he never repeated it. A few days passed by, when one day, the boy returned home with torn clothes and a few bruises on his face. But somehow, he had managed to return home on time. Perturbed by the son's appearance, the mother demanded to know the reason behind his dishevelled look. In a woeful tone, the son replied, "Actually, I was involved in a scuffle with some children in the school." Hearing this, the mother slapped him four to five times, and with a serious expression, told him, "Take this as a lesson. You go to school to study, not to fight!"

With the mother's slaps still ringing in his ears, the poor boy quickly learnt this lesson too. A few days later, the boy brought his quarterly results from school. Unfortunately, he had failed miserably in two subjects. Now, how could the mother tolerate this failure? As soon as she saw her son's mark sheet, she immediately slapped the boy and reprimanded him, "If you fall behind in your class, how will you ever win in the race of life? Remember, you must always excel in class!"

The son was quick to learn this lesson as well, and began studying diligently. His hard work finally paid off, and in the very next semester, he stood first in class! Brimming with happiness, he rushed home to show his report card to his mother. But, do you know what his mother did? Without even glancing once at the report card, she spanked him! Shocked and shaken to the core, the son began to sob. Sputtering between sobs, he asked his mother, "Have you gone insane? I have stood first in class, I deserve a reward, and yet you have slapped me! Why?"

Replying with a melodramatic flourish, she said, "My darling! Learn this lesson well; there is no justice in this world."

MORAL: Incredible, isn't it!? This is the treatment that most children have to endure. They are not being taught the right things even by those who love them. Nature revolves around justice, but children are being taught lessons which are not in tune with Nature. This being the case, how can children achieve success? To put it candidly, until you understand the psychological impact of your teachings and advice on a child, it will be prudent if you do not attempt to teach your child anything. Bear in mind, a child is Nature's gift, leave him in Nature's care to teach him and help him grow in life.

22 The Ticket to Heaven

Soon after my death, I was taken to the afterlife court where my life would be reviewed and I would have to account for my deeds. The court was teeming with souls; every soul's life on earth and its deeds were being minutely analysed, followed by discussions on whether to send those souls to heaven or hell. Joining one of the serpentine queues, I stood nonchalantly, awaiting my turn. The thought whether I would be sent to heaven or hell did not bother me at all. I had been a lawyer in my earthly existence, and knew that on the basis of my prowess at debating, I would definitely earn a place in heaven. Besides, I had diligently fulfilled all my social and religious obligations and was confident, that because of those deeds, I would be sent to heaven. While these thoughts were racing through my mind, it was soon my turn to account for my deeds. Before I knew it, the lists of both my good and bad deeds were being read out. But to my utter surprise, out of my numerous deeds, only one was listed as good! It was my heartfelt joy at a friend's success! All the other deeds performed by me throughout my life, including those I was proud of, had been listed as bad deeds!

Marshalling all my skills as a lawyer, I immediately voiced my objection and challenged their method of listing the deeds. Emboldened by my protest, the hundreds of souls standing in the queue with me also raised their voice in support. Perhaps, their deeds were similar to mine, hence they were supporting me so that they too, could earn a ticket to heaven if I succeeded in my arguments. In an attempt to stem the huge commotion that had erupted because of me, the court quickly gave me permission to present my case. In my opening statement, I asked the court directly, "I read the scriptures daily, frequently donated money and also visited religious places. Don't they count as good deeds?"

To my utter disbelief, the judge replied in a no-nonsense tone, "All of them were your bad deeds. No one ever benefitted from them. But you have already been punished for that in your lifetime on Earth – you lost your precious time, wealth and energy in doing all these deeds. We have nothing to do with that over here."

For a moment, I was at a loss for words. Then I said, "Alright, but what about all those people whom I had helped? Wasn't that a good deed?"

The judge instantly replied, "That is your misconception. This is not your court on Earth; this is the court of true justice. Physical deeds are of no consequence in this realm. It is only your intentions behind them that are considered. And your intention behind helping all the people was to portray a benevolent image, or use the deed as a balm for your ego, or to gain something in return. And you have already reaped the fruit of your actions on Earth in the form of respect that you desired from those you helped. So, you cannot reap the fruit of those actions either. As you have been told, this court appraises a soul only on the basis of its intentions behind its actions. Even if you had not actually helped someone, but had felt a genuine urge to do so selflessly and without any expectations, it would have sufficed to be counted as a good deed here. You read the scriptures every day and made numerous visits to the temple. Instead, if you had discarded your ego and had done something for the greater good with all your heart, then it would have been considered as one of your extraordinary deeds. Unfortunately, you continued to perform good deeds only on a superficial, physical level, which this court considers worthless. Come to think of it, you obtained no pleasure while performing them either. Therefore, understand clearly that you had been blessed with human life to live with good feelings and experience them. But you wasted the opportunity by getting involved in performing the so-called good physical deeds which are merely superficial in nature."

I finally understood that my sneaky ploys held no ground in this supreme court of true justice. This was not a court where what was wrong could be proved right by using brilliant arguments and lies. Truly, I had ruined my life by associating it with superficial physical deeds, instead of good feelings and intentions. Unfortunately, I lost my opportunity, but you still have time. So, whatever you do, do it with sincerity and with good intentions, otherwise, not only will you struggle on Earth, but you will be doomed in this afterlife court as well.

23 The Gurudakshina

Several centuries ago in ancient India, there lived a young boy in a small village who hailed from a poor family. His parents had to struggle hard to make both ends meet, but were happy that their son was highly talented and had great potential. So, they were not really surprised when the young lad succeeded in securing admission in a reputed *gurukul*[1] because of his talent. As was the trend in ancient India, the students living in the *gurukul* were either princes from powerful kingdoms or children from affluent families. Listening to them talk about their opulent lifestyles, the youth too felt an intense desire to earn wealth.

At that time, this young boy did not know that he was being closely observed by someone. Indeed, it was his guru, an extremely wise man, who always kept a close watch on all his students without making them aware that they were being watched. The guru had immediately sensed a growing desire in his young disciple to earn money. After completing his education, when the youth approached him to pay his respects and offer him his *gurudakshina*[2], the guru looked into his disciple's eyes and replied, "Become wealthy for my sake. That will be your *gurudakshina* to me. From this moment, earning wealth should be your sole objective in life." By saying this, the wise guru had allowed the young boy to give vent to his suppressed desire. The guru was aware that there was no sin greater than a desire that is suppressed.

The disciple was extremely elated. He had been granted permission to do exactly what he had wanted to. So, off he went to pursue his dream of becoming a wealthy man. To his good fortune, one day, he heard about a king who was exceedingly generous. He was told that the first person to enter this king's palace early in the morning would be granted whatever he desired. The youth felt his dream of

---

1. **Gurukul** - Traditional style of imparting education in ancient India where all students study under one teacher.
2. **Gurudakshina** - Hindu custom of paying a fee to the teacher by the disciple

becoming rich would finally be realised as he had discovered the key to the treasure trove. So, without a moment's delay, he set off on his journey to the generous king's kingdom. As it was a long journey, it was night by the time he reached his destination. But the youth was unconcerned. After all, dawn was not too far. He settled at a place near the royal palace, waiting for the night to pass. But soon, he felt time was dragging by slowly and the night was too long. I am sure, you too must have experienced this feeling when even an hour seems to stretch into eternity; especially when you are desperately waiting for a great dream to be realised, or for a great desire to be fulfilled. And here was this poor youth, who had to spend an entire night waiting for his dream to come true! Suddenly, a thought crossed his mind. 'Why not camp right outside the palace? Then I can walk in, as soon as the sun rises. If I wait here, I may not wake up on time and someone else will walk into the palace and take the reward! No! I cannot let that happen.' He immediately got up and walked towards the palace, and finding a small clearing near it, pitched a tent and eagerly waited for the sun to shine and usher in a new dawn in his life. As the first rays of the rising sun dispelled the remnants of the night, the youth was the first to walk into the palace.

True to his promise, the king was seated on his throne. When he saw the youth, he immediately asked him to express his desire. Unable to believe what he had just heard, the poor youth was speechless, his heart pounding loudly as he stood before the king and stared at him stupefied. He had travelled so far after hearing tales of the king's generosity, but had been rather sceptical about the veracity of these stories. At the back of his mind, he thought that they had been only rumours. The dazed youth suddenly realised that the king was speaking to him again. "Do not hesitate. Ask for whatever you want!" he urged.

The youth's heart began pounding hard against his chest. He was desperately thinking about things that he wanted. He was very poor, and his wants were many. 'A thousand gold coins would make me rich,' he thought happily to himself. But no sooner had he decided this, than avarice wriggled its way into his heart and mind. 'Why just a thousand? When the king is willing to give anything I want, why not ask for ten thousand gold coins?' he thought, as he bit his lip in uncertainty.

But, by now, greed had firmly entrenched itself within him, and under its spell, he even increased it to a million gold coins! However, even this, he felt was insufficient! Finally, it struck him! He knew exactly what he wanted. Feeling sure and confident about his wish, he demanded that the king give him his entire kingdom!

Much to the youth's surprise, as soon as the king heard his request, he joyously proclaimed, "Oh wow! I am finally free now!"

The youth was amazed at the king's response. He was, after all, a bright pupil of a wise guru. Alarm bells began ringing in his mind when the king immediately agreed to his request. He thought, 'There is definitely something wrong with this kingdom, otherwise, why would the king be so happy to give it to me? Why should I take the plunge into something totally unknown, just to relieve him of his burden?' As soon as this realisation dawned upon the youth, he immediately apologised to the king and turning back, took to his heels. In fact, he was so deeply affected by this experience that he lost his desire to earn wealth and power for good. He was also glad that his cautious approach and presence of mind had saved him.

MORAL: If you have a desire, you certainly must fulfil it, but you must also possess the presence of mind and intelligence to quickly free yourself from it. Greatness lies in becoming free from your desires. But yes, do bear in mind that both, suppressing a desire or living only to fulfil that desire, has a devastating effect on life. In fact, a human being's life is simple and straightforward and has no room for unhappiness. Life is governed by the mind, and this world has a very limited understanding of how the mind functions. A human being's mind is not complex at all. But, since it functions in accordance with laws which ordinary people do not have any knowledge of, the mind seems complicated. Once a person becomes familiar with these laws, complications will automatically come to an end.

In the present context, please understand this straight and simple law, that if the mind desires something, you cannot free yourself from that desire without fulfilling it and realising its futility. One can even fulfill it for a moment by experiencing it on a mental level and comprehending its futility. But freedom from a desire that has emerged from within at the moment can only be attained after it is fulfilled. This is a simple and clear truth, but despite this, everyone is attempting to become free of desires without fulfilling them; and the greater the effort to become free from those desires, the deeper they get entrenched. This is the reason why human beings are unable to attain freedom from a desire that has gripped them, despite the pain it causes them. But you are intelligent, so do not fall into the rut of attempting to become free of a desire without fulfilling it; instead, be conscious while fulfilling it. And soon, you will liberate yourself from every aspect that is meaningless in life. At the same time, do not get permanently caught up in enjoying the experience of a fulfilled desire. Otherwise, you will spend your entire life wanting for more. And when death arrives at your doorstep you will continue to remain in a discontented state of mind. Hence, if you find a desire rising within you, fulfil it and experience it, but also remain focussed on becoming free from it, after enjoying the happiness of a fulfilled desire. Additionally, be fully aware of yourself and ensure that no new desires emerge from within. This is the ultimate state which every human life must attain.

24 It's All in the Mind!

There once lived a woman with her teenage son. Suddenly, one day she suffered a paralytic stroke in her right hand. Several doctors made numerous attempts to cure her, but to no avail. As a last resort, her family took her to a psychiatrist, who hypnotised the woman and asked her to reveal all the important activities which she used to perform with her right hand before it became paralysed.

Recollecting events from the past, the woman started weeping copiously. Narrating an incident buried deep in the recesses of her mind, she revealed that she had once mercilessly beaten her son with her right hand when she had found that he had stolen something. Sobbing inconsolably, the woman said, "I felt so awful after beating up my child in this beastly manner, that I wished my right hand be severed right away."

Voila, the psychiatrist had found the root cause of her ailment! He realised that her malaise stemmed from the years of guilt that the woman had harboured within herself. Speaking in a soothing tone to the woman still under hypnosis, he consoled her and said, "Why don't you look at it this way, your beating him up has actually saved your son." The woman, still under the hypnotic trance, appeared puzzled by this remark. The psychiatrist continued, speaking softly. "Yes, you did the right thing, for, had you not beaten up your son that day, he would have, in all likelihood grown up to become a thief. So, your right hand has in fact, saved your son's life."

The woman was distinctly relieved on hearing this. With her guilt assuaged to a certain extent, she was completely cured of her paralysis within a few days!

MORAL: One's own state of mind and one's psychological experiences have a definite impact on one's health and they are often the root cause behind most physical ailments. Therefore, a mindful, conscious person is the one who can identify and understand the psychological force which is at work behind every impending disease, and based on his present state of mind, can even predict which illnesses he is likely to contract in the future. That is why, it is aptly said, "To lead a good life, it is better to know yourself first, instead of trying to understand the world."

25 The Story of Vishnu and Narada

When you are the God of your world, how can any other God have the right to interfere with your world? The law of the world states that you are responsible for your own psychological deeds and have to pay the price for them too. But man's inability to understand this straightforward and simple truth has made him behave in a ludicrous manner. He doesn't endeavour to do what he can, but depends on God and prayers to help him, without the realisation that the one he assumes to be God and worships, is powerless to do anything to make his life better!

Let me explain this by narrating an interesting story from one of the well-known Hindu *Puranas*[1]. Lord Vishnu, also known as Narayana, has been depicted as God in the story, and there is his devotee Narada,

1. Puranas - Sanskrit sacred writings on Hindu mythology and folklore of varying date and origin, the most ancient of which dates back to 4th century AD.

who keeps chanting God's name, "Narayana... Narayana.." day in, day out. Impressed by his own chanting, Narada gradually starts believing that he is the greatest devotee of Vishnu in the entire world. One day, to reinforce his mistaken belief, he pays a visit to Lord Vishnu. Narada prostrates himself before Lord Vishnu, and suffused with pride, egoistically asks, "Dear Lord, is there anyone who is a greater devotee of yours than I am?"

Laughing uproariously at Narada's vanity, Vishnu replies, "There are thousands!"

Hearing his dear Lord's response, Narada's arrogance takes a beating. But then, he quickly reassures himself with the thought that perhaps the Lord is saying this in jest, so he regains his composure and says calmly, "Surely, you are speaking in jest, O Lord!" When Vishnu realises that Narada has dismissed his statement in a light vein, he replies in a solemn tone, "I am not speaking in jest. I am serious! There are actually millions of people in the world who are far greater devotees of mine than you are."

Deeply shocked and hurt, Vishnu's words pierce Narada's ego like an arrow. Folding his hands in deep reverence, he says, "Please forgive me, my dear Lord, but I would certainly like to meet just one such devotee out of those millions."

The sarcasm in Narada's words do not go amiss, but Vishnu replies with a smile, "As you wish." So, off they go together. As the first rays of the sun pierce the remnants of the night, they reach a field where a farmer is tilling his field. Finding a suitable spot nearby, Vishnu and Narada settle down comfortably under the shade of a tree and quietly observe the farmer. Soon, it is noon but the sun, beating down relentlessly, makes little difference to the farmer who is toiling hard in the field. Meanwhile, with the passage of time, Narada's confidence increases and he begins to feel complacent, as the farmer has not uttered the name of Lord Narayana even once. Feeling overjoyed, he thinks that his dear Lord had been pulling his leg, after all. But he decides to keep quiet and watch the drama unfold for a little while longer.

In the meantime, the farmer's wife arrives with his lunch. Sitting under the shade of a tree, the couple eat their meal together.

Once they have eaten, the farmer rests for a while before resuming his work in the field, while his wife makes her way back home. Hours pass by, but the farmer continues to work in his field for the rest of the day. It is only when the last rays of the sun melt away into the approaching darkness, that the farmer packs his tools and heads home. On reaching home, he takes a bath, eats his meal and spends quality time with his children before turning in for the night.

At daybreak, the farmer is back in the field ploughing diligently, just like the previous day. This routine continues for the next three days as Vishnu and Narada observe him from a distance. Narada, however, is beside himself with joy as the farmer has not uttered the Lord's name even once in those three days! Unable to contain his happiness any longer, Narada finally loses his patience and in a bold tone asks Vishnu, "Dear Lord, why have you been fooling with me and making me waste so much time? In the past three days, this farmer has not uttered your name even once!"

Smiling benignly, Vishnu replies calmly, "You talk of three days, Narada? This man has not uttered my name even once in his entire life. I have been keenly observing him ever since his birth. Even when he faces adversities, he does not think of me, but instead, reflects upon his own mistakes. At times, even I am surprised at his behaviour! For, he never wavers from his path, but keeps creating and building his world. So, do you understand, Narada? He is my true devotee as he is aware that he is solely responsible for creating his world; therefore, he keeps working relentlessly towards this objective. Neither does he disturb me, nor does he ever expect anything from me. And, he most certainly never wanders around aimlessly, chanting "Narayana... Narayana" without shouldering any responsibility, like you!"

MORAL: According to Nature's laws, deeds and duties are the only true forms of worship. A truly pious person is the one who is immersed in the joy of performing his deeds and discharging his duties. In such a man's life, there is no necessity or place for any other form of worship, because every deed of his itself, becomes worship. Therefore, if you acquire an understanding of the most profound level of psychology, then you will understand that man can be religious, life can be religious, even teachings can be religious, but there is no such thing as religion by itself. So, read this statement over and over again and understand Nature's ultimate truth.

26 Kabir and the Dead Cow

It would be no exaggeration to say that the great saint, Kabir was Nature's gift to humankind. He is revered even today by millions in India who hold his verses close to their hearts. Each one of Kabir's couplets transcends time and reveals eternal spiritual truths far more engagingly and effectively than a thousand so-called religious scriptures put together. If there is a person who can be considered to be a prodigy in the world of philosophy and poetry, it is none other than Kabir, who lived in Benares, now known as Varanasi.

As a child, Kabir loved loitering around the tiny by-lanes of Benares, the ancient Indian city, keenly observing everything from his own unique perspective. And it was because of his sharp intelligence and extraordinary perception that he got the opportunity to train under the great saint, Ramananda Swami of Benares. Unlike other children, Kabir fearlessly voiced his doubts about almost everything that he was taught and also asked numerous questions at every opportunity.

One day, his guru had organised the *shraddh* ceremony to pay homage to his father who had passed away. This ritual, in which priests are invited for a feast is followed with great reverence; the common belief underlying it being, that when priests are fed, the food reaches the departed soul. The guru had, thus, invited several priests for the feast so that the delicacies fed to them could reach his late father. Preparations for the feast commenced early in the morning, and Kabir and the rest of the disciples were entrusted with different responsibilities. Kabir was assigned the task of fetching milk for the priests. So, early in the morning, he set off towards the market carrying an empty pail with him.

As milk is an important ingredient in the *shraddh* ceremony, the guru had asked Kabir to return quickly with the milk. But the guru was in for a surprise. Much to his dismay, even after an hour had passed, Kabir had not yet returned with the pail of milk. The guru became upset; he had not expected Kabir to be so irresponsible, but still waited patiently for him. Even when several hours passed by and Kabir had not yet returned, the guru became annoyed. He decided that he would take Kabir to task when he returned. However, Kabir had not arrived even after the sun was high up in the sky, and it was time to serve the meal to the priests. The ceremony was concluded, and the guru had to be content with feeding the priests everything except milk. As soon as the priests had left, the guru, now worried about Kabir's whereabouts, set off to search for him in the narrow by-lanes of Benares along with a few disciples. Soon, they found Kabir seated on the roadside beside a dead cow. Holding his head in his hands, he was intently observing the cow while the empty pail lay beside him. Taken aback by the sight, the guru could not understand what Kabir was doing near the dead cow. He went and stood beside him, to take a closer look at what it was that had kept Kabir preoccupied for so long. But Kabir was so engrossed in observing the dead cow that he did not notice his guru's presence. "What are you doing here?" demanded the guru. On hearing his guru's voice, Kabir was jolted back to reality. He replied innocently, "I am waiting for the cow to give milk, O guru!"

Surprised by the reply, the guru, affectionately stroked Kabir's head and said, "Since when do dead cows give milk, my dear boy?"

Kabir replied with a naughty gleam in his eyes, "If your dead father can have meals, then this dead cow can certainly give milk." Kabir's words struck Ramananda Swami like a thunderbolt. Embracing Kabir, he said, "My dear boy, you have opened my eyes today. Clearly, you have already taken the first giant step on the path towards wisdom."

MORAL: Well, Kabir had, even as a child, taken his first step on the path to wisdom, but when will you? If you really want to set forth on the path to wisdom, then, instead of blindly following age-old customs, use your inner intelligence to evaluate everything. After all, attaining wisdom is your birthright!

27 In Search of God

In 8th century Iraq, there lived a famous Sufi saint by the name of Rabia Basri. An enlightened soul, she had a unique but simple way of explaining even the most profound truths, which had won her the respect and adulation of the people of Iraq.

One evening, people noticed Rabia intently searching for something in the veranda of the *khanqah* (lodge). For a while, everyone watched her out of inquisitivenes while she was engrossed in her search. Finally, a man, unable to contain his curiosity any longer, went up to Rabia and asked her what she was looking for.

Without pausing a moment, her gaze focussed on the floor, Rabia replied, "I am searching for my lost needle."

Hearing this, several people came forward to help her search the needle. However, despite searching every nook and cranny for a long time, they could not find the needle. People soon became tired and in frustration, one of them asked her, "Are you sure you lost the needle here? Where exactly did you lose it?"

With her gaze still on the floor of the veranda, Rabia instantly replied, "Inside my bedroom."

Stunned on hearing this, the group of people looked at Rabia in disbelief. A few even laughed at her and called her dim-witted, while others pondered over her strange reply. Finally, one of them asked her in an acerbic tone, "How can you find the needle here in the veranda, when you have lost it inside your bedroom?"

Rabia replied confidently, "I am certain I shall find it here. I need to search for it a little more carefully." She then looked towards the bedroom and continued, "It is dark inside the bedroom, so I will not find the needle in the darkness. But here, in the brightly-lit veranda, I am sure to find it. All of you must now stop wasting time in idle talk and help me with my search! I am certain I shall find it very soon."

Most people stopped their search, thinking that Rabia had definitely lost her senses. Instead, they stood aside to watch Rabia make a mockery of herself. Only those who had blind faith in Rabia, continued to assist her in the search for the lost needle. But it was not long before they gave up, and Rabia was alone searching for the needle. Unaffected by the ridicule, Rabia continued to diligently search for the needle, confident of finding it. People stood watching Rabia's antics for some time with a smirk on their faces. Finally, a few took pity on her, thinking that she had certainly lost her mental balance and tried to dissuade her from searching for the needle in the wrong place. "It was lost in the bedroom, so let us all go there and search for it," one of them said.

Cutting him short, Rabia interjected, "It is pitch-dark inside the bedroom, whereas there is light in this veranda; it is better I search for it in the light than in the dark."

Exasperated with Rabia's behaviour, one of the onlookers spoke in a derisive tone, "You are insane, Rabia! It does not matter whether a place is in darkness or in light. Things can be found only in the place where they are lost."

Hearing this, Rabia broke into laughter and said, "At first, even I believed this. But your actions and behaviour have confused me. Since aeons, you people have been searching for God in the blinding lights of mosques, churches and temples, while you have lost Him in the dark recesses of your mind. So, I thought, why not try doing something similar? But, as I did not want to take a risk in matters related to God, I chose to experiment with a needle. If I find the needle in this well-lit veranda today, then I shall take the risk of seeking God in mosques and mausoleums; otherwise, I will quietly continue to search for him within the depths of my mind."

Rabia's words had a powerful impact on people. Standing motionless in the quiet still night, they tried to assimilate the truth in Rabia's words. None dared to refute her. They had realised the folly of their ways and fell at her feet in obeisance.

MORAL: Although we do not have Rabia in our midst now, we do have this wonderful anecdote that she has left behind, to understand and learn from. So, with the aid of this story, why don't we all begin searching for God within the depths of our mind, instead of visiting mosques, temples and churches? After all, we are human beings and we do possess the power to think! For how long can we keep ignoring these profound teachings imparted by saints and *fakirs*?

28 The Poor Woodcutter and Lord of Death

Once upon a time, in a remote village in India, there lived an old woodcutter. He lived alone in a small dilapidated hut with no family to call his own and no wealth to speak of. Getting on in years, his health too was deteriorating fast. But in spite of it all, he had no choice but to fend for himself by cutting and gathering wood from the forest. Besides, he had to carry the wood and sell it in the market in the evening to be able to afford a square meal for himself at night. Clearly, his life was filled with unimaginable hardships. During the monsoon, his plight would worsen. Often, the wood that he cut, would become wet, making it impossible for him to sell it in the market on the same day. Thus, he would be forced to go hungry to bed. So, during the monsoon, it was not unusual for him to go without food for several days at a stretch! Indeed, enduring travails in life at the ripe old age of seventy years, had left him deeply exhausted. Extremely distressed with his life, he would often cry out loud saying, 'O Lord of Death! Why don't you come for me? Are you angry with me? You have taken so many people far younger than me. So, why do you ignore me? Am I your enemy?' The pain he felt was clearly reflected in his poignant entreaties.

One day, there was an astounding twist to his mundane life. Sitting despondently under a tree, he was, as usual, invoking the Lord of Death to come and set him free from his sordid life. He kept beseeching the Lord of Death to release him from his miserable existence. As he continued with his rant, he suddenly felt a hand on his shoulder. Startled, the old man turned around to see who it was and nearly jumped out of his skin. A giant of a man was glowering down at him with eyes that resembled burning coals. With his heart fluttering with fear, the woodcutter fumbled for words, but finally managed to ask, "Who...who are you?"

In a booming voice that reverberated in the forest, the man replied, "I am the Lord of Death! I was just passing by, when I heard your poignant entreaty. The time of your death has not yet arrived. You still have many more years to live. But your pathetic condition has pulled at my heartstrings. Come, I will take you with me now."

Shocked, the woodcutter was jolted back to his senses on hearing these words. He was an experienced old man and instantly realised his folly. He fell at the feet of the Lord of Death and said, "Oh! Actually, you see, I have not eaten a morsel since the past few days, hence, I uttered these words in desperation. I am a very happy man. So, please understand that I have no intention of dying anytime in the near future. My outburst was merely due to my frustration. In the future, please do not heed my pleas, and do not take the trouble to visit me again. I will never call out to you, but in case I do so by mistake, please ignore my pleas."

Hiding a grin, the Lord of Death replied, "As you wish," and instantly vanished into thin air. It was because of the woodcutter's scary experience that his life underwent a remarkable transformation. Relieved that his life had been spared, not only did he walk with a spring in his step, but also stopped snivelling about his situation. Surprisingly, he never felt distressed after the incident. His mind and his life had changed forever. Although there was no discernible change in his circumstances and he still struggled to make ends meet, everything within him had changed. Why was this so? That was because, after having encountered death at such close quarters, the woodcutter had realised even though he possessed nothing, he was alive. And if one is alive and a sense of being alive still exists, then what else does one need?

MORAL: Life is the most valuable gift that Nature has bestowed upon humankind. Ironically, a person realises its value only when he is on the verge of death. A person who does not value his own life can never understand the value of the people or objects around him. Strangely, a human being considers all that he possesses as worthless, and what he loses seems priceless to him. But the undeniable truth is that he can only live with what he possesses.

29 Who Is the Fool?

This story dates back to about 800 years ago, when Mullah Nasruddin, a man of great wisdom, often roamed the desert regions of Turkey, Iran and Baghdad. He had a unique way of imparting knowledge; he would never sermonise or preach to people. Instead, he tried to impart wisdom using his formidable sense of humour. Mullah believed that wisdom imparted using wit and humour left a lasting impression on the minds of people. And, he was absolutely right in thinking so. In the entire history of humankind, Mullah is the only one who has been able to successfully interlace wisdom with wit and humour.

One day, Mullah was passing through the streets of Baghdad on his donkey. In keeping with his maverick personality, Mullah had a queer way of sitting astride his donkey; he would sit facing the hind side of the donkey! Needless to say, one glance at him riding his donkey was enough to send laughter rippling through the crowd.

Riding the donkey in his usual way, one day, Mullah travelled to the market. Needless to say, some people, looking at him smiled, while some were laughing aloud. When he was passing by a shop selling dates, Mullah alighted from his donkey and purchased some dates. In order to pay the vendor, he confidently inserted his hand inside the pockets of his pyjamas. But alas, the coins were not there. He immediately sat down on the floor, pulled his shoes out and bringing them close to his eyes, started peering inside them. However, the coins were not there either! Meanwhile, a huge crowd had begun to gather around him. His style of riding the donkey had already attracted enough attention. And now, his ongoing antics in the middle of the market square were drawing a large crowd. Soon, the crowd swelled in number, as they watched him, agog with curiosity, wanting to know what Mullah was doing, sitting in the middle of the road.

The stage was now set. On one hand, Mullah continued to search everywhere for the coins, and on the other, he was also eating the dates he had bought. This naturally did not go down well with the shopkeeper who angrily eyed Mullah and thought, 'Look at this man searching for coins in strange places! Besides, he is even eating my dates without paying for them! If he does not find the coins, how will I recover the dates from his stomach?' Mullah, in the meantime, had also pulled out his skull cap and expectantly began to search inside it. Seeing this, the shopkeeper could not contain his irritation any longer and yelled out in disgust at Mullah, "Why are you searching for the coins in such strange places, you fool? Why don't you just look inside the pockets of your waistcoat?"

Mullah's face broke into a gentle smile as he replied, "Oh! Why didn't you suggest this earlier?" He then inserted his hand inside his waistcoat pocket and found the coins he had been searching for all this while! Smiling gleefully, Mullah handed over the coins to the shopkeeper, nonchalantly adding, "I knew the coins were there all along. I was just taking a chance, you see!"

The crowd roared with laughter on hearing this. An old man from the crowd shouted out wryly, "This man seems to be insane. When he knew the coins were inside his waistcoat pocket, why was he searching for them in the unlikeliest of places?"

Now, it was Mullah's turn to react. It was time to deliver the message for which he had enacted this farce. Adopting a grave tone, he addressed the crowd, "Wow! How astonishing you people are! I am being called insane, merely because I was not looking for coins in the place where they actually were. But, please first observe your own lives. You know that God resides in your heart, but still, you continue to search for him in mosques. If I am insane, then all you people are totally deranged. My foolishness was confined to searching only for a few coins, but you people are far greater fools, as you are searching for the world's most important truth where it does not exist!"

MORAL: Even today, Mullah Nasruddin's rationale stands as a lesson and a warning to all of humanity. Mullah had become a laughing stock before a few people, but what about the futile exercise that people of all religions and communities have been indulging in, with great fanfare and pride for thousands of years, searching for God in places other than within themselves? Isn't this more hilarious?

30 The Farmer, the Mouse and the Snake!

Once upon a time, a mouse and a snake made a nesting hole in a farmer's field. Unbeknownst to the farmer, the snake and the mouse would hide in their holes during the day, while the farmer toiled in his field. They would only venture out in the field at night.

One day, it so happened that the farmer had gone to another village for some work. By the time he returned, night had fallen and he had to cross his field en route to his house. Meanwhile, the snake had just slithered out of his hole, and on seeing the farmer, bit him. Stung by the bite, the farmer peered down in the darkness to see what had bitten him, when he saw the mouse scurrying away. Assuming that it was just an insignificant mouse bite, the farmer dismissed it and soon forgot about it. Fortunately for him, the snake was not venomous, so the farmer remained unharmed by the bite.

A few months later, the farmer had to once again pass through his field at night, and this time, the mouse bit him. But when the farmer looked down, he did not see the mouse, but saw the snake slithering away. The farmer thought that he had been bitten by the snake and collapsed on the spot out of fear. Despite being treated by several physicians for months, the farmer showed no signs of recovery. After all, how could he recover? He was being treated for a snake bite when he had not been bitten by one! It was merely his delusion! He could recover only after freeing himself of his delusion.

MORAL: Take a closer look at your own life and mind; you will easily understand that it is not only your physical and mental ailments, but even the worries and pains that you harbour in life are the result of your own delusions. In reality, most of these do not even exist. So, throughout your life, you continue being treated for problems that are actually non-existent. How can a non-existent ailment be cured? How can a non-existent problem be solved? It is simply not possible! This is the reason why it becomes well-nigh impossible to free yourself from sorrows or mental and physical illnesses once you are afflicted by them. Even as you endeavour to become free from them by trying different forms of treatment, their grip over you becomes stronger with every attempt you make. Thus, if you really wish to free yourself from this endless cycle of struggles and problems in life, first, you need to find out whether you are actually in trouble or not. What if your troubles are merely an illusion? When you reflect upon your problems, you will realise that most of them are merely delusions that you have harboured in your mind. So, just break away from these delusions and you will be instantly free from most of your problems and struggles in life.

31 When Prayer Flows from Within

Fortunate are those who lead a life free of worries. But there are also those whose lives are fraught with extreme hardships. This story is about the great Indian saint, Ramakrishna Paramahansa. There was a phase in his life when he had to face untold difficulties and had led an impoverished existence. Some of his well-wishers could not bear to see him lead such a frugal life, so they had him appointed as the priest of the royal temple.

Over the years, the royal temple had acquired a formidable reputation for its meticulous arrangements and strict adherence to the timing of the *aarti.*[1] In accordance with the tradition of the temple, every day at seven o'clock sharp in the morning and evening, the sound of conch shells reverberated in the air, as the devout gathered to participate in the *aarti.* Thousands of devotees thronged the temple at that hour, and as the priest of the temple, Ramakrishna was expected to preside over the *aarti* at the scheduled hour.

But Ramakrishna was one of a kind! He could not be insincere in the execution of his duties. For him, the dictate of his heart was his command, and obeying that command alone was worship and duty for him. But, perhaps, the authorities who had appointed Ramakrishna as the priest were not aware of this facet of his personality. At seven o'clock sharp, a throng of devotees would religiously gather at the temple as they had been doing for the past so many years. However, this time, they were in for a rude shock. Ramakrishna was not present to conduct the famous *aarti* at the scheduled time! And if that was not shocking enough, Ramakrishna remained absent from the daily ritual for a few more days. While everyone was still mulling over this unprecedented development, Ramakrishna suddenly appeared in the temple one day in the afternoon, and began conducting the *aarti*. At that time, there were barely twenty devotees in the temple. But what happened a few days later was even more shocking and left everyone dumbfounded. In the wee hours of the morning, at 2 am to be precise, when there was pin-drop silence in the temple, with not a soul in sight, Ramakrishna's voice pierced the silence of the still, dark night, fervently

---

1. Aarti - a Hindu religious ritual of worship, a part of puja, in which light from wicks soaked in ghee or camphor is offered to one or more deities.

reciting holy chants in praise of the deity! This erratic schedule soon became the hallmark of the ancient temple.

Devotees who regularly thronged the temple every day were disconcerted by the irregular timing of worship at the royal temple. Unable to keep up with this unpredictable schedule, they soon lost interest, and gradually their numbers dwindled. They thought that if the rituals did not take place on time, what was the use of coming to the temple at all?

One day, the temple had an unexpected visitor for the seven o'clock *aarti*–the queen herself! But that was hardly a matter of concern for Ramakrishna. He did arrive at the temple at seven-thirty, but even on that day, Ramakrishna did not perform the *aarti*. The bewildered queen also noticed that the number of devotees in attendance had dwindled considerably. On enquiring what the matter was, she was informed that this had become a regular occurrence ever since the eccentric Ramakrishna was appointed priest. Apprising her of the situation, the devotees told her that Ramakrishna never conducted the *aarti* on schedule. They further informed her, that at times, he suddenly chose to conduct the *aarti* in the middle of the night. It was this irregularity in the timing of the rituals that had left the devotees confused and disappointed, hence they had stopped visiting the temple.

Shocked on hearing this, the queen demanded an explanation from Ramakrishna in the presence of everyone. Ramakrishna simply laughed and said, "One can worship only when one feels the urge to worship. One cannot fix a time for it. Sometimes, one feels the urge to worship five times in a day, and at other times, one does not feel anything even for an entire week at a stretch. So, who am I to conduct the rituals at the stipulated time? I am merely a medium that channels the prayers. I channel them as and when they come to me."

Reflecting upon his words, the queen was deeply affected by Ramakrishna's explanation. She looked into the saint's eyes and was stunned to see the truth in them. She suddenly realised what true worship was all about. Within no time, she had Ramakrishna appointed as the permanent priest of the temple. Simultaneously, she also did away with restrictions relating to the timing of the rituals. In fact, there were occasions when even the doors of the sanctum sanctorum remained shut, but Ramakrishna's prayers continued to flow from within. After all, a true devotee like Ramakrishna did not need to open those doors for his prayers to flow. The prayers of a person who is honest, inevitably bear fruit. So, he was bound to become the great saint Ramakrishna Paramahansa. And, by merely being in the company of this great saint, his disciple, Narendra was bound to metamorphose into the illustrious Swami Vivekananda.

MORAL: No matter what the deed is, if you have to force yourself to perform it, then it clearly means that the mind is not fully engaged in it. And when a man performs a deed reluctantly, it does not lead to a positive outcome. At the same time, it must also be understood that a person cannot immerse himself in a deed according to his will and at the time of his choosing. When we persuade others to 'apply their mind to work', it merely reflects our ignorance of psychology. The very idea that you can forcefully immerse yourself in performing a deed is erroneous. This, in fact, is a complex arithmetic. Actually, the mind can become engaged only at its own time and only in the field of its interest. If a person has a keen interest in music, it is not necessary that his interest in studies or business will also be at the same level. And the fact is, that even though this arithmetic is so unequivocal, it can neither be understood nor taught. It can only be experienced in the depths of one's own mind. The more one experiences it deep within oneself, the more awakened one becomes. Therefore, it goes without saying that the more awakened one is, the more one is entitled to happiness and success in life.

32 The Boy Who Made His Dream Come True

History, across the ages, is witness to the fact that there have been hundreds of kings who have captured kingdoms and have forced people into submission. But there have been extremely few who have managed to capture the hearts of people and cast a spell over them. This story is about one such emperor, who not only dared to dream big, but also ensured that the dreams of young children – and all those who were young at heart – came alive. He was none other than Walt Disney, who, even after a century, continues to rule over the hearts of millions across the globe.

Born on December 5, 1901, Walt Disney was one among the five children of Flora and Elias Disney. Although his father was a very hard-working man, success in business eluded him, and as a result, the family could barely make both ends meet. As a consequence, Walt Disney's childhood lacked the comforts that children of his age enjoyed. Playing with toys and wearing good clothes were luxuries he could only dream of. However, when he was seven years old, his life took an interesting turn. His aunt Margaret gifted him a sketchbook and a few colouring pencils. Now, for a child who had never played with toys before, this was a dream come true. The colours and the sketchbook opened up a glorious new world in the life of Walt Disney. He became fascinated by the art of sketching.

When Walt Disney grew up, he was duly enrolled in a school. But due to his family's poor pecuniary condition, he was compelled to sell newspapers and eggs every morning before leaving for school. By the end of the day, this hectic schedule left the young Walt Disney extremely fatigued. However, with the family fortunes dipping even further, Walt had to drop out of school and work full-time with his father. Not surprisingly, he had to endure several bitter experiences while selling eggs and delivering newspapers, when he ran into many of his school friends on the street, or in the homes that he visited. Undoubtedly, these encounters were extremely embarrassing for him, but Walt bore them all with a smile. At times, the smile would become clouded by sadness for a few fleeting moments, as he would forlornly watch other children play with toys. He would, however, quickly shake himself out of his despondency and come to terms with the reality of his life. Unfortunately, however, it was not just toys that were missing from his life; he did not have friends to play with, either. To keep up his good spirits, he would watch the trains that passed by his house and sketch them. Very soon, sketching turned into his hobby, and the train became his dream.

However, difficulties seemed to have a special affinity with Walt's life; they snatched away even these two things that gave him happiness. On the threshold of youth, Walt was burdened with even more work and had to hold multiple jobs to make both ends meet. At the age of seventeen, he joined the Red Cross and travelled to France with its medical team for a year. It was during his stint in France, that he finally found the time to once again pursue his passion for sketching. He spent his spare time in sketching portraits of his colleagues, but soon tired of it, became dissatisfied and yearned to explore his art further.

On Disney's return from France, he decided to give vent to his passion and turn it into a source of livelihood. He managed to get himself a job as a cartoonist in a newspaper, and even learnt animation. Eventually, he set up several animation studios of his own, but they all shut down due to some reason or the other. Despite the setbacks, Walt Disney never let the flame of his passion die. With full confidence in his talent, he did not give in to depression, but plodded along with an optimistic attitude. At the age of 23, he decided to try his luck in Hollywood. No doubt, it was an uphill task to establish himself with neither money nor a godfather to back him. But eventually, Hollywood had to doff its hat to Walt's passion and talent, and today, the world is witness to the history that he created.

This was just the beginning of his journey, for, the best was yet to come! The days of penury had now become a distant memory. Walt Disney's passion for drawing had already catapulted him to the pinnacle of success as the king of animation. It was at this point that a long-forgotten dream began to haunt Walt Disney once again–the train. Nothing could stop him from fulfilling it now. Soon, he purchased a large farm and laid the foundation for a 1400 ft long track on which his dream train chugged ahead along with his dreams and aspirations! This train was no ordinary train. It was built with the latest technology and was equipped with ultra-modern facilities. Walt often used to have his dinner on the moving train. In fact, among the celebrities and iconic stalwarts of Hollywood, it became a matter of great prestige to be seen having dinner in it.

Walt Disney, however, was unstoppable. He had fulfilled his dream, and now, wanted to do something for the world. How could he forget his childhood, when, as a child he had been bereft of the joys of playing with toys? Therefore, as an ode to his childhood and to all the children of the world, he decided to construct the world's biggest playground on 160 acres of land and called it Disneyland. Since then, the place is considered to be a veritable children's paradise which has cast a spell over every child across the world, bringing cheer and happiness into their lives.

MORAL: This is the greatest example of how a person can not only dream and fulfil his dreams, but also share them. After reading this story, why shouldn't Disney be called the 'Emperor of Dreamers'? In spite of having faced adverse circumstances, Disney could realise his dreams and scale the pinnacle of his passion. Walt Disney's life is an exemplary model of diligence, determination and unwavering focus. Truly, if one nurtures a passion, harbours a dream and immerses himself in fulfilling that dream with diligence, then is there anyone who cannot become like Walt Disney? As for the rest of us, who nurture a thousand passions and a million dreams, well our condition is hardly a secret.

33 The World's First Robot

Did you know that the world's first robot was created 5000 years ago in Egypt? And, do you know who invented the first robot? If you don't, then read on.

Five millennia ago, the Egyptian religious leaders felt that they needed to wield absolute control over the people of their land. There were many things they wanted people to do and believe in, without asking questions. In order to force people to obey their diktats, they fabricated a robot using cotton, clothes and other available materials. The end product was a huge robot with the body of a human being and the face of a fierce jackal.

In the darkness of the night, the religious leaders installed the giant robot in the center of the village. The next morning, the robot attracted a huge crowd, who curiously eyed the creature that had appeared out of nowhere. According to their plan, one of the religious leaders hidden inside the robot, began instructing them on everything that the leaders wanted them to do. Guileless and innocent, people did not realise that it was their religious leader who was inside the robot reading out instructions to them. Easily taken in by the ploy of their leaders, the people believed it to be the divine command of God and felt compelled to follow its dictates. Today, years later, the situation is no different. Religious leaders are still ruling the roost, and we are blindly following them without even a murmur.

MORAL: This was the story of how robots were first created. But this small incident actually sheds light upon two deeply significant facts. First, it demonstrates the low intelligence of people 5000 years ago, who were so easily duped by a simple robot. This incident, therefore, proves that the mental evolution of a human being has also been a gradual, step-by-step process, just like his physical evolution. The second most important fact is the exploitative mentality of religious leaders, which drives them to manipulate people for their personal gains, and is an age-old phenomenon which is prevalent to date.

As man continued to evolve, religious leaders too, continued to discover increasingly advanced robots in different forms to ensnare human beings. Some examples of these robots are introduction of new gods, or a new set of rites and rituals and so on.

Religious heads have only one motive behind this hypocrisy; to coerce gullible people to part with their hard-earned money by proclaiming that they are in direct contact with God, and will put in a good word with Him for their well-being. Of course, certain terms and conditions apply here too. In return for their 'service', they will partake of all the offerings made to God by the people, because, they claim with mock innocence that it is God's decree!

Unfortunately, even today, people continue to be taken in by their charade. Even the intelligent human race of the present era is easily lured into the scheme they've been running for ages – 'We Will Flourish at The Expense of Your Hard Work'. This clearly implies, that in spite of 5000 years of mental evolution and tremendous scientific progress, the common man is compelled to dance to the tunes of new, attractive robots created by religious leaders.

It is also clear, that unless the common man frees himself of these robots created by religious leaders, it is futile to dream of prosperity, happiness and success of the human race. So, in order to ensure that the human race makes progress and prospers, there is an industry which needs to be shut down immediately. And, I am sure, all of you are sensible enough to understand, which one.

34 The Turning Point in Steve Jobs' Life

This story is culled from an incident taken from the life of the legendary entrepreneur and visionary, Steve Jobs. Many are aware of his success story, but very few know that as a child, Steve Jobs could put even the naughtiest child to shame. Famous for his pranks and mischievous behaviour, Steve was also quite inquisitive by nature and highly steadfast in his intentions. The following incident also gives us a glimpse into his caring nature and intelligence.

When he was thirteen years old, Steve chanced upon an issue of *Life* magazine that had a picture of two under-nourished African children on its cover. He looked at the picture in shock and became extremely perturbed by the pitiable state of the African children. Overwhelmed by emotions, tears welled up in Steve's eyes. He could not accept the fact that these innocent young children were suffering in spite of the existence of God. So, with the magazine in hand, Steve rushed to the church and confronted the priest with a straightforward question, "Does God know everything?"

The priest duly replied, "Yes, my son."

Steve then showed the magazine to the priest and asked him pointedly, "Does God know about the misery of these children too?"

The priest instantly replied, "Certainly!"

Enraged by the reply, Steve said in a reproachful tone, "Then why doesn't God help improve the condition of these children?"

Flustered at this unusual query, the priest fumbled at first and then mumbled a vague reply that he had obviously learnt by rote. But the intelligent Steve was far from satisfied by it. He stomped out of the church, vowing never to step into its premises again! After all, the priest's ambiguous response had answered his question, loudly and clearly!

MORAL: A person has to carve his own destiny through hard work and intelligence. And one must certainly salute the intelligent

Steve Jobs, who has amply proved this philosophy right by establishing the iconic company, Apple. At the same time, you too must awaken such intelligence in yourself to progress in life. After all, success eludes human beings because in spite of their actions leading to negative experiences umpteen times, they foolishly continue to repeat the same mistakes over and over again.

35 The Bell and the Bone Experiment

The word 'conditioning' is a psychological term that has been explained through a fascinating experiment which will help us understand the intricacies of the term. In addition, it also helps us understand the power of conditioning.

In this experiment, every evening, a dog was taken near the church and made to sit outside its gate. When the clock struck seven, the church bell was rung and simultaneously, the dog was fed a bone. Now, it was quite natural for the dog to salivate on seeing the bone. But the interesting development here was that when this 'coincidence' was created regularly for the next fifteen to twenty days, the dog became conditioned to the sound of the bell and the appearance of the bone.

The next day, as usual, the church bell was rung at seven in the evening, but this time, the dog was not fed a bone. And surprisingly, in spite of not seeing a bone in front of it, the dog began salivating, merely on hearing the sound of a church bell. This meant that the physical response of the dog – salivating, which was earlier triggered by the bone, was now connected to the tolling of the church bell by ringing it regularly at a fixed time.

MORAL: Religion and society have conditioned the human mind in a similar manner too. By persistently employing brainwashing tactics, joy, happiness, peace and knowledge, which were naturally attainable for man, are now connected to a number of useless things. As a consequence, a human being has been reduced to a puppet, always at the beck and call of religion, society and the educational system. He just cannot accept that none of them are giving him anything useful. However, those who have broken the barrier of this centuries-old conditioning and have stopped running around, and those who are interested only in attaining something that is worthwhile, continue to scale the peaks of happiness and success on a daily basis, even today.

36 The King Mosquito and the Elephant

Once upon a time, a swarm of five thousand mosquitoes, led by their king lived together in peace on the branch of a tree. The mosquitoes adhered to their routine in so strict a manner, that they would leave every morning to suck blood, and would not return until late evening. Once back from work, they would spend a fun-filled evening with their family and friends, and share their daily experiences with each other. Their standard of living was far superior to those of other mosquitoes. And the credit for this went to their king. He not only brought them together, but had also explained the benefits of living together, to them.

Very soon, within a few months, the swarm doubled in size and in no time, the crack of the branch in which they had settled became crammed due to overcrowding. Being far-sighted, the mosquito king took it upon himself to relocate the whole swarm and began his search for a new place. Day in, day out, the mosquito king would set out relentlessly searching for a new place, until one day, his eyes fell on an elephant. As soon as he saw the elephant, he was instantly attracted to its huge ear. Eyeing the ear wondrously, he thought, 'Oh! Just look at his huge ear, it can even be made into a palace! It is not only bigger than our crack in the branch but unlike any other branch, the elephant's ear can even move and take us to different places! What an experience it would be, living in that ear and owning a palace that could move!'

Undoubtedly, the mosquito king had given a lot of thought to his new home, and because of his intelligence, had found the ideal place to settle in. Now that he had made up his mind, he thought it would be better to first seek the elephant's permission before relocating in the elephant's ear with his swarm. After all, besides being intelligent, the king was particular about etiquette too! He did not want his swarm to settle in the ear without the elephant's permission. So, the mosquito king went buzzing deep into the elephant's ear and shouted, "Listen, dear elephant! I am the king of mosquitoes and you will be quite pleased to know that I have taken a liking to your ear, and would love to build my palace in it. I know this is a matter of pride for you, but still, I do not wish to build my palace in your ear without your permission."

However, to the mosquito king's surprise, the elephant did not utter a word in response. So, he repeated his request two to three times, but failed to elicit any response from the elephant. Finally, even after repeated attempts, when the elephant did not respond, the mosquito king misconstrued the elephant's silence as a sign of approval. He thought, 'Maybe, the elephant is so elated by the news of our arrival that he has become speechless. After all, as the old saying goes, 'silence is another form of agreement.' So, the mosquito king started living in the elephant's ear with his entire swarm. But soon, the swarm grew exponentially in number, and now, even the elephant's ear was inadequate to accomodate everyone. So, the mosquito king once again began scouting for a new palace and soon managed to find one.

Finally, it was time for the swarm to leave the elephant's ear. So, while the entire swarm vacated the ear, the mosquito king decided to stay back a little longer to thank the elephant, who had graciously permitted them to stay for so long. Once again, he flew deep into the elephant's ear and shouted in it, saying, "Listen, dear elephant, I know it is quite heart-wrenching for you to see us depart. But what can we do? We have no other option as your ear has become too small for us to live. Otherwise, trust me, we would have never left you at all!"

Surprisingly, this time too, the elephant did not utter a single word. The mosquito king repeatedly shouted in his ear, but it appeared as if the elephant was totally unaware of him. Stunned, the mosquito king thought, 'Why is the elephant behaving so rudely? Perhaps, he has not heard me.' So, finally, he decided to make a final attempt. Mustering all his strength and shouting at the top of his voice, he screamed, "Listen, my dear elephant, we have been staying in your ear for a very long time, but we have to leave now. I know that our departure will dishearten you, but what can we do? We have no choice but to leave."

This time, the elephant responded. Expressing utmost surprise, he said, "Oh, so you have been staying in my ear all this while... a whole swarm, you say? And you are leaving now? Well, I was not even aware that all of you were living in my ear!" Dumbfounded by the elephant's words, the mosquito king's smugness melted away in an instant. He thought to himself, 'Forget about our activities, the elephant was totally unaware of our presence! He did not have a clue of our stay or departure!'

MORAL: This is exactly what happens with us as well. The Supreme Soul is so colossal and expansive that only pure feelings can reach him. But we find it difficult to connect to the Supreme Soul through our pure feelings. Therefore, we seek and worship it in temples, mosques and churches. Sometimes, we observe fasts, or pay obeisance to Him in the form of offerings. But even after diligently following these rituals for years, there is no positive impact on our minds and in our lives. Then we cry and wail in protest, "O God! I have fasted, visited the mosque regularly, but you have turned a deaf ear to all my supplications! You haven't alleviated my pain and suffering." But your laments go unheard. And sometimes, when you really cry out loud, the Supreme Soul does reply, "Oh, you have been going to the church for so many years, you say? I did not know! Actually, only the vibes of pure emotions are able to reach me." So, there is still time for us to bring our life back on track. You must understand that the only way to connect with God is through pure feelings. In fact, there is no other way, but this.

37 Pandemonium at Sea

Once upon a time, there lived a benevolent merchant, who was not only rich, but also very generous. His main business was to transport cargo across the seas. Therefore, at any given time, he had numerous ships sailing on the seas, en route to different ports of the world.

One day, he realised that the number of ships sailing on the high seas was growing exponentially and facing several difficulties during their trips. Some ships faced shortage of fuel, while others ran out of food supplies. A few ships required urgent medical supplies, while others lacked clothes and blankets. The merchant, a man of benevolent disposition, decided to step in and help these ships in distress. So, he immediately assigned four of his largest ships to sail out into the seas equipped with essential materials such as foodstuff, medicines, blankets and clothes to help the ships in distress. A special flag bearing a sign of peace was hoisted on them to help other sailors at sea identify these ships with essential supplies. The four ships had a specific objective - to supply materials free of cost to the ships that needed them. Since he had sent the ships on a noble mission, it was inevitable that the merchant's fame spread far and wide.

Soon, the benevolent merchant was hailed by everyone for his noble deed. However, even the noblest of deeds cannot evade the attention of evil people. News of the four ships laden with essential supplies soon reached four dreaded pirates who had gained notoriety for plundering several ships over the years. These pirates now set their sights on the four ships on a noble mission, thus heralding the approach of a storm that would jeopardise the lives of the sailors at sea. Blissfully unaware of the intention of the pirates, the four ships continued sailing across the seas together, discharging their noble duty.

Suddenly, there was a huge commotion on the decks of the four ships. The sound of the waves was now interspersed with the sound of gunshots and the cries of wounded crew members. And within no time, the four ships were captured by the pirates and their gangs. It was decided that each pirate would take control of one ship each and later divide the entire loot equally amongst themselves. But just when they were about to sail, one of the pirates noticed the flag with the insignia of peace on the ship and asked, "What should we do with it?" One of the pirates suggested, "It is the flag that identifies the ship. So, I suggest we add a small, unique symbol of our own to these four flags for identification and continue carrying them." Agreeing unanimously to the plan, the pirates made their own small signs on the flags and sailed off in different directions with the loot. Needless to say, this sounded the death knell for the ships that needed help on the high seas. Sighting the flags of the four ships from afar, these ships would expectantly approach them, seeking help, but would end up being plundered by the pirates. Thus, the ships which had set off on a noble mission to provide succour to the men at sea, were now being nefariously used for ignoble deeds.

MORAL: This precisely is the present state of affairs in the world too. Ships bearing compassion, love, wisdom and noble feelings of Christ, Buddha, Krishna and Muhammad have been plundered. These ships still have their original flags fluttering on them, but most of them have been taken over by pirates. Unaware, when we reach out to them, expecting to receive wisdom and compassion, our hands are ruthlessly cut off by these pirates, disguised in the garb of religious leaders. But all is not lost yet. If we understand the modus operandi of these pirates and take appropriate measures in time, there is a chance we can save ourselves. Otherwise, these pirates will steal everything we possess and leave us with nothing but worries and sorrows. We must bear in mind: we can have only two kinds of relationships with great people like Christ, Krishna, Buddha and Muhammad. We can either place them in our hearts, then there will be no need to visit temples, mosques, and churches. Or, we can transform our minds by imbibing their wise teachings, and set ourselves on the path to attain a higher state of mind akin to what they had attained. Apart from this, everything else that we are doing in their name will only make us even more vulnerable to exploitation.

38 The Disciple's Awakening

There once lived an obstinate youth, who, in his thirst to acquire knowledge, approached a Sufi saint. The saint looked at him thoughtfully for some time and decided to accept him as his disciple.

When his training began, the saint told the youth, "I want you to sit under this tree by yourself and allow your thoughts to flow. When you get tired of sitting under the tree, feel free to walk around. You may eat when you feel hungry, sleep when you wish to, and even take a stroll if you feel the need to walk. And if you wish to ask a question during this period of time, you can come to me."

Perplexed by these instructions from the master, the disciple not only obeyed him, but also brought himself in tune with his 'Psychological Happening'. For the next two days, he diligently followed his master's instructions. However, on the third day, unable to hide his bewilderment any longer, he approached his teacher and asked him, "I have followed your instructions, but for how long should I continue in this manner? I have come to you to obtain knowledge."

The saint gently nodded and replied, "You are right indeed, but I know nothing more than this. Let me also tell you that apart from the art of being in tune with your own psychology, there is no other knowledge to be obtained." Unable to comprehend the saint's words, the youth stood with a look of astonishment on his face. The saint saw that the youth was staring at him with a blank expression, trying to comprehend what he had heard. Looking at the puzzled expression on the youth's face, the saint smiled and continued, "Tell me something, were you troubled in any manner during these past two days?" The disciple replied instantly, "No. I was not troubled at all." The saint then asked, "Did you feel re-energised during these two days?"

Reflecting upon his routine during the past two days, the disciple's face suddenly lit up with a radiant smile. He realised that his energy level had certainly increased several notches higher in the past two days. Falling at his teacher's feet, he said gratefully, "You are absolutely right; I did not feel troubled even for a moment, and there was a tremendous surge in my energy level in the past two days."

Hearing this, the saint, with a twinkle in his eye, smiled and quipped, "Then why do you need knowledge? The aim of knowledge is to free ourselves of difficulties. And the magnificence of knowledge lies in its ability to leave a person brimming with energy. These two things are possible only by being in tune with one's own Psychological Happening." The saint then paused, looked into his disciple's eyes and continued, "Just think for a second, had you not felt the need for knowledge during these past two days, then what would have happened? You would have become a king! Because, in the past two days, apart from your desire for knowledge, everything else occurred exactly as you wanted it to! If you had not harboured the desire for knowledge, then you would have already reached the zenith of happiness."

MORAL: Instead of getting distracted by a number of useless things and frittering away life, attempting to seek knowledge, if a person learns to fulfill the simple desires of one's own mind and body, then he can surely attain greater happiness and success. By sacrificing simple desires and actions, human beings have neither gained anything in the past, nor will they ever be able to do so in the future.

39 The Ascetic and the Scorpion

One day, an ascetic and a few of his disciples were meditating on the banks of the river Ganga in Varanasi. There was a lot of hustle and bustle near the river bank, with some people bathing in the river, others chanting mantras, and a few women washing their clothes.

Oblivious to the chaos around them, the ascetic and his disciples were sitting absolutely still with their eyes closed. Deep in meditation, they were unaware of the danger lurking beneath the calm, still waters of the river. A deadly scorpion was crawling out of the water, moving slowly towards the ascetic. And before anyone around could notice, the scorpion, which was within striking distance of the ascetic, stung him hard on his leg. But the sequence of events that followed was even more astonishing. Instead of screaming in pain or killing the scorpion, the ascetic gently picked it up with a cloth and dropped it in the flowing waters of the river, and quietly returned to his meditation as if nothing had happened. However, the scorpion quickly crawled back on the bank and stung the ascetic again on the same leg. Although in terrible pain, the ascetic did not lose composure. Instead, he picked up the scorpion and once again set it free in the waters of the river.

The scorpion, however, was determined to destroy the ascetic's meditation, for, it crawled back and once again stung the ascetic on the same leg. This time too, although writhing in pain, the ascetic gently picked it up and put it back in the water. Meanwhile, the ascetic's disciples had finished their meditation and opened their eyes. Unable to believe the sight that met their eyes, they speechlessly watched this terrible game between the ascetic and the scorpion. Every time the scorpion stung the ascetic on the leg, he would calmly put the scorpion back in the water. Needless to say, the ascetic's leg was now throbbing with unimaginable pain and had also turned blue. On one hand, the disciples were extremely worried about their guru's health, on the other, they were astonished to see their teacher treat the scorpion with such extraordinary compassion. Anger and resentment at the scorpion began to build up within them. Eventually, one of the disciples, unable to control his anger anymore, exclaimed, "If this scorpion stings you once again, I will kill it!"

Hearing this, the ascetic immediately placated his disciple and gently replied, "Will you make me lose to a scorpion? If the scorpion is not abandoning its psychology of stinging me, then why should I abandon mine, which is to protect it?"

MORAL: This is precisely what everyone needs to understand. A person's character cannot be considered strong and stable if he changes his innate nature under external influence or by emulating others. A person with a fickle nature can never instil confidence in others or make claims regarding himself. However, in spite of this, everyone not only harbours false opinions about themselves, but even claims to be decent, guileless, simple and religious. But once provoked, all their tall claims of being decent and religious collapse like a pack of cards. So, when an arrogant person hides behind a façade of humility, there comes a time when the demon rears its ugly head at the slightest provocation. A person with an unstable nature can never become successful and happy in life, irrespective of the tall claims he makes.

40 You Are Fooling Yourself, Not Me – Christ

One day, I, Jesus Christ, was passing by a village when I saw a farmer ploughing his field with a pair of bulls. The farmer appeared exhausted and so did the bulls. But this was understandable since it was summer and the sun was beating down relentlessly on both, man and beast. But as I was walking past the field, there was something else that caught my attention. The farmer, while goading the bulls to plough his field, was also cursing and abusing them in a loud voice. I could not be a mute spectator to this abuse of the poor animals. So, I approached the farmer and, in a calm tone, explained to him that what he was doing was wrong. Feeling repentant at his behaviour, for, after all he was a simple farmer, he immediately folded his hands and said, "Forgive me, Jesus. I realise that I have erred. I promise you, I will never curse the bulls again." I went along my way happy with the thought that I had succeeded in helping the farmer realise his mistake.

About six months later, I happened to pass by the same village and remembered the farmer. I was keen to learn whether the farmer had mended his ways, so I deliberately changed my path and went by the farmer's field to find out how he was treating his bulls. I could clearly see him from a distance, toiling in his field with his pair of bulls. But to my utter shock, as I neared the field, I could see that the farmer had not changed at all. Compelled by his old habit, he continued to shower a volley of abuses at the hapless animals who were panting and gasping for breath, buckling under the burden of all the hard work they were being forced to do. I was pained by the fact that his attitude towards his animals had not changed at all, and so I decided to meet him once again. As soon as the farmer saw me approaching him, he was stunned. Embarrassed and alarmed, he fumbled for words. However, he soon gathered his wits together, and told his bulls in a tender voice, "My dear bulls! Did you hear the manner in which I cursed you? This is precisely how I used to curse you before I met Jesus Christ here," he said gesturing in my direction. "It was only to remind you of those days, that I cursed you right now. You must thank Jesus Christ, who has saved you from my errant behaviour."

The farmer, of course, was feigning affection for his bulls only for my benefit. Hence, I simply told him, "By putting on this act, neither are you fooling me nor these bulls; ultimately, you are deceiving only yourself." Today, I wish to reiterate the same to you, dear readers. By visiting a church or reading the Bible and celebrating Christmas, you are trying to deceive me into believing that you remember me. But let me tell you, I am not misled by this pretence. In fact, it is you who have ended up being deluded about me. So, instead of attempting to mislead me, if you follow and imbibe my teachings in your life, you will definitely flourish and prosper.

MORAL: Actually, every person's 'Soul' dwells within him as a witness and as his conscience. While lying to someone, or living in falsehood, you might succeed in deceiving others, but you are always aware and conscious of your own lies. This is because you are accountable to your Soul. Remember, nothing can be hidden from the soul, and it is impossible to deceive it. So, why should you unnecessarily hide things from people or deceive them?

41 The Right Treatment

In a small, nondescript village in India, there once lived a carefree young man. His fun-loving disposition was the envy of many people in the village. Whether it was working in his field, managing household chores or running an errand for the elderly, this young man did everything happily with an infectious smile. Villagers, weary of the rough and tumble of life, made it a point to spend some time in this young man's company. And sure enough, he could raise their sagging spirits within no time.

One day, the villagers were shocked when the young man, the life of the village, suddenly became morose and depressed. No one had a clue about the cause of his sudden despondency. His despair became the main topic of discussion among the villagers. But when this spell of dejection continued for a prolonged period, it became a matter of grave concern for the young man's family. Alarmed on seeing their son in a disturbed state of mind, his parents prodded him to reveal the reason behind his unhappiness, but the youth maintained a stoical silence.

Seeing no solution in sight, the parents decided to seek the advice of a religious leader. Taking the youth to a quiet corner, the priest encouraged him to confide in him his problem. Reluctantly, and in great apprehension, the youth finally spilled the beans, and nervously replied, "Actually, I have been fantasising about befriending women." Aghast at what the youth had divulged, the priest immediately chastised the hapless boy and recommended several religious rituals to be followed to cure him of his deviant thoughts.

How could such a treatment ever work? How could religious rituals wipe away his thoughts of women? On the contrary, the youth's fantasies continued unabated, while the stern voice of the priest also echoed in his mind, repeatedly admonishing him that these were impious thoughts and must be quashed immediately. So, instead of being cured of his fantasies, pangs of guilt and remorse had caught the youth in their vice-like grip. Alarmed on seeing his condition deteriorate even further, his parents eventually consulted a psychiatrist. As soon as the psychiatrist heard their son's problem, he laughed uproariously. Seeing the stunned expression on the parents' face, the psychiatrist excused himself and explained the nature of their son's problem. "This is a natural desire! In fact, it would have been a matter of grave concern had he, at his age, not fantasised about women. Then, he would have certainly required treatment. But your son is absolutely normal!" Needless to say, with his feelings of guilt assuaged by the psychiatrist's words, the youth soon became his usual cheerful self.

MORAL: Before hastily assuming that you have been afflicted by a mental illness and making a beeline to these religious leaders, it is absolutely essential to clearly understand this: are your present feelings, thoughts or desires truly the signs of mental perversion? Very often, a person evaluates himself according to people's perception of him. And people always have varying opinions about everything. There is absolutely nothing bad or negative about flowing with natural processes and enjoying the simple joys of life. Besides, these natural joys can vary from person to person. So, do not needlessly harbour a guilt, for, when it becomes deep-rooted, it leads to scores of mental and physical ailments.

42 Practice What You Preach

"If someone slaps you on one cheek, turn the other one to him as well." You may have heard this famed quote by Jesus Christ. Many of you may have even understood this quote and Christ's sentiment behind this profound saying. But how can one explain the wisdom underlying this famous quote to priests?

One day, a priest's sermon on this quote by Jesus set the stage for an interesting scene. The sermon was a well-publicised event which attracted a sizeable crowd of devotees to the church. A local miscreant, loitering around the streets with nothing better to do, happened to read the announcement. But when he read the quote by Jesus Christ, he was baffled. "If someone slaps me, how can I offer him the other cheek?" he wondered in puzzlement. To clear his doubts, he decided to attend the sermon and find out for himself. So, the miscreant, dressed in his best clothes, reached the church just in time for the sermon.

Beginning the sermon at the designated time, the priest took his position on the podium. With passion running high, he explained Christ's quote with such flourish and earnestness, it appeared as if it was his own dictum. The miscreant was awed by the priest's sermon. But he was a person who could not believe anything without ascertaining its veracity. He wanted to clarify his doubts about the practical feasibility of Christ's saying in the real world. He sat deep in thought, wondering how to prove the authenticity of this statement, when suddenly an idea struck him. The idea was far from pleasant, nonetheless, he decided to put it to practical use. So, he quickly got up from his seat and walked up to the altar under which the priest was standing. When he saw the miscreant walking towards him, the priest realised that he did not belong to his parish, and felt proud that new devotees from other places had also come to attend his sermon. Expecting a question from this new devotee, the priest smiled benevolently at the miscreant, who was now standing close to him. The next moment, before the priest could even blink, the miscreant had dealt him a resounding slap on his cheek. There was pin-drop silence as the sound of the slap resonated in the church's hallowed precincts. Time suddenly came to a standstill, as the congregation looked askance. Only the sound of the birds sitting on the rafters could be heard, while the priest stood rooted to his spot, absolutely dazed. He could feel the sting of the slap on his cheek. Everyone waited with bated breath for the priest to react. Seething with rage from within, the priest actually wanted to teach the miscreant a lesson he would never forget. But the priest was smart. He knew very well, that he had to practice what he had just preached. Feigning a smile, with great difficulty, the priest offered his other cheek to the miscreant.

It was now the miscreant's turn to look at the priest in bewilderment. He could not believe that the priest was actually offering him his other cheek to be slapped. He quickly regained composure and thought, 'In for a penny, in for a pound. Why should I not allow myself to be convinced completely? It is not good to leave a task incomplete.' So, the miscreant dealt a blistering slap on the other cheek of the priest as well! Now, this act of the miscreant had surpassed the priest's level of tolerance. And before the miscreant and the congregation realised what was happening, the enraged priest pounced on the miscreant and thrashed him with all his might. Crying for mercy, the hapless man protested, "Why are you hitting me? Did you not give a sermon a few minutes ago on Christ's quote eulogising the virtues of non-violence?"

In no mood to forgive, the priest continued to rain blows on the miscreant, and bellowed, "I obeyed every word of what Jesus said, and offered you my other cheek. But guess what? Jesus did not say what to do after someone slaps your other cheek too!"

MORAL: Human life is all about the Mind. And the arithmetic of the Mind is very clear. There is nothing wrong if you believe or don't believe in something. It is the attempt to present an image that is contrary to reality, which is the root cause of all perversions of the Mind. The desire to project a false image or falsely magnifying the image of something which is not, are the creations of the Brain. If you want to stay mentally healthy, let your Mind soar freely; interference by the Brain will cost you dearly. In fact, it is precisely this interference by the Brain which is the main reason behind a warped mentality evident in human beings today. But in order to stop this process, it is imperative for you to first grasp the difference between the Mind and Brain. Bear in mind, that without knowing the difference between these two, a human being can never lead a happy or successful life. However, in the present context, let me broadly explain the difference between the Mind and the Brain to you. The Mind's beliefs, understanding and actions are characterised by depth and intensity. But the Brain is not concerned with depth and intensity; it excels in doing everything at a superficial level.

43 The Truth of the Matter

Discourses by enlightened sages like Buddha always drew large crowds in ancient India. Indubitably then, sermons by Buddha were not only known for their large attendance, but also for their interesting conversations between Buddha and his followers and his unique advice to each one of them. At times, Buddha's advice to certain people baffled even the oldest of his disciples, making them realise that they still had a lot to learn. During one such discourse, people who were listening to Buddha in rapt attention were distracted by an obese man plodding along slowly towards the gathering. Breathing heavily, the man walked in with an unsteady gait and looked as if he would lose his balance and fall any moment. Finally, the man reached the spot where Buddha was seated. Wheezing heavily, the man, with his hands folded beseeched Buddha to take him into his fold as his disciple. Buddha looked at him, smiled and in a gentle tone replied, "We will talk about initiation later, but you must first abstain from food for seven consecutive days. Then you can come back to me." The obese man readily agreed to follow Buddha's instructions and left, trudging slowly back in the direction he had come from. A few hours later, another man approached Buddha requesting to be initiated. This man was frail, pale and appeared very weak. Buddha glanced at his lean frame, smiled affectionately at him and told him, "I will definitely initiate you at the right time, but first, I want you to enjoy four meals a day and you must eat to your heart's content." The lean man agreed to obey Buddha's instructions and left.

Listening in to these conversations was Ananda, Buddha's disciple of many years. Baffled and unable to hold his curiosity any longer, Ananda looked at Buddha and asked, "O guru, this is quite puzzling. Two men wanted to be initiated but you asked one to feast, and instructed the other to abstain from food for a week. Which then is the most comprehensive path to knowledge?" Hearing this, Buddha assumed a solemn expression and asked, "Ananda, did I instruct you to do any of those two acts? I did not, right? Therefore, clearly understand that these are of no concern to you. The instructions I gave to those two men were given considering their immediate needs. As for you, just continue to follow your own routine."

MORAL: You must clearly understand that the purpose of religion is to infuse a person's life with happiness, peace and enjoyment. To attain this, wise people speak two kinds of truths. One is, 'The Truth of The Moment,' which is revealed to a particular person, or at a specific point in time. This truth is not eternal in nature, as it becomes meaningless when the time or the person changes. In the above story, Buddha was addressing a specific person and hence was speaking 'The Truth of the Moment'. The other kind of truth is 'The Eternal Truth,' which is beneficial to all people at all times; like the famous exhortation by Buddha, "Be the light unto yourself!" This means that, as a human being, instead of seeking refuge in and assurances from different people, you must tread the path to your destination on the strength of your own endeavour and intelligence. Unfortunately, no one pays heed to these 'Eternal Truths' spoken by wise people, while everyone continues to carry the dead weight of the 'Truths of The Moment', which are totally irrelevant in the present age. Honestly speaking, this is the biggest reason behind the ruin of human beings. Well, you are intelligent enough and I hope that you will be able to comprehend the difference between 'Eternal Truths' and 'The Truths of The Moment,' articulated by these wise people, and thereby steer your life in the right direction.

44 When Size Does Matter

Once upon a time, a poor boy arrived in the city from his village. Over the years, it was through perseverance and hard work that he had now become a successful businessman. Naturally, his family was extremely pleased at his success. However, there was a teeny-weeny problem with the man which was a cause of worry to his parents. He had become so involved in his work and business that he had paid scant attention to marriage. His parents were worried that their son, in his late thirties was still unmarried. So, they began pressurising him to marry. Initially, the son turned a deaf ear to their constant nagging, but finally acceded to his parents' wishes and agreed to marry a woman of their choice. In due course, his parents fixed his marriage and the wedding was solemnised with great fanfare. Celebrations continued for several days, and his parents welcomed the bride to her new home.

However, much to his chagrin, the wife's weight was double that of the man. To make matters worse, his wife put on an additional two kilos within two years of their marriage. Naturally, the husband and wife made a very odd couple, which irked the man to a great extent. He would often get annoyed at his wife and would not spare a single opportunity to criticise her. He wanted his wife to lose weight, but in spite of her earnest efforts to please her husband, she was unable to shed the extra pounds. It was hardly surprising then, that the rift between them widened as time went by. Gradually, the husband became convinced that his wife was more of a burden than a life-long companion.

One night, when the couple was fast asleep, two burglars were lurking behind a tree outside their compound wall, keenly watchful for any movement in the house. When they were convinced that everyone inside the house was sound asleep, the burglars broke in and ransacked the house. One of the burglars stealthily stepped into the bedroom and quickly opened the locker in their closet, while the other kept a keen watch for any movement. Delighted to find the locker full of valuables and money, one of the burglars exclaimed in excitement, "Oh, my God!" Hearing the burglar's voice, the couple woke up with a start. Switching the light on, they found themselves staring at the two burglars looking back at them in a menacing manner. Without thinking, the wife jumped out of the bed, rushed towards the burglars and pushed them with all her might. Startled at what had hit them, both the thieves lay sprawled on the floor. In a jiffy, the wife plonked herself on them, squashing them under her weight. Then she asked her husband to immediately fetch the police from the police station nearby. Stunned at the sudden turn of events, the husband, completely beside himself with fear, nervously searched for his slippers. Seeing this, the wife shouted, "What are you doing? Why don't you go quickly?"

Fumbling for words, the husband replied, "I...I am searching for my slippers..."

Hearing this, one of the burglars who was being crushed under the wife's weight squealed out aloud, "Brother...forget the slippers! Just go barefoot, and get the police as soon as possible. Otherwise, you will soon find us crushed to death beneath your wife!"

MORAL: When the appropriate occasion arises, each person plays an important role, no matter who or what kind of a person he or she is. Hence, it is not right to find faults with someone or to indulge in nitpicking and humiliate them repeatedly without reason. So, before considering anyone inferior in any way, it should be understood that no matter what kind of an individual the other person is, he is a precious gift of Nature. As you can understand in the story above, it was the wife's obesity - which the husband considered a burden - that saved their lives and valuables!

45 Can Anger Be Suppressed?

In a large joint family in a remote village in India, there lived two brothers with an age difference of fifteen years between them. The elder brother was employed with a local firm and would return home from work in the evening, feeling fatigued. On seeing his elder brother back from work, the younger brother, who was still a child, would become mischievous. The elder brother, longing for some much-needed rest, would get extremely annoyed by his younger brother's mischief. But, despite wanting to scold his younger brother, he would always suppress his anger. He knew that if he reprimanded the child, the family would not take kindly to it and chastise him instead.

A few days later, when the elder brother returned home from work, he noticed that the situation at home was different. The entire family had gone out, leaving his younger brother alone in the house. Noticing the fatigue on his elder brother's face, the younger brother innocently enquired if he wanted a glass of water. The poor boy, however, had no clue about the price he was about to pay for his innocent query. With no one else at home, the elder brother could not have found a better opportunity to vent his suppressed anger on his younger brother. Instead of replying or being grateful for his thoughtfulness, the elder brother, seething with anger, grabbed his brother by the collar and callously flogged him. Now, was there any reason for the elder brother to beat his kid brother in such an inhuman manner? Well, the answer lies in all the pent-up anger which the elder brother had borne in his heart over the years. Waiting for an opportunity to release it, it had manifested itself in all its fury!

MORAL: When you suppress your anger against a person, it inevitably finds release on that same person, who has to invariably bear the brunt of your anger. But this suppressed anger is released at the wrong time and without a valid reason, and is expressed in a volatile manner. It is precisely this ill-timed manifestation of anger that creates bitter feelings in relationships. So, what does one gain by suppressing anger?

Why don't you understand that all the laws of Nature are equally applicable on human beings as well? It is the law of Nature that no one has the power to create or destroy even a speck in this universe. The same law applies to a person's anger as well. In spite of this, because of improper conditioning, a person keeps suppressing his anger whether the occasion demands it or not. Later, this suppressed anger erupts in a volcanic outburst. In fact, this is the cause behind growing instances of misunderstanding in interpersonal human relationships.

46 Is Man Really Free?

In ancient India, education was imparted through the guru-disciple system, wherein children were required to live with their guru in a *gurukul* (an ancient form of boarding school) till the completion of their education. In order to make education more interactive and gauge the progress of students, *gurukuls* held a weekly question-answer session during which disciples were encouraged to get their queries answered by the guru.

During one such session in a *gurukul*, a disciple stood up and asked his guru, "Is a human being absolutely free?"

The guru replied, "Yes."

Hearing this, another student enquired, "Is a human being bound by anything at all?"

The guru replied, "Yes, he is."

There were twelve disciples studying in this *gurukul* at that time. Hearing the guru's reply, all of them were flummoxed. One of them got up and asked, "O guru, we are confused; on being asked if a person is free, you said 'Yes'; then you were asked if a person is bound, you replied in the affirmative. How can a person be free and bound at the same time?"

Breaking into a smile, the guru asked the disciple to come near him and stand facing the students. The disciple readily complied. The guru then instructed him, "Lift one leg up."

The disciple immediately raised his right leg up. The guru then said, "Now, lift your other leg up."

Hearing this instruction, the disciple was even more puzzled. How could he lift the other leg, when he was already standing on one? Watching the disciple's predicament, the entire class broke into laughter. Amidst the mirth, the teacher explained, "This, in essence, is what human life is. A person is absolutely free to take the first step." Pointing at the disciple, he continued, "When I asked this boy to lift one leg, he had complete freedom to lift either his right or left leg. He also had absolute freedom to simply refuse to lift any leg at all. But the moment he raised his right leg, he was bound. This precisely is what the game of life is; a person is absolutely free to act, but the moment he does so, he is bound by the fruit of his action."

47 Pride Has its Fall

Mr. Verma had recently retired as the Managing Director of a bank. Having held this high post for several years, he exuded a personality that was supremely confident and refined. He had only one child, a daughter, and talks of her marriage to the scion of a reputed business empire were underway. He had arranged for a meeting to finalise all decisions regarding the marriage with the boy's family at five o'clock in the evening.

Since Mr. Verma was a stickler for punctuality, he had planned to leave the house well in advance to be on time for the meeting. He knew it in his heart, that this evening could turn out to be the most auspicious evening of his life. The entire family was in an upbeat mood, especially his daughter who was floating on cloud nine, feeling ecstatic about her future! Their happiness, however, was tinged by a sense of anxiety. The Vermas were keen on the alliance due to the boy's family background. Hence, everyone in the family was on tenterhooks, even as a teeny-weeny doubt niggled at the back of their minds: what if things did not work out as expected? So, when Mr. Verma stepped out of the house, they all bid him adieu, wishing him luck. Waiting impatiently for him to return after the meeting, the family was, however, ill-prepared for the jolt they would receive.

Mr. Verma, who was expected to return late at night was back home within an hour. He stormed into the house with anger writ large on his face. Unable to fathom the reason behind the sudden turn of events, the family started speculating on the possibility of what might have transpired. Several questions lingered on their lips, but they were unable to muster the courage to ask the reason for his foul mood. All that they could do was assume the cause of his anger. 'Did the talks of the alliance fail? Well, even if they did, what was the need to become so angry about it? It would have been understandable had he felt dejected. But why was he angry? Maybe they had insulted him. But they were such well-mannered and respectable people. It is one thing to reject an alliance, but they could not have stooped so low to insult him. So then, what could have possibly happened?' These questions were on everyone's mind, and they were all busy speculating the answers to them!

Meanwhile, throwing his coat on the sofa, a furious Mr. Verma began to pace up and down the room. Livid with rage, he even refused to drink the glass of water that was proffered to him. His family could not understand the reason behind his vexed behaviour. Watching her father in this agitated state, the poor daughter, whose alliance he had gone to discuss, felt her heart sinking and a sense of anxiety gripped her. Finally, it was the wife who mustered enough courage, and cautiously approached him. In a gentle tone, she asked him, "What happened, dear? Why are you so angry?" Waiting for the opportunity to vent his anger, Verma bellowed, "This world has come to naught, and maintaining cordial relations with people has become a worthless exercise. Helping someone has become pointless!"

Bewildered, the wife looked at him, unable to comprehend what her husband was talking about. Softly, and in a cautious tone, she asked him, "What exactly do you mean?" Verma replied angrily, "That Tom Alter, he is such an ungrateful, lowly creature! Everyone knows that I had helped him get his first loan from my bank. I had also helped him get several loans after that. But today, he thinks he has become so big, that when I met him at the sweet shop, he did not even care to respond to my greeting!"

The wife was not interested in hearing her husband rant about an old acquaintance. She was more concerned about her daughter's future. Impatiently, she told her husband, "Forget Tom Alter's behaviour! That is the harsh reality of the world. Tell me about your meeting with the boy's parents. What happened when you met the boy's family for our daughter's marriage?"

Feeling guilty now, Verma looked down at the floor, unable to meet his wife's gaze and replied meekly, "Actually, after what happened at the sweet shop, I was so upset that I did not go for the meeting at all!"

Numbed with shock, the wife stood dazed, unable to react. Her husband had sacrificed their daughter's happiness at the altar of his ego, just because an old acquaintance had not acknowledged his greeting! Not only had the retired Managing Director missed a golden opportunity in life, but he had also failed in his duty as a father. He could not even shoulder the simple responsibility of ensuring a secure future for his dear daughter, the apple of his eye and his very heartbeat.

MORAL: This is what a weak inner personality inevitably leads us to. It does not matter how strong your outer personality is; in the absence of a strong inner personality, everything else in life falls apart in an instant. Throughout his life, a human being concentrates on developing and refining his outer personality, but he does not pay heed to his inner personality. He forgets the fact that it is his inner personality which plays a major role in enhancing his life. It is only because of a weak inner personality that everyone today is able to utilise only ten per cent of their capability and talent throughout their life. And all of us are well aware of the restlessness of those unable to live up to their full potential. So, if your ego does not trouble you, look within for a moment; once you realise that you are compelled to lead a life whose standard is way below the potential of your talent and capability, you will instantly stop doing everything else and first dedicate yourself to enhancing your inner personality. If your inner personality is weak, your talent and everything else is rendered useless. A person, then continues to wallow in resentment all his life, unable to do anything worthwhile.

48 The Three 'Brilliant' Magicians

On the outskirts of a small village, bordered with dense forests, there lived three talented magicians who were also the best of friends. They lived near the forest, but for some reason had never ventured inside it. One fine, sunny day, they decided to go on an adventure trip and explore the forest.

With the first rays of the Sun casting a golden glow on the verdant countryside, they took a chariot along with a charioteer and excitedly set out on their journey. As the chariot entered the dense forest and moved deeper into it, the early morning brightness and the sounds of the village were suddenly lost in the eerie silence and the thick foliage. As the shadows lengthened with the approaching dusk, the magicians, who were earlier chatting and frolicking throughout the trip, stopped talking. Realising the dangers of moving further into the forest, they decided to wait till the morning and pitched a tent under a tree for the night.

At daybreak, the magicians could feel the warm rays of sunlight peering from between the branches of the trees, casting their glow all around. They woke up to the sounds of the chirping of the birds. Soon, the three magicians instructed the charioteer to venture deeper into the forest. The sunlight, filtering through the canopy of trees, had created a surreal atmosphere and the forest looked enchanting as well as mysterious. The magicians were stunned by this ethereal scene created by Mother Nature and were lost in admiration. However, suddenly, one wheel of their chariot struck something hard, making it lurch wildly. Thinking it to be a large rock, the magicians jumped out of the chariot to remove it from under the wheel. But an ear-shattering shriek escaped their lips at the sight that met their eyes. Under the wheel of the chariot, now tilted to one side, there lay the skeletal remains of a dead tiger. Relieved, the magicians said a quick prayer. "Thank God it is not a live tiger, otherwise, we would have become his sumptuous breakfast!" one of them exclaimed in relief.

The sight of a dead tiger suddenly made them boastful of their magical prowess and brimming with confidence, they started bragging. One of them said proudly, "With my magic, I can put flesh and skin on this dead tiger." Hearing this, the second magician shot back, "If you can do that, my friend, then, with my magic, I can make the blood flow inside the animal's veins!" On hearing this, the third magician could not contain his excitement, and, not wanting to be outdone, interjected, "If you two can actually accomplish what you claim, then I will bring the dead animal back to life with my magic!"

Hearing the three magicians, the poor, uneducated charioteer became alarmed. He was well aware of the consequences of what the magicians were planning, and pleaded with them in a nervous tone, "O skilled magicians! Even if you can do what you claim to, it is imprudent to indulge in such a rash behaviour. I am sure you will find countless other opportunities to prove your skills, so why experiment with this dead tiger?" The three conceited magicians, who were now determined to display the power of their magic to each other, laughed disdainfully at the charioteer, and humiliated him, calling him a coward. The poor charioteer had no choice but to quietly watch the drama unfold from a distance.

Meanwhile, just as he had proudly declared, the first magician came forward and with his magical skills covered the skeletal remains of the tiger with flesh and skin. The charioteer instantly stiffened with trepidation on seeing this. It was now the turn of the second magician. As he had announced, he used the power of his magic and infused blood in the animal's veins. The charioteer, though speechless, became alert. His survival instincts took over and his hair stood on end in fear. He was smart enough to understand his gut feeling. So, before the third magician could display his prowess, he hopped onto the chariot and fled from the scene.

The three magicians stood near the tiger, which was now covered with flesh and skin, and also had blood flowing in its veins. The first two magicians were beaming with pride after proving their mettle. Now, it was the turn of the third magician to display his skill. So, without wasting a moment, he breathed life into the animal's body. Lo and behold! To the glee of the three magicians, the dead tiger stood on its paws and roared with life! But little did the foolish magicians realise that they had just sounded a death knell for themselves. The tiger, which had been dead for so many years, was ravenously hungry. So, what did it do? Even as the three arrogant magicians were basking in the glory of their feat, it pounced upon them and gobbled them up in a jiffy!

MORAL: You must clearly understand the difference between being brilliant and intelligent in life. By merely studying, seeing, hearing and understanding, a person may become brilliant; whereas human intelligence is inborn. It is natural and one of the centres of the power of the human mind. You must always remember that to be happy and successful in life, one requires ninety per cent intelligence and only ten per cent brilliance. Unfortunately, in the case of most human beings, the proportion of intelligence and brilliance is inverse to what is required. And this is the main reason leading to a human being's failures. Now, you are sensible enough to understand whether you need to enhance your intelligence or brilliance. You have this example right before you to learn from. The magicians were brilliant, but were devoured by the tiger. The charioteer, on the other hand, though uneducated, was intelligent, hence fled the scene before a mishap could occur. So, you must realise that more often than not, brilliance without intelligence can put you in grave trouble.

49 Where God Resides

There was a quaint, picturesque village situated on the banks of a river, surrounded by lush green mountains. A small church nestled in the heart of the village, which was built with great love and labour by the villagers, who would begin their day with a visit to the church. As most villagers depended on agriculture for their livelihood, they were eagerly awaiting the monsoon. The pleasant pre-monsoon breeze and the dark clouds only enhanced the beauty of the village and the mountains around it. And then, to the sheer delight of the villagers, a drizzle not only brought the temperature down, but also left behind a divine fragrance of wet mud as a gift.

A few days later, there was a heavy downpour in the village. The villagers could not contain their joy. They had been desperately waiting for the rains. But by evening, their joy turned into a nightmare. The downpour continued incessantly till the next afternoon. By then, the entire village was submerged. Gradually, the downpour reduced to a drizzle and then stopped completely. With their homes devastated by the flood, the villagers wandered about assessing the damage to their village. It was then that an amazing sight caught their attention. While every other village building was destroyed or was under water, the church stood in its magnificent glory and had suffered no damage at all!

The villagers were stunned on seeing this. Everyone felt it was a miracle; soon, news of the purity and sanctity of the church spread far and wide. Millions of dollars poured in as donations for the church, and people from distant lands began flocking to the tiny village to worship in this miraculous church. Gradually, the small village church was transformed into a grand, world-famous church. But there was something about the church which had not changed. It was the head priest, who had been elected by the villagers when they had built the church. He continued to preside over the newly transformed church as well, with a large amount of money under his sole control. As the flood had devastated the entire village, the villagers decided to seek help from the head priest to rebuild their village. But when they approached him, they were stunned to hear his reply. Not only did the head priest refuse to accede to the villagers' request, but also told them in no uncertain terms, that the money belonged to God, so it could not be used to rebuild the village. To make matters worse, the devotees, who came to visit the grand church from distant places, paid no heed to the villagers' plight. They would only donate money to the church and leave. Left with no other option but to fend for themselves, the villagers marshalled their resources and with the assistance of a few Non-Governmental Organisations (NGO), managed to reconstruct their village.

Nature, however, had decided to make the village and the surrounding region a target of its wrath. Barely had a year elapsed after the flood, when Nature once again unleashed its fury on the hapless villagers. One night, when the villagers were fast asleep after a hard day's work, an earthquake rocked the entire village, sending everyone into a tizzy. Fortunately, it was a mild tremor and did not cause much devastation. But, the aftermath of the earthquake had wreaked its havoc on something that left the villagers utterly shocked and bewildered. While the earthquake caused minimal damage to their houses, it had reduced the grand church to rubble! It was a grave catastrophe indeed. How could the church now be considered miraculous?

The news of the devastation of the church also spread like wildfire. Soon, the number of devotees visiting it dwindled by the day. Even its rich patrons, who had earlier sent millions of dollars in donation, did not evince interest in reconstructing the church. Dejected and defeated by this sudden turn of events, the otherwise arrogant head priest was left with no choice but to approach the villagers for help. But this time, the villagers turned a deaf ear to his request. They told him bluntly, "We now know that God resides in the heart of the NGOs who help hardworking people, and not in churches. So, henceforth we would rather help these NGOs instead of churches."

50 A Father's Love

The Mughal emperor, Akbar had ascended the throne at a very young age, and soon became an extremely powerful emperor, who was also quite popular among his people. He had everything that a person could dream of, but was still unhappy. The cause of his sorrow was that he had not sired a son. It was only after years of prayers and supplication to the Lord that he was finally blessed with a son. An extremely overjoyed Akbar lovingly named his son, Salim. He was enamoured of his beautiful child and his playfulness. One day, Akbar proudly asked Birbal, "Have you ever seen a child as beautiful and naughty as Salim? Don't you think he is extraordinarily beautiful and mischievous?"

Laughing at the emperor's words, Birbal said, "Your Majesty, honestly speaking, I don't think so, for, I have seen thousands of other children like him."

Without taking umbrage at the comment, Akbar laughed and said, "Birbal, your sense of humour has not diminished, has it?"

In a firm tone, but with head respectfully bowed, Birbal replied, "Your Majesty, I am not joking! I have really seen many children like Salim."

This time, Akbar replied in a commanding tone, "Alright then, present one such child before me!"

"Sure," Birbal said, "As you wish, Your Majesty. I shall present the child in the court tomorrow."

After Birbal had left, Akbar became restless and anxious. Unable to sleep a wink at night, he tossed and turned in bed, ruminating over his conversation with Birbal. He thought, 'Could Birbal be right? Can there be a child more beautiful than my darling Salim? Besides, Birbal had also said that he had seen thousands of such children!' Well, the night passed quickly, and early the next day, Akbar was seated on the throne in his court, waiting in anticipation for Birbal to arrive. He knew Birbal always lived up to his promises and would soon reach the court with a child. And sure enough, Birbal entered the court at the scheduled time. Accompanying him was a small child with a dark complexion, pockmarked face and a runny nose. As soon as he saw the child, Akbar was furious and growled at Birbal. "What kind of a joke is this, Birbal? How could you even think of comparing my beautiful, darling Salim to this child you have brought here?"

Birbal replied calmly, "Your Majesty, if you believe that this child is not beautiful, I beg you to come with me. I will prove to you that this child is no less beautiful than your Salim, if not more."

Hearing this, Akbar immediately got up from his throne and left with Birbal and the child. After a long walk, they reached a slum. Birbal then asked one of the soldiers, who had accompanied them, to take care of the child and requested Akbar to follow him towards one of the huts. Once they reached a dilapidated hut, they could see a woman crying inconsolably. Birbal walked towards her and asked her in a sympathetic tone, “What happened, mother? Why are you wailing?”

The woman replied between sobs, “Because of my son! My dear son is lost.”

Birbal prodded on gently, “Oh! Could you describe him for me so that I can help you find him?”

As soon as the woman heard this, she wiped her tears with the back of her hand. Her face lit up as she spoke to Birbal, “What can I say about my son? My son is like the moon... just as radiant and pure! I don’t think there is anyone more beautiful than him in this entire kingdom. If you come across an extremely beautiful, naughty child wandering all by himself, you can be assured that he is my son!”

Akbar was shocked to hear the mother’s description of her child. With an expressionless face, Birbal gently told the woman, “Please stop crying. This morning, people from the royal palace found a child who fits the description you have provided. It is possible that he might be your child. I will go and fetch him.”

The woman could not believe her ears. Her heart throbbed in anticipation, as Birbal called out to the soldier to bring the child in. When she saw that the child with the soldier was her own baby, the woman became overwhelmed with joy. Rushing towards her son, she picked him up in her arms and smothered him with kisses. With tears of joy streaming down her cheeks, she embraced him and repeatedly intoned, “My son...my moon!”

Perplexed at the spectacle before him, Akbar headed back towards the palace, leaving the child with his mother. On the way back, Akbar looked enquiringly at Birbal and asked, “What was that all about, Birbal?”

Birbal replied with a smile, “It is a very simple and universal emotion, Your Majesty. All parents feel that only their child is the best. Hence, what you feel about Salim is nothing new at all.”

Akbar was quick to understand the import of Birbal’s message. Patting Birbal’s back in praise and beaming at him, the emperor said, “Birbal, today, you have opened my eyes and made me see reason.

Indeed, when I look at Salim as a father, my immense love for him surely enhances the beauty of my child."

MORAL: In fact, it is a natural human tendency to be biased in favour of one's own possessions or loved ones. Therefore, before you express your opinion about them, it is always prudent to check whether your opinion is impartial or not. You must check if your obstinacy or bias is exaggerating your opinion, whether it is about your offspring, academic degrees or your religion. The Truth remains unalterable under all circumstances. To perceive this Truth, it is necessary that you see it through unprejudiced eyes, because, the Truth is visible only to those who are intelligent and unprejudiced. So, until you are able to view people and objects from an unbiased perspective, nothing positive will happen in your life. It is Truth that delivers results in life, not your beliefs!

51 Who Is the Stingiest of Them All?

In a village, there once lived a miser, so stingy and tight-fisted that he abhorred parting with anything. Word of his stinginess gradually spread throughout the village. Although this man was wealthy and had been living in the village for many years, no one had ever seen him give anything to anyone.

Impressed by his extreme miserliness, some people started visiting his home to learn the art of being miserly. Seeing his popularity soar among the villagers, he took this as an opportunity to earn money, and began delivering lectures on 'The Art of Miserliness' at the village square. Soon, these lectures became so popular that people from nearby villages also started flocking to his village to listen to him. The miser was riding on a wave of popularity, with the crowd of listeners growing by the day. But as they say, time and tide wait for no man.

One day, he heard that there was another miser, from a distant village, who had also started gaining popularity for his lectures on miserliness. The differentiating factor, however, between his lectures and the second miser's lectures was the set of pointers and strategies that the second miser provided to the listeners, which instantly appealed to them. Gradually, people from nearby villages stopped attending the first miser's lectures. In fact, the situation came to such a pass that the second miser was fast becoming popular in the first miser's village too. As time went by, the first miser became increasingly frustrated as he could not think of a way to draw his audience back to his lectures. Initially, he adopted a persuasive stance and warned the people. "Mark my words," he told them, "The other fellow is an imposter! I was born a miser! Miserliness is in my blood! Come to me!" But alas, all his attempts to convince them failed!

With everyone ignoring his implorations, the entire issue had now become a matter of prestige for the first miser. Clearly, his pride had been hurt. He thought, 'The villagers refuse to believe me, so why not visit this so-called miser and expose him as a fake? Once we confront each other, people will see for themselves which one of us is a bigger miser. After I defeat him, people will have no choice but to return to me.' With these thoughts in mind, he set out to confront the second miser. However, since he was going to visit him for the first time, he decided to observe etiquette by carrying a gift for the second miser. 'What can I give him?' he wondered. Thinking hard, he came up with a wonderful idea. He took a piece of paper and drew four large mangoes on it with green ink. Smiling at his artwork, he said to himself with great satisfaction, 'It is not polite to go empty-handed when you are visiting someone for the first time.' He put the paper in his pocket and set out on his way to the second miser's home.

Unfortunately, when he reached the second miser's home, he learnt that the miser had gone to another village on an errand, leaving his son at home. As soon as the first miser introduced himself, the second miser's son seated him respectfully and then requested him to wait for his father to return. The son had obviously heard great stories of the miserliness of this visitor. The miser thought, 'Since I have travelled so far, I will not leave without meeting this impostor.' He made himself comfortable on the sofa and waited patiently for the second miser to return home. The hours ticked by slowly, and he could see the sun setting in the distant horizon. When the second miser did not return home even by dusk, the first miser's patience began to wear thin. After all, he had to return to his village too. So, he thought,

'Well, if I could not meet the miser, then so be it. But I can certainly leave behind a proof of my miserliness. That will cut him down to size.' And so, with a sly smile on his lips, he called the son and handing him the piece of paper with the drawing of mangoes on it, cunningly told him, "Please give this gift to your father on my behalf, and convey my regards to him."

Feeling pleased with himself, as the miser turned to leave, the son, on seeing the gift, called out to him at once, "Please wait, sir. My father has given me strict instructions that if someone comes with a gift, they should not leave empty-handed."

Hearing this, the miser felt elated and thought, 'Hah! What sort of a miser is he, if he believes in giving a return gift! I gave him a piece of paper with a drawing of mangoes, but he obviously will gift me something good in return. Let him! As soon as I reach my village, I shall show his gift to everyone and expose him as an impostor. Then they will finally come to know, who the true miser is!'

However, it turned out be wishful thinking on his part. The second miser's son drew four mangoes in the air and said, "Take these and share them with your entire family."

Seeing this, the poor miser's pride was smashed to smithereens. He scurried out of the house as fast as his legs could carry him, and stopped to catch his breath only after he had reached his village. He thought, 'If the son is such a miser, one can only imagine the level of his father's miserliness!'

Meanwhile, the second miser reached home late at night, and his son informed him of the other miser's visit, showing him the drawing of the four mangoes which he had left as a gift. The son then narrated the entire incident and told his father proudly, "And do you know what I gifted him in return?"

"What gift did you give him?" frowned the second miser, consternation writ large on his face. At this, the son sprung up on his feet and proudly drew four mangoes in the air, expecting to be praised by his father. But the poor boy was in for a rude shock. Instead of praising him for his ingenuity, as he was hoping, his father lost his temper. Glowering at his son, he slapped him hard and screamed, "You fool! Couldn't you have drawn smaller mangoes?"

MORAL: Very often, a person holds on to his negative traits and over a period of time, begins to consider them to be his virtues. In fact, he even passes on these traits to his own children, under the false notion that he is instilling positive qualities in them. A child not only imbibes positive qualities of his parents, but also learns their negative traits in equal measure. So, the sooner we change our negative thoughts, the better it is for our future generations.

52 The Lion Cub's Complex

This is the story of a lion cub, who, like a few humans, became the victim of an inferiority complex. This was because the quiet-natured cub was constantly being compared to other cubs who were aggressive and ferocious by nature. A hapless victim of low self-esteem, the lion cub believed that he was really weak and inept at hunting in the jungle. Several days went by and he continued to feel miserable, especially when he saw his brothers and cousins go hunting with the elders and savagely attack their prey like true lions. There came a time, when the little cub found it difficult to tolerate the constant taunts and comparisons, and one day, this deep-seated inferiority complex assumed the form of a superiority complex. With an inflated ego and a puffed-up chest, off he went on a trip into the jungle, alone, determined to prove how fierce he really was. He had barely walked a few steps, when he chanced upon a deer hurriedly passing by. The cub growled menacingly and said, "Hey! Puny deer! Stop and answer me! Who am I?"

Hearing the cub's command, the deer froze with fear. He could not believe his ears that a lion was actually talking to him. This was an unprecedented event in the history of the jungle. The deer thought, 'Since he has ordered me to stop, I have no choice but to obey him. If I run, he will certainly shred me to pieces and devour me. But if I stop, then perhaps he will spare me.' Regaining his composure, he stuttered, "You... are...the lion... the king of the jungle."

Hearing these words, the cub was intoxicated with pride. This made his vanity soar to the skies! He had just been called the king of the jungle! Raising one paw in the haughty manner of an emperor, he gestured to the deer to leave, while he jauntily strutted into the jungle. A little further, he spotted a jackal foraging for food. The cub, already inebriated with pride, roared as loud as he could, and asked the jackal in an assertive tone, "Hey! Dumb jackal! Answer me! Who is the king of the jungle?" Now, the sly jackal instantly realised that the cub was a victim of an inferiority complex. Pandering to the cub's feeling of low self-esteem, the jackal said, "Why, you are the future king of this jungle. And frankly speaking, I can already see that you have all the qualities needed to become a great ruler of this jungle." On hearing these gratifying words from the jackal, the cub's vanity skyrocketed. Already intoxicated with pride, he shooed away the jackal in a haughty manner and walked further into the forest with a distinct swagger.

Soon, a few yards away, he could see an elephant walking slowly towards him. Assuming an arrogant tone, the cub imperiously asked the giant beast, "Hey, Jumbo! Tell me, who is the king of this jungle?"

The mighty creature did not pay much heed to the cub. Not in a mood to pander to the cub's vanity, the elephant simply ignored him. Surprised at being snubbed by the elephant, the cub sobered up to some extent. But then, in order to maintain his air of supremacy, he finally leapt up close to the elephant's ear and shouted, "Tell me, who is the king of the jungle?"

The elephant, who had been ignoring the cub became irritated at the cub's audacity. He instantly grabbed the cub with his trunk and flung him far into the distance. The poor cub suffered multiple injuries, but still managed to get up and crawl towards the mighty elephant. Standing on both his hind legs, he muttered meekly, "O brother elephant! If you did not know the answer to my question, you could have told me so. What was the need to fling me with such fury?"

MORAL: In Nature's scheme of things, each human being is not only special but also unique. Therefore, one should never try to alter his original personality under the influence or pressure of others, as all such attempts ultimately lead to ludicrous outcomes. The only person who becomes successful in life, is the one who does not develop a complex based on 'what others say' or 'what others are like' and forges ahead on the power of his own convictions.

The Demon Who Tricked God

This is an incident from our ancient past when gods and demons freely roamed the Earth. There once lived a demon who was an absolute maverick, and had acquired a formidable reputation for his strange, unpredictable behaviour. For several days, he had been thinking of doing something dramatic to bring some excitement into his monotonous life. Suddenly, he remembered some scriptures that he had read, and a strange idea occurred to him. He thought, 'Why not give up my demonic ways and instead perform penance, just like those silly sages and gods? If I am blessed with a boon, as mentioned in the scriptures, it would be a great way to take a break, wouldn't it?' Chuckling mischievously, he told himself, 'Indeed! What could be more dramatic than a demon performing penance and getting a beautiful reward in return?' So, he began to meditate with earnestness. He was barely a month into penance, when the great God of the Hindus, Lord Shiva, known for his innocence and for being easily appeased by devotion was pleased with the demon's sincere efforts, appeared before him to bless him with a boon.

The demon was shocked to see Lord Shiva appear before him. Instead of being happy, he appeared a little upset. He said, "O Lord, why have you appeared? I had read in a scripture that when sage Vishwamitra performed penance, celestial nymphs like Menaka and Urvashi had descended on Earth to distract him. Actually, I was expecting to see the nymphs."

Shiva was momentarily stunned to hear the demon's words. He had never faced such a peculiar situation before. Quickly regaining his composure, he addressed the demon in a compassionate tone and said, "Forget Urvashi and Menaka, my son! They are mere illusions. I am standing here, before you. So, go ahead and ask for a boon that could enrich your life." Hearing the Lord, the demon quickly understood what had to be done. He thought, 'The nymphs will not come anyway. But now that Shiva is insisting on granting me a boon, let me at least make up for the loss.'

So, after giving it some thought, the demon looked straight at Lord Shiva and said, "Please grant me a special bracelet with the power to reduce anyone to ashes as soon as I place it on their head!"

Startled on hearing such a request, Lord Shiva thought to himself, 'Look at this demon. Even after performing such austere penance, his demonic nature is still intact. He wants a weapon, an object of violence and destruction, as his boon. Well, so be it!' and quietly produced a bracelet out of thin air and handed it to the demon. But, far from being satisfied, the demon, now wanted to be assured of the effectiveness of the bracelet. He impertinently asked Shiva, "This bracelet looks good, but what is the guarantee that it will work?"

Taken aback by the demon's discourteous remark, Lord Shiva quickly recovered and laughing at the demon's naivety, smilingly told him, "I am God! And I give you my word that it will work. What more guarantee do you need?"

Unconvinced, the demon reluctantly agreed, "Okay, but do not go anywhere. As soon as someone comes along, let me first try out the bracelet on him. If there is any problem, you can solve it before you leave."

Left with no option but to acquiesce to the demon's demand, Lord Shiva was forced to stay back. Keeping a watchful eye for a victim to come along to verify the efficacy of the bracelet, the demon soon became impatient when no one turned up even after a long wait. Irritated, he began moving the bracelet towards Shiva's head and said, "Listen, I cannot wait any longer. No one seems to be coming along this way, so let me test the bracelet by placing it on your head. If you are reduced to ashes it will prove that the bracelet works. Otherwise, you can repair it."

Aghast on hearing the demon's words, Lord Shiva turned on his heels and instantly fled the scene!

MORAL: The most amazing aspect about a human being is that both Shiva and the demon reside within him. Whenever the demon in him rears its ugly head, his words and actions turn vicious. Just think, if this demonic form of a human being can spell trouble for God himself, you can imagine the plight of mere mortals like us. Therefore, men must not harbour expectations from each other at all. If they do so, their expectations will inevitably remain unfulfilled. Human beings must also be cautious in their interactions with each other, interacting only when necessary. Always remember this eternal truth; only those people whose behaviour with others has been honest, have attained happiness. They are the ones who have not let expectations dictate or drive their behaviour.

54 Be 'Aware' of Your Desires

In the sacred Hindu *Puranas* (ancient Hindu scriptures), there is a reference to a tree called *Kalpavriksha* (a wish-fulfilling divine tree) which instantly fulfils every wish of the person sitting under it. And, if a human being finds such a tree, he cannot attain anything greater than this in life. However, this raises a pertinent question: even if you do come across this tree, would it really help?

One day, an exhausted traveller lost his way and was trapped inside a forest. The forest was so dense that this man could not find a way out of it even after wandering aimlessly for four days. Extremely fatigued after walking continuously without food and water, the man was in a pitiable condition. As he dragged his weary legs in search of the right path that would lead him out, he saw a big tree ahead of him. Feeling dejected, having lost all his energy and without a hope of survival, he collapsed under the dense canopy of the tree. The man tried to sleep, but how could a thirsty man who had been starving for days be able to sleep? Wearily, he thought, "If I could just get some water to drink, how wonderful it would be." He had not realised that he had taken refuge under the *Kalpavriksha* tree. But whether he was aware of it or not, the great tree, in accordance with its nature, was bound to do what it was meant to, and fulfilled the traveller's wish. So, the moment he expressed a desire to drink water, lo and behold, a miracle unfolded before his eyes! Before the traveller could understand what was happening, two beautiful damsels appeared out of nowhere, and holding a jug of water and a silver cup walked towards him. Dazed at the sight of the damsels, the traveller instantly grabbed the jug and gulped down the water in one huge swig. With his thirst now quenched, he felt hunger gnawing at his stomach. No sooner had he wished for food, four beautiful damsels appeared, carrying a huge platter containing various delicacies and began serving him. The traveller ravenously wolfed down everything, leaving the platter clean. Now that his thirst and hunger had been satiated, several thoughts entered his brain. Needless to say, a scary notion crossed his mind. 'Wait a minute!' he said. 'What is happening here? Are there some ghosts around who are playing tricks upon me?' The moment the traveller thought of ghosts, they instantly appeared before him. Shocked on seeing them, the man, scared out of his wits, collapsed and died on the spot!

MORAL: The truth is that every human being gets precisely what he has desired. However, he lacks awareness required to harbour the right desires. Since a human being is unconscious, his thoughts, understanding, desires and actions are not in tune with each other. It is this dissonance between his thoughts, understanding, desires and actions, and the huge gulf between his desires and achievements, which deludes him into thinking that his desires always remain unfulfilled. If a man is fully aware of his thoughts, understanding, desires and actions then nothing that he receives can ever harm or hurt him. As for the people who live in a state of unawareness, even if they find the *Kalpavriksha,* all they will choose for themselves is death.

55 The Magician Tricks the King

One day, a magician, driven by greed to receive a handsome reward from the king, decided to visit the palace and impress him with his magic. The king welcomed him and gave the magician an opportunity to perform. Eager to show off his prowess, the magician thought, 'Instead of conjuring the usual magic, why not perform a trick on the king himself? He will be so impressed that he will reward me instantly.' So, using his spectacular powers, the magician made the king's crown disappear in the presence of everyone in the court.

Astounded, the king's council of ministers and others present could not believe what had transpired before their eyes. Staring at the magician in awe, they soon began talking among themselves, murmuring that the king would surely reward the magician generously. Feeling proud of his feat, little did the magician realise that his happiness was short-lived. The king was certainly not pleased by the magician's impudence. The latter had made his crown vanish in his own court, in full view of all present. This was an audacious act intended to humiliate him, the king! 'How dare he!' The king fumed and immediately ordered his soldiers to arrest the magician, and proclaimed the death sentence on him, stating that the magician would be executed after seven days. Stunned, the magician stood rooted to the ground, trying to come to terms with the sudden volte-face his luck had taken. Little did he know that showing off his prowess would cost him his life.

Sobbing inconsolably, as soon as news of the magician's imprisonment and the death sentence reached his wife, she rushed to meet her husband in prison. But, to her surprise, her husband, the magician showed no sign of fear or disappointment. Shocked to see her husband looking composed, the wife, in between sobs, enquired the reason behind his calm demeanour. The magician replied cheerfully, "My dear, I have six days to live before the death sentence is carried out. A lot can happen in these six days. So, why should I waste this precious day worrying about the punishment?" Bewildered by her husband's response, the wife was certain that the fear of impending death had affected his mind. Shedding copious tears, the wife returned home at the end of the visiting hours. This routine, however, continued for the next five days. The wife would visit her husband, and with tears in her eyes return home, confused after seeing his perfectly calm countenance.

Finally, the day when the death sentence would be executed dawned. However, even on that day, there was no sign of fear on the magician's face. Soon, the king arrived on horseback to meet the magician. When the magician saw the horse, an idea took shape in his mind. He immediately pulled a long, sad face and began to weep. Seeing the magician break down like this, the king's happiness knew no bounds. He taunted the magician, saying, "The other day, in full view of my people in the court, you made my crown vanish in great style. Now that you are facing the death sentence today, you are wailing like a child. Where have your style and swagger disappeared all of a sudden?"

The magician said, "Your Majesty, I am not afraid of death. I am crying over its timing. Actually, for the past two years, I had been training my horse to fly. By next year, I would have trained it to fly like a bird. Unfortunately, my time has run out and that is why, I am feeling dejected." With his presence of mind, the magician had astutely aroused not only the king's interest, but also his greed. The king thought, 'If I could own this flying horse, I would never lose a single battle.' So, to lure the magician, he said, "What if I give you a year to live?"

Seeing the king swallow the bait, the magician felt a huge wave of relief wash over him. Slyly, but calmly, he replied, "Then I will gift the flying horse to you, Your Majesty!"

The greedy king said, "You are free from today, but remember, this is only for a year. If you are unable to give me the flying horse by the end of the year, then nothing can save you from the gallows."

Released from prison, the magician happily made his way back home. However, on reaching home, he was shocked to witness the scene before him! His relatives and neighbours had gathered at his house. Loud sounds of wailing reverberated in the air, as everyone had assumed that the death sentence had been executed. Relatives and neighbours were consoling his wife who was shedding copious tears, lamenting her husband's demise. But when they saw the magician, they were taken aback to see him return alive, hale and hearty. When the magician apprised them of the king's decision, the mourning instantly gave way to celebration and everyone rejoiced with the couple before leaving for their homes.

Unable to contain her curiosity any longer, the wife asked her husband how such a miracle had come to pass. The magician proudly told her the story of the flying horse and the king's ultimatum. On hearing this, the wife's smile vanished and her brow creased with worry. She knew that her husband had gained freedom on the basis of a false story, and that once the year passes by, her husband would inevitably be sentenced to death. So, she started wailing loudly and between sobs, told the magician that she would now spend the entire year in great anxiety.

The magician stroked his wife's head lovingly and said, "Don't worry my dear, a year is a very long time; so many events can occur during this period. So, let us spend this one year that we have in peace and happiness."

The shrewd magician's foresight was commendable indeed. Within six months of his release, the king died, followed by the death of his own horse three months later. As a consequence, his death sentence was automatically revoked.

MORAL: The fact is that every event that occurs in this world is the sum total of millions of past events. Therefore, its occurrence depends entirely on those millions of events. This being the case, can there be anything more foolish than worrying about something that has not yet occurred? If you observe carefully, then you too will instantly realise that most of your worries are imaginary, and they do not exist in the present moment. Instead of focussing on genuine matters of concern, you fritter away the most precious time of your life caught up in worries that are a figment of your own imagination.

56 The Prayer of an Innocent Child

There was a religious organisation, famed for its unconventional programmes, as well as for its huge following. Events organised by it invariably drew large crowds, received a lot of media attention, and were much-talked about in social circles. Emboldened by the success of its previous ventures, the religious organisation began to hold a number of similar events, on a large scale. It now decided to hold a global prayer competition, the first of its kind to be ever held. But that was not all. This time, the organisation had managed to achieve the impossible. It had succeeded in inviting a very special judge for its prayer competition – God Himself! Heads of several religions were participating in the event. The prize money for the winner was substantial too. So, naturally, scores of people from far and wide flocked to watch this mega event.

As soon as the competition began, renowned religious leaders of different religions came forward to recite their prayers which were full of praises, eulogising their revered form of deity. Interestingly, among all these learned religious personalities, there was a participant who stood out from the rest, surprising everyone. He was a small child who had decided to participate and compete with the religious leaders. So, when it was his turn, he stepped forward with his hands folded in reverence and told God, "O Lord! I am going to read out only the letters of the alphabets from A-Z. After all, how can a child like me know how to weave these letters into flowery words to describe your glory? So, on my behalf, please pick the most suitable letters from the alphabet for a fitting prayer of your glorious self." Saying this, the child began reciting the letters of the alphabet from A to Z. Delighted by the child's prayer, God declared him the winner, much to the astonishment of the gathering.

MORAL: You need to understand that God is omniscient. He knows what is suitable and beneficial for you, better than you do. So, you cannot ask Him for anything. You can only express your gratitude for whatever you receive from Him and you can only trust Him wholeheartedly. He has already been graceful and benevolent enough to bestow upon you all that you possess at present. Therefore, demanding something from Him or whining and complaining before Him, reflects nothing but ignorance on your part.

57 The Secret of Buddha's Effulgence

This incident occurred during the time when Buddha used to hold discourses in villages across India. Once, a group of religious mendicants and people from nearby villages had gathered to hear Buddha's discourse. Peace and a pleasant feeling of contentment pervaded the air. The crowd was silent and only Buddha's voice could be heard loud and clear, interspersed by the calls of birds on the tree under which Buddha sat. People were listening to him with rapt attention and great joy.

Suddenly, the peace was rudely shattered and the villagers were jolted out of their trance by a strange man. He had suddenly stood up from the crowd and was running towards Buddha, shouting profanities at him. People were stunned, but as expected, Buddha remained unfazed by the commotion and the man's obscenities. He ignored the man and continued with his discourse. Seeing that he was being ignored, the man, who was already very angry, became livid with rage. Unable to think clearly because of his rage, he became confused about what to do next. But he was hell-bent on venting his ire on Buddha. So, stepping close to him, the man spat on Buddha's face in the presence of everyone. Instantly, his disciples were on their feet, enraged at their guru's humiliation. But Buddha merely smiled, and gestured to the disciples to remain seated and carried on with his discourse as if nothing had transpired. In other words, Buddha's joy and concentration remained unaffected by the incident. Meanwhile, the strange man had now vented his anger, so he left quietly and the incident was soon forgotten.

But what happened the next day was totally unexpected. Buddha had begun his discourse as usual and people were listening to him with rapt attention. An atmosphere of serenity and peace had descended upon the gathering. The birds on the trees were quiet, as if they too, were listening to Buddha's sermon. However, the joy of the crowd was short-lived. Like the previous day, once again the discourse was interrupted by the loud sound of a man weeping bitterly. When everybody turned to see who it was, they were stunned to see the same man who had spat on Buddha the previous day! The man who was sitting amidst the crowd, stood up and was once again running towards Buddha. But this time he was pleading incessantly, "Forgive me, Lord! Please forgive me!" Before anyone could realise what was happening, the man fell at Buddha's feet, weeping like a child. But, just like the previous day, Buddha did not pay heed to him or his entreaties and continued with his discourse, oblivious of the man's presence. Unable to elicit a response from Buddha, the man pleaded even louder, but to no avail. Finally, realising his tears were not enough to evoke a response from Buddha, the man started banging his head at Buddha's feet crying for forgiveness. Sobbing uncontrollably, he said, "I am ashamed of my conduct yesterday, so please forgive me! Until you do so, I will not let go of your feet!"

Left with no option, Buddha was compelled to respond to the pleading man. So, he pulled up the wailing man at his feet and told him, "I did not take offence when you spat at me yesterday, so for what should I forgive you today? In fact, yesterday, I understood that you were very angry with me and were unable to express it in words, so you vented your ire by spitting on me. And the matter ended there. Today, the manner in which you are weeping and asking for forgiveness, I have understood that you are regretting your past behaviour. But both of these are your problems. What do I have to do with them?" Now, isn't this the ideal inner personality. Is it possible for anyone to perturb an exalted personality like Buddha? You too must learn the art of taking the reins of your life in your own hands. Until you lay the foundation for a strong inner personality, you cannot dispel pain and suffering from your life.

MORAL: We have been hearing about Buddha's effulgence for many years, but perhaps the thought may have never crossed your mind to learn about the secret behind it. A person's external effulgence is a reflection of his inner personality. The more a person remains unaffected by other human beings, their ideas or their influence, the more radiant his face appears. The radiance on Buddha's face, who remained unperturbed under all circumstances, was beyond description. This is the reason why, whosoever saw him, instantly sought refuge in him.

58 Who Is the Real Master?

During the medieval period in India, there lived a *Sufi fakir* (a Muslim ascetic), known for a strange habit. He would suddenly accost any passerby to stop and answer his questions. Although people were naturally taken aback at his request, they did not want to disrespect an ascetic. So, they stopped to answer his questions. If their answer did not satisfy the *fakir*, he would provide the answer, shed light on the truth in his own unique manner, explaining to them where they had gone wrong.

One day, while he was sauntering around a busy area, he saw a washerman with a load of clothes dragging his donkey with a rope, which was tied to its neck. As soon as he saw him, he rushed towards the man and asked, "Brother, can you please help me?"

The man replied instantly, "Of course!"

The *fakir* said, "Actually, I am a little confused. I see you and the donkey tied to the opposite ends of the same rope, and I want to know who the master is. Are you the master of this donkey, or is this donkey your master?" A few passers-by also heard this question, and surprised by the query, stopped in their tracks and instantly glanced at the washerman, curious to hear his reply.

Flustered for a moment by this strange question and the public attention it had drawn, the washerman quickly regained his composure and looked closely at the *fakir* and thought, 'Is he a mentally challenged man wandering in the guise of a *fakir*?' But since people were watching him intently, the washerman thought it better to reply in order to avoid further embarrassment. He said brusquely, "Can't you understand such a simple thing? I am the owner. You can see that the donkey has the rope tied around its neck, and I am pulling it along with the other end of the rope in my hand."

Instead of replying, the *fakir* silently stared at the washerman, his donkey and the rope between them, observing closely for a few moments. Then, without warning, he cut the rope from the middle. No sooner was the rope cut, than the donkey took to its heels with the washerman in hot pursuit.

With a look of amusement on his face, the *fakir* shouted after the washerman, "See, you were wrong! You are not the master of the donkey. It is the donkey who is your master. That is why you are running after it."

MORAL: Does this story ring a bell? Our life and our thoughts are similar to the donkey and the washerman. You think you own your car, house, money and jewellery. But, if you observe carefully, you will realise that these inanimate objects have become your master. For, you are the one who is chasing the car or the house; they are not chasing you! But remember, the day you learn the art of truly owning all these things, they will begin to chase you and will also bring immense joy into your life.

59 The Friend Who Did Not Change

In a mega-city like Mumbai, lack of time generally takes a toll on friendships, with people finding it difficult to spend time with each other. But there are always exceptions to every rule.

Four friends, Albert, Tim, John and Peter were fortunate that they could revel in each other's company despite their hectic work schedule. Not only did they spend evenings together, but they also worked together in the same firm. They made a merry foursome and every evening, after office hours, the friends would meet at a local bar and bond together over three pegs of whiskey before making their way back home. To avoid any kind of acrimony, each would pay his own bill.

This routine continued for several years and by now, they had become the best of friends, sharing joy and sorrow together. But a sudden, unexpected development hit them like a bolt from the blue changing everything in a flash.

It was late in the evening as the four friends were about to leave their favourite watering hole after a long session of gossip, exchanging jokes and ribbing each other. There was a call on Tim's mobile phone. Feeling tipsy after his drinks, Tim looked at the mobile screen to see who had called him. His vision was blurred because of the drinks. So, he held the phone close to his eyes and checked again. Realising that the call was from the USA, he smiled and showed the phone to his friends. He told them that a distant relative had finally remembered him. He put the phone to his ear, and before he could even complete his greeting, he was cut short by the person on the other end. In an instant, his face tensed and his jaw dropped. A little while later, he disconnected the call and looked at his friends with a strange expression. "What happened? Why do you suddenly look as if someone has just slapped you?" Albert asked. "I thought it was my distant relative who had remembered me. But it was a friend of his. He called to say that my relative has passed away!" Tim announced. Hearing the news, his friends did not know how to react. Then Tim told them something that left everyone with mixed feelings. He told them that the relative had no children or close relatives, so... "So? What?" Peter asked impatiently. "So, he has willed his entire wealth to me, including the responsibility of running his business," Tim spoke slowly. Hearing this, John, Peter and Albert looked at him in stunned silence for a minute. Recovering soon from the astounding news, they expressed sorrow at his relative's demise and also congratulated Tim on the unexpected windfall. Suddenly, the three friends realised something else. Though Tim would lead a far better life abroad, they would have to part with him. Tim, too was feeling dejected at the thought of leaving his friends and settling in a strange, new place. However, he assured them saying, "Going abroad is a compulsion. But, my dear friends, all of you will always remain close to my heart. Even I cannot stay away from you for long. So, I will make it a point to come at least once a year to meet all of you."

After Tim left for the USA, he continued to stay in touch with his three friends. Soon, a year passed by since Tim had left India. One fine day, to their utter delight, they received a message from Tim. He was visiting Mumbai the following week. On hearing the news, Albert, Peter and John became delirious with joy. For the entire week, all they could think of was a joyful reunion with their good friend. Finally, Tim landed in India, and the first thing he did was, make a call to his three friends. They decided to meet the same evening at the bar. But there was a change of venue. This time, Tim invited them to a bar at a five-star hotel, instead of their regular haunt. The three friends were overjoyed. Excited about their impending reunion, Albert, John and Peter spent the entire day praising their old friend who, they said had not changed a bit despite his good fortune.

In the evening after work, the three friends rushed to reach the bar of the five-star hotel. The moment they saw Tim, they ran to him, and the four of them boisterously embraced each other. Within no time, the celebrations began and they even ordered their customary three pegs of whiskey right away! When their drinks arrived, the friends raised a toast in honour of Tim, "The first peg is for the man who, in spite of having become so successful, did not change at all as a person." The second and the third rounds were also dedicated to the success of their friend. Soon, they were at the end of the party and were about to finish the third round of drinks. But to their surprise, Tim immediately ordered a fourth peg for everyone, and also called for the bill. Tim's enthusiasm had had a heady effect on the three friends too. Nestling their drink, they sank deeper into the plush sofa, loudly congratulating Tim for his success and thanking him for this unexpected treat. Tim gestured them to hold on, and lifting his glass, he placed his own share of the bill amount on the table and said, "I have not changed at all! So, cheers to that once again!"

Suddenly, there was an embarrassed silence. The laughter of the three friends fizzled out. The heady effect of the drinks had almost vanished now, and they sobered up instantly, staring at their friend in disbelief. The fourth glass of whiskey lay suspended in their hands, as the golden liquid scorched their throat making it difficult for them to swallow. They were under the impression that Tim would be treating them at the five-star hotel. Had they known earlier that they would have to pay for their drinks, they would have refused to meet him at the five-star hotel. With their meagre salary, they could not dream of drinking at this expensive, high-end place. But nothing could be done now. Meanwhile, seeing the consternation on their faces, Tim asked cheerfully, "What are you all thinking about? Tell me, has your friend changed?"

Albert, John and Peter feebly replied in unison, "No, my great friend, you haven't changed at all!"

"Okay, so let's down the drink in a gulp. Bottoms up!" said Tim. The three friends quietly finished their drinks. In one stroke, an entire month's salary had been wiped out in settling their share of the bill. And they ended up broke for the rest of the month. Needless to say, the three friends spent the rest of the month cursing Tim, wishing he had not returned from the USA!

MORAL: Man, by nature, considers change to be a painful experience, but resistance to change also creates problems for him. Isn't this the height of complexity? That is why it is easy for a human being to deal with God, but to deal with a fellow human being – it's well-nigh impossible!

So, the lesser the expectations and hopes that a person has from other people, the happier he will be.

60 King Janaka and the Wise Disciple

Several centuries ago, the ancient kingdom of Mithila was ruled by the great King Janaka. He was also known as the father of Sita, wife of Rama, the fabled prince of Ayodhya, who is worshipped by millions in India even today. Janaka was a supremely wise king, revered for overcoming the perversions of his mind instead of conquering other kingdoms. As a consequence of this internal victory, all of his mind's latent powers had not only been awakened, but functioned at their peak.

Janaka's supreme accomplishment was that he had completely overcome involvement in his life. That is why he was also addressed as *Videha* or the 'non-involved man'. He was totally detached from people as well as objects. In fact, he remained absolutely unperturbed even when his beloved daughter Sita was forced to spend fourteen years in a forest in exile, and was subsequently abducted by Ravana. He was of the firm opinion that a person's life and his karma would take its own course.

Since Janaka had completely overcome all kinds of involvement, word of his great wisdom spread far and wide. Many notable scholars, hermits and sages of the time considered him to be their ideal. Interestingly, since King Janaka always remained uninvolved with any object or person, he did not need to hold on to or renounce anything. Therefore, even on gaining wisdom, he neither thought of forsaking his palace nor did he change his routine; he did not feel the need to do so. Another special trait of King Janaka's personality was that he was a connoisseur of alcohol and dance. There were several occasions when, late in the evening, his palace resonated with the sound of music combined with scintillating performances by dancers and free-flowing alcohol. He lived in style, and just like his wisdom, his lifestyle and passions were also the topics of animated discussions in and around Mithila.

Far from Janaka's kingdom, in another ancient city, there lived a great guru, who had disciples flocking to his *ashram* in hordes from far-flung places to gain wisdom. One of the disciples was a young man who had become a cause of great concern to his guru. He had been training this disciple for a long time. But in spite of all the guru's attempts, the disciple was unable to detach himself from involvement, even though he was keen and willing to. He had left his home and was now staying at the guru's *ashram*, but would often feel homesick. The guru was not the one to give up easily and was determined to help the disciple overcome his involvement with his family. But, when all his attempts proved futile, the guru finally instructed the disciple to approach King Janaka and seek wisdom from him. On hearing this, the disciple was flustered. He had heard innumerable accounts of King Janaka's lavish indulgences. He thought, 'Janaka himself is in need of wisdom! How can he impart it to me?' But he could not disobey his guru's instructions. So, he reluctantly set out on his journey, carrying with him a pair of clothes and a letter addressed to King Janaka from his guru. Throughout the journey, all that he thought about was his meeting with the king. He could still not come to terms with the fact that a man like Janaka could impart wisdom to him. In complete control of his ego, he thought, 'What wisdom can Janaka impart to me! In fact, I will put him in his place! I swear I will make him give up his passion for dance and alcohol! In this way, I will not only free my guru from his delusions regarding Janaka, but I will also prove to him that I am quite wise.'

Basking in his inflated ego, the disciple finally reached King Janaka's palace. His guru was a highly revered person in Mithila's corridors of power. So, the moment he showed his letter, the disciple was immediately ushered into Janaka's court. After reading the letter the disciple had brought, King Janaka looked at him and immediately understood what had to be done. He ordered the court officials to arrange for the disciple's stay in one of the palace rooms and asked the disciple to meet him in the evening after some rest. It was an indication that the spiritual discussions would take place in the evening.

The egotistic disciple became afflicted with self-righteousness on seeing King Janaka's opulent palace and splendour. He became even more resolute that he would change his teacher's opinion about Janaka, and this thought only added to his smugness. Actually, it was not entirely his fault, for, most sages and ascetics in India are under the delusion that religion only talks about renunciation, sacrifice and austerity. Women are anathema to those who possess such a mindset, and they live at odds with life itself. This disciple too, was no different from others of his breed. So, considering his definition of religion, it was natural for him to be filled with self-righteousness. Seething with indignation, the disciple, however, could do little but wait patiently for an audience with the king. When the last rays of the sun had faded away, and dusk had cast its long shadows, the disciple was ushered into the entertainment chamber of King Janaka. As usual, the king was enjoying the performances of dancers and singers. King Janaka offered the disciple a seat beside him and asked him to enjoy the performances. But the disciple considered such indulgences a sin, so he could not sit for long, and requested the king to grant him audience the next morning. Agreeing to his request, Janaka asked him to come to his chamber in the wee hours of the morning. Seeing the disciple hasten out of the chamber, Janaka smiled and thought, 'If he really was not fond of singing and dancing, then why did he rush out like this? His scurrying out in a hurry indicates that this disciple was in some way influenced by these acts of entertainment.'

Janaka was surprised at the disciple's involvement with music and dance, which had made him scamper away in such haste. Spending a restless night in the huge chamber, the disciple waited impatiently for the night to end. At the break of dawn, the disciple entered the king's chamber. Relaxing in his royal bed, King Janaka invited the disciple to sit peacefully by his side for a few moments. However, the disciple had become weary of the king's lifestyle in just a day. He requested him, "Your Majesty, my guru has sent me to seek wisdom from you; therefore, kindly impart it to me so that I can head back to the *ashram*. The grandeur and luxury of your palace is making an asectic like me feel uneasy."

Looking straight into his eyes, King Janaka replied, "Alright, I will impart my wisdom to you, but first let us go and bathe. There is a beautiful, natural pond behind the palace. Let us go there for a swim. After that, I will definitely impart wisdom to you."

The disciple contemplated for a while, 'There is nothing wrong with taking a dip in a natural pond; if it had been a swimming pool instead, then I would have had to think about it, because a pool would have been a luxury. After all, what does an ascetic have to do with luxury?' So, having convinced himself thus, he left with the king. Before heading out, King Janaka called his general and gave him some instructions. The king then proceeded towards the pond along with the disciple and started swimming in the cool water. Meanwhile, not a word had been exchanged between the two; but even while both were swimming silently, each immersed in his own thoughts, there was a marked difference in their state of mind. While King Janaka was enjoying his bath, the disciple, on the other hand, was anxious to finish his bath quickly. As he was swimming, his gaze suddenly fell on the palace and the blood drained from his face. King Janaka's majestic palace had caught fire and the flames were rapidly engulfing parts of it. Deeply shaken by the sight, the disciple looked at the king who looked relaxed and was luxuriating in the clear water of the pond. He shouted in nervousness, "King Janaka! Your palace is on fire! And by mistake, I have left my clothes in there!" The king did not respond. Instead, he continued to be engrossed in enjoying his bath, letting the cool water of the pond wash over him with gay abandon. The disciple was dumbfounded. He also realised that even while his grand palace was burning, the king continued to enjoy his bath with equanimity, whereas he was so anxious to save his single set of clothes. The moment this realisation hit him, the biggest obstacle to his progress – the tendency to become involved – was removed. He had finally gained the wisdom his guru had sent him to attain. He realised that the value of an object, its quantity or the interest of a person in it is of no consequence. What really matters is whether a person is involved with an object or not. If he is, then neither will he be able to enjoy it completely nor will he be able to bear the sorrow of losing it. The disciple was also trapped in the vortex of involvement with worldly objects. Hence, he was unable to enjoy his swim and also had to endure the pain of losing his clothes in the fire.

MORAL: The disciple was liberated from his involvement because he had met a wise king like Janaka. As for us, we will have to take inspiration from this story and liberate ourselves from involvement. Actually, a person's possessions, or his activity, occupation or vocation have nothing to do with the heights of his mind or life. That is because, the root cause of man's sorrow does not lie in his possessions or his actions. It lies in the extent of his involvement with his possessions or actions. So, if you can do something or enjoy something without involvement with it, then you can indulge in any kind of activity and enjoy anything you wish to. It will never lead to pain or sorrow. And when there is no sorrow in your life, then you are not a sinner! You will not need to perform 'pious deeds' to wash away your sins! You are aware that the entire world is engaged in extremely pious deeds but is still suffering from pain and sorrow. Now, such people may be religious according to their own definitions of religion, but according to Nature's definition, they are anything but pious!

61 The 'Honest' Villagers

The great Mughal Emperor, Akbar had nine highly accomplished men in his court. He called these men his *Navratnas* or the Nine Gems. One of them was Birbal, who held a special place because of his quick and sharp wit. Akbar enjoyed long discussions with Birbal on varied topics, which he invariably found intellectually stimulating.

One day, Akbar and Birbal were debating on the most sublime human trait - honesty. Akbar was of the view that generally most people were honest by nature, whereas Birbal was of the opinion that honesty was an individual's compulsion and most people blatantly resorted to dishonesty the moment they got an opportunity. With both of them vehemently defending their views and refusing to relent, the debate remained inconclusive. Now, the question was, how could they verify the truth of their statements and determine whose view was correct? Well, as was the norm, the onus fell on Birbal to find a solution to this question. And soon, he did come up with a solution. Birbal proposed that a royal decree be issued to the common people, ordering them to pour a litre of milk into a dry well in the centre of the city. Akbar was baffled. "How would this help?" he quizzed. Birbal replied, "Your Majesty, why do you worry? You will get the answer by tomorrow evening. Not only will our debate be resolved, but the veracity of all the points raised in our discussion will also be proved."

Akbar was not really convinced by Birbal's proposal. However, since Birbal had ably proved his intelligence on numerous occasions, Akbar let him have his way. And so, the royal decree was issued instantly, ordering people to pour a litre of milk into the well. Early, the next morning, people began to queue up to pour milk into the well. This continued the entire day, and at dusk, Akbar and Birbal arrived to check the well. When he peered into it, Akbar was astounded. The well was filled with water and had no trace of milk in it! It was obvious that everyone had poured a litre of water into the well, thinking that it would hardly be noticed in a well full of milk! The answer was loud and clear. Akbar realised that the moment people were presented with an opportunity, they would resort to being dishonest.

MORAL: If you think you are honest, then please understand this clearly: acts done out of compulsion cannot be considered as a mark of your honesty. If you behave honestly out of fear of losing respect or because you fear the law, religion or society, then you cannot be considered an honest person. Let me elucidate this further with the help of a story. Some years ago, a city in the USA faced a major breakdown in power supply and was engulfed in darkness for two consecutive days. As a result, hundreds of incidents of theft were reported from all over the city. Where were all these thieves, who had suddenly emerged in the darkness, hiding during the day? Obviously, they were quietly sitting at home out of fear of the law and the fear of losing their respect. But there was a thief lurking within them waiting for the opportunity to come to the fore. This kind of honesty is absolutely useless in life. And the day you understand this lesson in honesty, your life will be suffused with peace and joy.

62 When Kabir Turned into a Thief

Kabir was a simple, good-natured Indian mystic, poet and saint who lived in the 15th century in the ancient Indian city of Varanasi. Kabir was a weaver by profession, and weaving rugs was not only hard work, but time-consuming too. In spite of this, Kabir would often give them away to the needy for free. As a result of his habit, there was a perennial shortage of food in his household. To aggravate the situation further, when people came to his house to listen to his hymns in the evenings, he would offer them food and serve them too. Consequently, his wife Loi and son Kamaal were often forced to sleep on a hungry stomach. They would express their disapproval of his habit and try reasoning with Kabir saying, "You know that we never have enough to satiate our hunger, then why do you offer food to everyone?" Kabir did understand that his habit was creating problems for his family, but as soon as his devotees gathered to hear him, he would instantly forget everything else. So, it was hardly surprising when Kabir's incorrigible habit created a tense situation at home.

One day, Kabir had just finished feeding his followers and they had left soon after eating. Just then, Kamaal reached home, tired and hungry after a hard day's work. When he searched for something to eat and saw the empty vessels, he lost his patience. Seething with anger, he yelled at Kabir, "Father! If you do not get rid of your habit of feeding people, then we might have to start stealing to feed ourselves!"

As soon as Kabir heard this, he clapped his hands in excitement and exclaimed, "Wow, my dear son! This is such a wonderful idea! Why did you not think of this before?" Kamaal was speechless. He could not believe his ears, regardless of how determined Kabir sounded. His father, the great saint Kabir, was not only supporting the idea of stealing, but was excited about it too! Kamaal thought, 'Is he testing me? Is he thinking that I deeply regret having made such a suggestion? Well, he does not know that I am quite serious about it. So, why don't I make my intentions clear to him and also gauge his seriousness on the matter? Everything will be clear then.' Looking straight into Kabir's eyes, he said, "Father, I am talking about stealing, not about singing hymns! Are you saying that you are ready to go out and steal with me?" Kabir replied enthusiastically, "Of course!"

Shocked to hear the eagerness in his father's tone, Kamaal asked, "When?" Sounding very determined, Kabir casually replied, "What do you mean when? Right now! In fact, I just cannot wait to steal. I have never done it before, and I am sure it is going to be an exciting experience!"

Kamaal was an eccentric boy, just like his father. Although he still could not believe Kabir, he was in no mood to let him off the hook so easily. He decided to take his father to steal something and watch him do it. Setting off on their mission, the father-son duo sauntered around the deserted lanes of Varanasi in the middle of the night, until they stumbled upon a rich merchant's granary. Leaning close, Kamaal whispered in his father's ears, "Father! Come! Let us carry off two sacks of wheat from here."

Kamaal was sure that Kabir would now back out, but to his surprise, the saint was so eager to steal that even before he had finished speaking, Kabir had entered the granary. And within no time, he returned with a sack of wheat on his shoulders! Kamaal was at his wits' end, unable to fathom his father's deviant behaviour. He had spoken about stealing only in a fit of anger. He had absolutely no intention of walking on the wrong side of the law. But now he was left with no other option. So, he reluctantly went inside the granary and quickly came out, carrying another sack of wheat. But, no sooner had they taken a few steps ahead, than Kabir suddenly put his sack of wheat on the ground and said, "Oh! We have made a mistake, Kamaal. We forgot to inform the merchant that out of helplessness, 'God' had come to the granary and has taken away two sacks of wheat from 'God'. So, go back immediately and inform the merchant before he wonders in the morning where his two sacks of wheat have gone and punishes some innocent person for it."

MORAL: How could Kabir, who saw divinity in every person and object, ever feel like stealing? According to him, one form of divinity – the poor man, was running short of another form of divinity – food. The third form of divinity – the merchant, had a surplus of it. So, one form of divinity was taking another form of divinity from a third form of divinity! All actions are immaculate in themselves. There is nothing good or bad about them at all. All that matters are a person's sentiments behind the action and his psychological maturity. Actions of ordinary people – even if they indulge in kind acts, perform charity or engage in religious practices – will still lead to negative outcomes. But when we talk of people like Kabir and Krishna, even their act of stealing is no less than an act of devotion. Therefore, if you want to fill your life with joy and happiness, then pay heed to your sentiments, not your actions. And similarly, focus on other peoples' sentiments, not on their actions. No action is ever right or wrong. It is only the sentiment hidden behind the action that determines whether it is right or wrong.

63 An Unforgettable Lesson in Happiness

Once upon a time, there was a man who was not only blessed with a great amount of wealth, but also led a happy life with his family in their village. A man of friendly disposition, he stood like a rock, always willing to share the joys and sorrows of the people of his village. Needless to say, he was much loved by one and all in the village.

While life moved on smoothly, suddenly for no reason, he began to feel forlorn and dejected. There was no apparent cause of his unhappiness, but he could not shake off this feeling of despondency. Gradually, his situation worsened to such an extent that he stopped speaking to everyone. Slipping deeper into depression, he isolated himself from the world, and spent most of his time in solitude. His deteriorating condition naturally became a matter of great concern for his family and the villagers. His wife and sons asked him the reason for his gloom, but the man was clueless about it, hence was unable to give them a reply. But what really worried everyone and became a matter of grave concern was that his despondency was growing with each passing day.

Meanwhile, an ascetic who was passing by the village one day, was impressed by the serenity the place exuded, and decided to pitch his tent on the outskirts of the village. This ascetic was a great psychologist, and adept at solving any problem in his own unusual way. The methods he employed to solve these problems were often unconventional and people usually found it difficult to comprehend them. But that hardly mattered. What was important was, that he could effortlessly treat any malaise. And within no time, he had become a revered figure among the villagers. Some of them felt that when the ascetic had successfully treated many people, then why not get the rich man treated by him for his depression? The villagers went to the rich man and advised him to seek the ascetic's help to cure him of his illness. Now, I am sure, everyone is familiar with the adage, a drowning man will clutch even at a straw to save himself. Likewise, the rich man, nurturing a ray of hope in his heart, instantly agreed to meet the ascetic, and left to meet him on the outskirts of his village. The moment he saw the ascetic, the rich man fell at his feet and pleaded with him to pull him out of this endless spell of depression and help him return to his usual, cheerful self.

The ascetic attentively and calmly listened to all that the rich man had to say. He also gazed deep into his eyes to gauge the rich man's personality. After the rich man had finished speaking, the ascetic thought for a while and then, in a calm and reassuring tone, told him, "I can definitely help you regain your happiness, but for that, you will have to donate some of your wealth. So, tell me, how much wealth are you willing to give away to attain happiness?"

The rich man promptly replied, "O wise one! If you help me regain my happiness, then I will do anything you say. I am ready to donate ten thousand gold coins."

The ascetic scoffed at his answer and said, "That is hardly anything! Do you expect to regain your happiness at such a low price?"

After thinking for a while, the rich man made another offer, "Alright. I will donate ten thousand gold coins, and a small pouch filled with diamonds and jewellery."

Adopting a serious tone now, the ascetic replied, "It seems that you do not really value your happiness. This amount will not suffice. I can fill your life with happiness once again, but only on one condition: you will have to agree to donate your entire wealth."

Desperate to cure himself of his malaise, the rich man thought, 'What will I do with all the wealth if there is no happiness in my life?' Accepting the ascetic's terms, he agreed to donate his entire wealth. "Please tell me, O wise one! Where and to whom will I have to donate my entire wealth?" he asked.

The ascetic laughed and replied, "What kind of a question is that? You have to give it to me, of course! Put your entire wealth in a sack and place it at my feet tomorrow morning. I will then instantly cure you and you will once again brim with happiness."

According to the deal, the next day, the rich man collected all his wealth and valuables in a sack and went to the ascetic. Handing over the sack to him, the rich man requested, "O wise one! I have donated all my wealth to you as promised. It is your turn now to make me happy."

The ascetic, with a gleam in his eyes, smiled enigmatically at the rich man, and before the rich man could comprehend what was happening, the ascetic lifted the sack, swung it on his back and began running at great speed. Seeing this, the rich man stood rooted to the spot for a moment, too stunned to react. Momentarily dazed, his brain had stopped functioning when he realised he had been conned. But he quickly gathered his wits and shouting at the top of his voice, began chasing the ascetic. But by now, the ascetic was far ahead of him and had begun running towards the forest which was far from the village.

The rich man's condition was pitiable. He had never even walked a short distance before, let alone run the long distance to the forest outside the village! He was not only getting on in years, but the sedentary lifestyle he had led so far had also taken its toll on his health. He had hardly run a few yards, when he began panting heavily, gasping for breath. But he could not give up the chase. After all, it was a question of his life's savings, which he could see disappearing before his eyes. It was his determination to get all his wealth back that was propelling him forward, and he continued chasing the ascetic. However, the slow pace of the man was no match for the lightning speed of the young ascetic. Sprinting nimbly ahead, the ascetic had already reached the dense jungle. Although he was trailing far behind, the rich man had not yet given up the chase. The ascetic knew that the rich man would not give up his entire life's earnings so easily. He decided that now it was time for the cat-and-mouse game to end. Dropping the sack containing the rich man's wealth on the ground, the ascetic hid behind a tree. Gasping for breath, the rich man soon reached the spot where the ascetic had dropped the sack. A wave of relief washed over him on seeing it lying there. He picked it up instantly and checked if it contained all his wealth. It was intact. Elated beyond measure, he now looked around for the ascetic. 'Why did he drop the sack after making me run so much?' he wondered. 'Anyway, I have got my wealth back.

What have I got to do with the ascetic now?' he thought. And holding the wealth close to his chest, the rich man thanked God.

All this while, the ascetic, who was hiding behind the tree, now spoke in a loud, reverberating voice, "Are you happy now?"

Startled, the rich man quickly regained his composure and simply replied, "Yes!"

Now, the ascetic, adopting a theatrical tone, said, "Run along with your sack now. Otherwise, I'll snatch it from you and take off again! And remember! If you become despondent again, then I assure you, your wealth will be gone forever! So, now tell me, will you ever feel dejected again?" he demanded.

The rich man replied, "Definitely not. There is no question of that!"

Staying true to his promise, the rich man never entertained gloomy thoughts for the rest of his life. He had, indeed, learnt his lesson the hard way.

MORAL: What was the secret of happiness that the rich man had found again? This is precisely what you must understand. He always had wealth, but in spite of it, had been feeling depressed for a long time. However, when the ascetic snatched away his life's earnings, the same wealth now became the source of his happiness. Our attitude in life is similar to that of the rich man. We do not value what we possess, whether it is a person or an object. But the minute that person or object – whether it is the TV, electricity, car, wife, parents or a friend – is snatched away from us, its absence not only makes us realise its value, but we also begin to miss it. In fact, we have the same attitude towards our physical self too. We take all our organs for granted. We are not even aware of the existence or importance of an organ until it malfunctions. Indeed, it takes a headache or a fractured leg to realise we have a head and legs! Indeed, this is the state of our 'unconsciousness' and this precisely is the root cause of all our sorrows and misfortunes. Most people feel that whatever they possess is worthless. But the moment they lose it, that same object becomes their most priceless treasure! A wise person is the one who, instead of being driven by the desire for something new, first enjoys what he has to the fullest, cherishing and nurturing it.

The Disciple with a Difference

In India, several conceited ascetics hold prejudiced and sexist views on women. They believe that a woman is the sole cause of a man's downfall; it is a woman who entices man to commit sin, and because of her, he has to suffer in hell. Blinded by arrogance, these ascetics forget the eternal truth that they owe their existence to a woman! In ancient India too, there were several ascetics who belonged to this ilk. They had established their own *gurukuls* (ancient forms of boarding schools), wherein they imparted knowledge to their disciples. On the other hand, there were several *gurukuls* too, which were run by exceptionally wise sages. One such wise guru, who ran a well-known *gurukul,* had a unique style of imparting knowledge to his disciples. To inculcate the virtue of non-involvement, he would instruct the disciples to choose a new emotion every month and refrain from becoming involved with it. The disciples in this *gurukul* had been training for several months, and were now ready to move on to a more rigorous level of training. So, as the next step, the guru instructed them to abstain from any kind of involvement with women. The disciples could not dare disobey their guru's decree, because a unique characteristic of these ancient *gurukuls* was that the guru's command was the final word. Therefore, involvement with any woman was now out of question for the disciples.

A few days after receiving this instruction, five disciples set out on an excursion. The monsoon had set in and it was pouring heavily. Passing by the banks of an overflowing river gushing at great speed, they noticed a woman standing alone, drenched to the skin, looking fearfully at the swirling waters. She wanted to cross over to the other side, but afraid of the strong current, could not muster the courage to cross it. When she saw the disciples, she was relieved and requested them to help her cross the river. To her utter surprise, one of the disciples squared his shoulders and haughtily declared, "We cannot help you. Our guru has instructed us to avoid involvement with any woman for a month. And we cannot disobey our guru." The woman looked at the other disciples, her eyes beseeching them to help her. But all of them shrugged their shoulders, expressing their helplessness.

However, there was one disciple, standing at a little distance from his group, silently listening to their conversation. He now stepped forward and looked at the woman. Then he looked at the tumultuous waters of the river, and silently lifting the woman on his strong shoulders, quickly waded into the river. His friends gaped at him in disapproval, but the disciple bravely continued, pushing through the powerful current of the river. Holding the woman on his shoulders with one hand, and using the other like an oar, he finally managed to reach the other bank, where he eased the woman off his shoulder. Before his friends could recover from the shock of what they had just witnessed, the disciple had joined back into the group. However, his noble deed did not win him praise. Instead, his blatant disobedience of the guru's instruction earned him severe rebuke from his fellow disciples, and on their way back to the *gurukul*, they continuously chided him for his misconduct.

The matter, however, did not end there. Once they were back at the *gurukul*, they were so eager to complain about the disciple's misdeed, they immediately met the guru and narrated the incident to him. They were confident that the guru would reprimand the aberrant disciple. But, hey, what is this? They were in for a rude shock. The guru not only praised the disciple for his 'audacity', but also embraced him. "Thank goodness!" the guru exclaimed. "At least one student has finally rid himself of involvement." The disciples could not believe their ears. Taken aback by the contrary effect of their complaint, the disciples looked at their guru in disbelief. Noticing their bewilderment and burning curiosity to know the reason behind his remark, the guru explained why he had praised their friend for saving the woman. "He was able to help the woman cross the river only because he had truly risen above his involvement with women. Had the woman's presence affected him in any way, he too would have refused to help her, like you all did. Besides, my observation tells me that he helped the woman cross the river safely and left her there, but the rest of you are still carrying her on your shoulders!"

MORAL: Attraction towards an object or a person is not the only indication of involvement. But attempting to escape or abstain from an object or a person, also indicates involvement. In fact, running away from something denotes an even deeper involvement. If you observe yourself carefully, you will realise that you are equally concerned about your loved ones as well as others. The only difference is that while you are concerned about the progress of your loved ones, the progress of others too is of great concern to you. You are only too well aware of your tendency to keep track of friends and foes alike. Therefore, you must understand that whether you label an object or a person as 'good' or 'bad', interaction with either of them will invariably lead to sorrow. Happiness is attained when one rises above mundane emotions and follows the middle path, in a thought-free, unbiased state of mind. This objective state of a human being's mind is the 'golden mean' between two extremes which can lead to happiness.

65 The Lost Chance

This story sheds light on a profound truth and tells us how the world missed out on a golden opportunity to carve out a glorious destiny for itself.

Around 2000 years ago, mankind was blessed by the birth of a wonderful child. His parents, who were poor shepherds, named him Jesus. As he grew up, the child turned out to be an extremely simple, good-hearted, lovable and wise person. His prime motive was to spread the Truth in the world, for the benefit and prosperity of mankind. But changing the mindset of society is a mammoth task. So, it was hardly surprising that, to achieve his aim, Jesus had to oppose several prevalent teachings and beliefs that were erroneous. The clergy took offence at his teachings and rousing the sentiments of the fanatics, they mercilessly crucified Jesus. In their ignorance, little did they know that, by crucifying Jesus their plan would backfire. To their horror, Jesus' beautiful and radiant face, his infinite love and teachings were indelibly etched on the minds of the people. Contrary to what they had expected, Jesus' popularity soared after His crucifixion.

The fanatical preachers of that time became anxious at this sudden development. They were alarmed, because people had begun to disregard them. In a desperate attempt to save their identity and maintain their relevance in the rapidly changing society, the preachers immediately called for a meeting to discuss the crisis that had befallen them. However, even after several hours of deliberations, they were unable to come up with a plan to stem the tide of Jesus' growing popularity. In this group was a smart, young priest who sat on the sidelines, quietly watching the elderly preachers with their foreheads creased with worry lines. Realising that the meeting was turning into a futile affair, he finally lost patience and stood up to address the gathering. "All of us have seen the repercussions of crucifying Jesus. We must refrain from doing anything to stem Jesus' growing popularity. Trying to curtail his popularity could have adverse effects, and the situation could deteriorate even further. So, it will be in our best interest if we ride the wave of his popularity and declare him as the 'Son of God'."

Hearing this, an old and experienced priest immediately scoffed at the suggestion saying, "But Jesus' teachings are going to ruin our business! If we lend credence to his messages, it will pose an even greater threat to our existence!"

The young priest laughed on hearing this and explained, "Actually, you haven't really understood my plan. We will present Jesus to the world as the 'Son of God', but we will not adopt his teachings. Instead, we will replace them with our own scriptures. And naturally, all the teachings in these 'scriptures' will be oriented towards the enhancement of our business. We will advocate our teachings in the name of Jesus."

Even though the old priest could see merit in this idea, he continued to express his doubts, saying, "But everyone is familiar with the teachings of Jesus."

Countering his argument, the young priest retorted, "So what? They will soon forget them. In any case, Jesus' teachings are so pure it will be difficult for people to adopt them. Instead, we will create such an exciting Bible in his name that people will vie with each other to possess it. We will also construct elegantly designed and imposing churches and place grand statues of Jesus in all of them. Seeing the splendour of these churches, people will become so enamoured of them, that they will soon forget Jesus' teachings. Besides this, we will also address ourselves with a new title. Instead of priests, henceforth, we will call ourselves 'Fathers' so that people will accept us as the true devotees of Jesus. Even after all this, if a few people remember some of Jesus' teachings, what difference does it make? How much can they really harm us? So, heed my advice and adopt this strategy – let churches belonging to Jesus endorse the Bible written by us. It is only a matter of time before we regain our supremacy in the world!"

MORAL: Today, we can see this is exactly what is happening. Due to the shrewd manoeuvres of religious heads and our own foolishness, we lost the opportunity that Jesus had created to enable us to lead happier and more prosperous lives. But better late than never. There is still time! Carefully reflect on what Jesus taught, and once you do that, you will forget the church and the Bible. You will find Jesus' simple and straightforward messages far more profound than the written word. Soon, you will truly reach that particular state where Jesus envisioned every human being to be – where there is neither sorrow nor failure. Now, it is up to you to choose the path on which you wish to tread.

66 The Magic of Acceptance

In ancient Turkey, there lived a famed *fakir* who had set up a unique school, similar to an ancient Indian *gurukul*. He was well known for his unconventional but highly effective teaching methods. So, naturally, several local students and those from distant regions flocked to his school to gain knowledge and benefitted immensely from his wisdom. The *fakir* led a happy life with his two children and a beautiful wife. He loved his children dearly and would never eat his meals without them, no matter how late they were in returning home. The children, too would never eat without their father and always waited for him to return home.

One evening, just before sunset, the children were playing outside their house, waiting for their father to return, who had gone to the city for some work. Realising that their father would be late, they decided to race each other. So, they ran at an incredible speed outside the house and through it, with the younger child chasing the elder one. Soon, the younger child was fast closing in on his brother. Realising this, the elder brother, not wanting to be overtaken, thought that if he stepped up the game to surprise his brother, it would slow him down. So, he sprinted out of the house and suddenly climbed the wall of the well in their courtyard. His brother was surprised by the unexpected move. However, not to be outdone easily, he also climbed the wall of the well. But unfortunately, the moment he did so, his foot slipped and he fell into the well. On hearing the loud splash of water, the elder brother, still standing on its wall, looked down to see what had happened, lost his balance and also fell in the well. Hearing the commotion outside the house, the mother came out to see what had happened. Fearing the worst, she looked around in panic, calling out to her children. When there was no response, she darted towards the well, her heart thumping with fear. She screamed in horror and felt the blood drain from her body at the sight of her children's bodies floating lifeless in the well.

By the time the *fakir* had returned exhausted after the long journey, it was late evening. The wife was traumatised by the death of her children, but realised that it was not the right time to break the sad news to her husband. She thought it would be better to let him eat before she told him about the tragedy. So, she served him dinner. The *fakir* was surprised at his wife, for, the children had not yet returned. His wife knew that he had never eaten without them. He wondered why his wife was behaving strangely today. Puzzled, he looked at her and said, "My dear, have I ever eaten without my children? Never! So, why have you served me dinner in their absence today?"

What could the wife say? Hiding her pain with great effort, she said, "You look weary after the long journey. The children have gone with their friends to the neighbouring village and may return home late. It is quite likely they might eat something on the way. That is why I have served you dinner today." Saying this, she instantly looked away so that the *fakir* could not see her unshed tears.

The *fakir* nodded and said, "Of course, I am tired, but I can surely wait for my children. And even if they do eat something on the way, at their age, I am sure they can eat with me once again. And I am certain that no matter how much they eat, or how late they come, they will definitely have dinner with me."

Now, what could the wife say or do? Reluctantly, she had to break the sad news of the death of their children to her husband, seated before the untouched plate of food. After she finished speaking, she expected her husband to feel distressed, but his action took her by complete surprise. The *fakir*, instead of being shocked at this heart-wrenching news, simply sat quietly for a few seconds, and then began to eat his food. His face reflected no trace of shock or sorrow for his dead children. And to the wife's utter disbelief, he not only finished his own meal, but also ate the food from his children's plates! What was even more shocking was that during his dinner, and even after it, he did not enquire of the cause of the accident. In fact, he even went out for his customary stroll after dinner and on returning, calmly went to bed. Perplexed at her husband's strange behaviour, the wife, unable to control her tears now, lay awake; her husband's behaviour had only added to her woes.

The next day, she confronted her husband and demanded to know the reason behind his abnormal reaction to the news of their children's death. Looking into his wife's eyes with compassion, the *fakir* lovingly made his wife sit beside him and spoke to her in an endearingly tender tone, "Listen, my dear, loving, living with and deriving joy from what you have is an art; but to enquire about, to miss and to mourn what you have lost, or what you do not possess is an illness. The children were a gift from God and now, God has taken them away; they were guests in our lives. But we have to admit, till the time they were with us, they gave us immense joy. But my dear, our happiness does not depend on just a couple of blessings of God, for, he has blessed us with the art of deriving happiness from whatever we possess at any given point of time. Think with a calm mind, even today, I have you, the *gurukul* and all the children who study there to infuse my life with joy. What I mean to say is that God has blessed me with so many gifts, that even if I can derive joy from each one of them in this lifetime, it will be enough." Listening to these profound words of wisdom from her husband, the wife's sorrow was allayed to some extent, and she realised the futility of her remorse.

MORAL: You must learn the great lesson that this wonderful story teaches and free yourself from sorrows. On losing something, acquire the ability of immediately accepting the loss. One cannot consider oneself to be intelligent and yet grieve over something that has been irrevocably lost. Understand this clearly: how religious a person is, cannot be determined by the number of times he visits a temple, mosque or church. His religiosity is determined by how quickly that person can accept what has happened.

67 When Imagination Runs Wild

Two centuries ago, in a remote village in India, there lived two friends, Salman and Akram, both aged fifteen years. They had been friends since the age of five and were an inseparable duo. In fact, their names had become synonymous with 'friendship'. They would spend all their waking hours together; eat their meals, study, play and even roam the streets of their village happy in each other's company. In the years they were together, they never fought, argued or disagreed with each other.

One day, Salman and Akram were sitting under a tree and chatting away indolently as usual, while villagers who were passing by, looked on indulgently, waving at them. Gradually, their leisurely chat took on a serious tone, and then, to the surprise of the passers-by, it turned into a heated argument. Curious to know what the matter was, the villagers stopped in their tracks, shocked to see the friends arguing so bitterly. They had never seen Salman and Akram behave in this manner before. But before the villagers could realise what was happening, Akram delivered a resounding slap on Salman's cheek. Stunned by the sudden attack by his friend, Salman looked at Akram in shock, while the onlookers stood aghast as the two friends fought bitterly. They could not believe what was happening and rubbed their eyes in disbelief. But before anyone could react, Salman retaliated with all his might. Soon, the brawl ended up in a serious fight, with each hitting the other mercilessly. Incredulous villagers quickly gathered their wits, intervened and managed to stop the ugly fight. Since the matter was serious, they took the boys, who were now bleeding profusely, to the village council. Even the council was stunned to see the condition of the two boys. Meanwhile, news of the bitter fight between the two best friends spread like wildfire across the village. Everyone who heard about the incident rushed towards the village council.

Stunned at this unexpected development, the village council demanded an explanation from both Salman and Akram, "Tell us in detail, why did you both hit each other in this callous manner?" But, the two friends remained quiet. Not a word escaped their lips as they stood before the council with their heads hanging in shame. Even after repeated questioning, the council was unable to elicit a response from either Salman or Akram. It was only after the council issued a stern warning that the two finally spoke. But instead of replying to the council, they began mumbling to each other. "You tell them what happened," Salman said, obviously embarrassed. "No, I won't. You tell them," Akram replied, unable to look directly into his friend's eyes. Really, what a peculiar situation this was! They had not felt ashamed when they had fought. But now, they were too embarrassed to even speak about it!

Irritated by their behaviour, the village council reprimanded the two and ordered Salman to quickly explain the reason for their fight. Feeling terribly embarrassed and with head bent down, Salman mumbled, "Both of us were sitting under a tree and chatting, when I casually said, 'Akram, I was just thinking, for how long can we live off our parents' money? Why don't we set up a small business venture, and take care of our school fees and pocket money by ourselves?'"

Hearing this, the council was puzzled, trying to comprehend how a positive thought could have led to a bitter fight between the two. So, they asked Salman to shed more light on the incident. "Actually, Akram loved the idea and said that he was also thinking on the same lines. He even said that it was as if I had expressed his thoughts aloud. So, we excitedly began deliberating upon the idea. I told Akram that I was thinking of buying two buffaloes. I would sell the milk that the buffaloes would yield in the market for a neat profit. It would involve only a couple of hours of work. At this, Akram said that he was thinking of buying a small plot of farmland. He said that if he worked on the farm for three-four hours, he could easily grow enough crops to cover his school expenses and pocket money. As soon as Akram mentioned this, I told him that it was a wonderful idea, as I would not have to take the buffaloes too far for grazing, instead, I would bring them to his field to graze. But the moment I said this, Akram vehemently opposed the idea. He put our friendship on the line over such a trivial matter and warned me not to bring my buffaloes to his field. I did not like his tone and indignantly, I thundered, 'My buffaloes will definitely graze in your field. I'll see how you stop them!' Enraged on hearing this, Akram retorted in a menacing tone, 'I will kill your buffaloes if you even bring them near my field!' Unable to tolerate this belligerence from a close friend, I became furious, and warned him that if he dared to even touch my buffaloes, I would smash his head! That was it. Both of us lost control over ourselves and came to blows! We never realised that our fight had escalated to such an extent that we would end up injuring each other." Saying so, both the friends stood with their heads hanging in shame, too embarrassed to even look anyone in the eye.

MORAL: Whether a person has more friends or enemies depends on the extent of perversity of his own mind, rather than on other people's behaviour and nature. It is the individual's mind which is responsible for all the external conflicts and confrontations. If a person's mind is free of these convoluted thoughts, he will hardly see anyone as 'bad', let alone as an 'enemy'. He will not harbour a negative perception of the world, but see everything in a positive light.

Kabir's couplet expresses this message in an apt manner:

'I went out looking for the bad, but no bad could I see,
And when I looked within my mind, none was as bad as me!'

68 The Donkey's Shrine

In a village in India, there once lived a poor washerman whose sole worldly possession was a donkey, which toiled hard and served him well. The poor man, unfortunately had no family. The donkey meant everything to him – his friend, family and his entire universe. The washerman never travelled anywhere without his four-legged friend, and they would often travel together for long distances.

One day, the two set out on a long journey to a distant village, basking in each other's company. The washerman fussed over his donkey, feeding him at regular intervals and giving him plenty of rest too. He was so busy taking care of the donkey that he did not even realise when they had reached their destination. On the second day of their stay in the unknown village, the washerman noticed that the donkey was not as energetic as it usually would be. Worried about the donkey's health, the washerman thought that the donkey was probably exhausted and would recover after some rest. But, to his horror, the donkey's condition deteriorated even further. And before the hapless washerman could do anything, his four-legged friend collapsed and died. Traumatised at the loss of his beloved donkey, the washerman sat by his side, sobbing uncontrollably, and lovingly caressed the dead donkey. He felt his entire world had fallen apart with the death of his sole companion. Feeling utterly dejected, the poor man managed to bury his donkey in this distant village and also built a grave for his beloved companion. But even after completing the last rites of the donkey, he could not tear himself away from the grave and head home. Indeed, it was well nigh impossible for him to imagine life without his donkey. Ten days passed by, but the washerman still sat morosely by the grave. So overwhelmed was he with sorrow that he even lost his voice and ability to speak. In other words, in one stroke, his life had suddenly become mired in misery and grief.

Meanwhile, some villagers passing by every day had seen the washerman mourning over someone's grave. Soon, news about this grieving stranger in the village spread like wildfire. Every person who saw the woeful washerman would ask him, "Who has passed away?" But having lost his ability to speak, the washerman was in no condition to respond to their queries. So, whenever someone enquired, he would only cling to the grave of the donkey and weep inconsolably. Seeing the man's pathetic condition, the entire village became anxious. The villagers wondered whose grave it was for the poor man to be reduced to such a state, that he was unable to overcome his grief.

Now, when a question like this arises, some 'smart' person invariably comes up with an answer. That is precisely what happened in this case too. A smart aleck told the villagers, "Surely, a great person must have died here. That is why the poor man is so grief-stricken!" This seemed to be a sensible explanation and the villagers were convinced that this was definitely the reason for the man to be reduced to such a plight.

They decided to contribute money and build a magnificent shrine over the grave! Soon, news of this shrine spread and people from nearby villages flocked to it for worship! Now, the entire situation had taken a strange turn. On one hand, the semi-conscious washerman continued to mourn over his dead donkey, and on the other, the number of visitors to the shrine swelled by the day. But their foolishness did not end here; after a few days, the washerman was dressed in the garb of a *maulvi* (a priest), and the villagers even conferred on him the title of a *maulvi*! After all, it was the washerman alone who had spent time with the 'great person'.

Now, as the news of the magnificence of the shrine spread far and wide, people from far-flung places began visiting it in the hope that their wishes would be fulfilled. As the footfall of devotees increased, a grand market sprung up around the shrine.

The donkey was truly amazing and so was its destiny! And even more amazing were the people who had now begun living in the hope of receiving blessings from a dead donkey!

MORAL: This story is not about a particular religion, but encompasses all religions. Thousands of similar incidents have occurred in the history of every religion and nation, and continue to occur even today. You are well aware that there are numerous such 'enterprises' thriving in all religions, who, in the name of divinity, peddle false hopes and assurances with impunity. But you are intelligent; you do not depend on blessings of saints to lead your life. You rely only on your emotions and your karma. Then, why should you worry? No matter how many shrines are being built or how many people are flocking to them for worship, why should it concern you?

69 Was Krishna Really a Deserter?

Krishna's life has been an enduring enigma not only for his devotees but also for his critics. His actions have always been differently interpreted. But there is one aspect on which everyone unanimously agrees – there is hardly any other life in human history, that has been as tumultuous and as awe-inspiring as that of Krishna.

The following episode clearly illustrates this point. When Krishna's uncle, Kansa, who was also his sworn enemy, invited him to the annual celebrations in Mathura, Krishna immediately set off from Vrindavan with his brother Balarama to attend the festival. No one could have imagined that this trip by the two brothers would rewrite the history of Aryavarta. But, due to certain reasons, Krishna was compelled to kill his uncle in the midst of the celebration for the greater common good. During this period, Kansa's father-in-law, Jarasandha, the King of Magadha was the most powerful king in the entire region of *Bharatvarsha* (as it was then known). Both his daughters were married to Kansa and with his untimely death, their lives were ruined. Naturally, Jarasandha could not bear the pain of seeing his daughters' misery. His pain soon turned into uncontrollable fury, which was directed towards the root cause of his daughters' agony – Krishna. Jarasandha's only aim was to mercilessly kill the slayer of his son-in-law. In order to realise his goal, he ordered his formidable army to attack Mathura, where Krishna lived.

Earlier, Krishna had managed to foil Jarasandha's attack by employing his shrewd war strategies. However, Krishna was shaken to the core when he learnt of Jarasandha's vicious plan to attack Mathura. This was definitely terrifying news for any ordinary mortal. Krishna marshalled his mental prowess and strength to think of an effective way to thwart Jarasandha's attack without bloodshed. However, even after days of intense thinking and with no solution in sight, Krishna chose what he felt was the next best option – to flee from Mathura, taking his brother Balarama along with him. Balarama accompanied Krishna, but was extremely annoyed by Krishna's decision. Balarama could not accept the fact that due to Jarasandha's fear, Krishna had beaten a hasty retreat from the battle even before it was fought. He even reprimanded Krishna for it. But all that Krishna replied was, "At present, 'Time' demands that we flee." Profound words indeed, for, was there any sense in defying 'Time' and getting killed needlessly?

It is precisely because of this decision that Krishna quickly acquired notoriety as *rannchhod* or 'the one who fled the battlefield'. Interestingly, many years later, Krishna vehemently objected when a petrified Arjuna wanted to quit the battlefield after seeing the humongous army of the Kauravas during the epic battle of the Mahabharata. In fact, it was Krishna who convinced Arjuna to fight after revealing and explaining to him the secrets of human life and creation. This contradiction in Krishna's personality has always remained an enigma to most people. But to explain it simply, it is all about Time. When the two armies were ready for the battle of the Mahabharata, it was certainly not the appropriate 'Time' for Arjuna to flee from the battlefield.

MORAL: There is nothing good or bad about engaging in, or performing an action, or avoiding it. Actually, physical actions of any kind cannot be termed as good or bad. Whether an act is good or bad can only be determined by the situation and circumstances controlling it at that moment. Different circumstances demand different actions. An act committed in a certain circumstance can become great or historic, but that same act committed in the very next moment in a different set of circumstances can prove disastrous. Therefore, only the one who knows and understands the arithmetic of 'Time and Space' can invariably perform appropriate actions leading to positive outcomes. It is to explain this profound truth, that I have narrated this story behind Krishna's reputation as a *rannchhod.*

70 The Washerman and His Donkey

In ancient times, when there were no motorised vehicles and washing machines, it was the washermen who washed people's dirty clothes. These washermen would carry the clothes of their customers on donkeys to the riverbank and wash them.

One morning, a washerman was walking towards the riverbank with a pile of clothes on his donkey's back. He held the rope at one end, with the other tied around the donkey's neck. A passer-by saw the two and smirked at the washerman, saying, "What a fool this man is! In spite of owning a donkey, he is on foot!"

The washerman felt that the man was right, so he immediately climbed on the donkey's back and placed the heap of laundry on his lap. He was passing by a roadside eatery when a few people seated there were astonished at the sight of the washerman seated on the donkey with a pile of clothes. One of them commented, "What kind of a person is this man? He is devoid of any compassion or humanity! He is not only seated on the donkey, but has also placed the bundle of clothes on the poor animal!"

The washerman overhead their barbs and felt that what they were saying was also true. Indeed, he had blindly followed the other person's suggestion and was being cruel to the donkey by forcing it to carry such a heavy load. Feeling guilty, he not only alighted from the donkey's back, but also picked up the bundle of clothes from its back and placed it on his head. After he had walked a short distance ahead, he crossed a few people standing and chatting on the street. Seeing the washerman with the bundle of clothes on his head and the donkey trailing behind him, one of them sneered, and in a derisive tone said, "Look at this man! His intelligence level seems to be lower than his donkey's! He has such a sturdy animal, but the fool is still carrying the load all by himself!" On hearing this, the man's friends laughed with disdain at the washerman.

The poor man! Deeply disturbed and confused by the taunts and comments, the washerman stopped taking the donkey to the riverbank. As a consequence of this, he now had to carry the heavy load of clothes all by himself to the riverbank and back!

MORAL: We frequently find ourselves in a similar plight too, because we give undue importance to the opinions of others. As a consequence, our own inherent qualities and achievements in life are buried somewhere deep within ourselves. We become puppets in other people's hands, carrying unnecessary baggage in our mind. Always remember, it is our intelligence and emotions that are of prime importance to us. If they keep functioning at their optimum level and in the right manner and there is nothing wrong with them, then why should we bother about other people's opinions about us?

71 When Socrates Defied Death

The Greek philosopher Socrates was an extremely wise and learned man. His messages were laden with profound meaning. Socrates was fond of holding long discussions on a variety of topics and loved to advise people. Since his words always bore the ring of truth, it was not surprising then that his opinions and ideas often went against beliefs prevalent in society during his time. As a consequence, he drew the ire of not only common people but also of the local administration. He was warned to refrain from saying things that were considered offensive and went against the prevalent norms of the society. But the incorrigible Socrates continued to raise their hackles at every opportunity.

Finally, the administration was left with no other option, but to arrest Socrates and produce him in court for a trial. Everyone was eager to see the outspoken and insolent Socrates in the dock. So, a large number of people gathered in court to witness the trial. A list of transgressions committed by Socrates was read out by the prosecutors, accusing him of instigating common citizens against prevalent customs, beliefs and social norms and for forcing people to listen to him. Hearing this, the judge, who was a conservative and a staunch follower of the prevalent traditions, became livid with rage. He was also familiar with Socrates' antics and bore a grudge against him. Unleashing his fury at Socrates, he thundered, "Do you plead guilty to these charges?"

Socrates simply laughed and replied, "Yes, Your Honour."

Taken aback at this unusual reply, the judge spoke to him in a grave tone, "Alright then, let us forget whatever has happened till now, but if you can convince the court that you will reform your ways, the jury might consider showing you some mercy."

But Socrates was incorrigible. His sole purpose in life was to dispel the darkness of ignorance among people and to help them see the light of truth. So, he humbly replied to the judge, "Sorry, Your Honour, but I don't think I can change."

No sooner did the judge hear this audacious reply, than his face turned livid with anger. Struggling to control his anger, he glowered at Socrates, and said in a menacing tone, "Think it over; because if you do not give this assurance, then I shall pronounce the death sentence on you."

Without hesitating even for a moment, Socrates immediately retorted, "What is there to think about, Your Honour? I will definitely not change my ways. You are free to use your discretion and sentence me as you deem fit."

On hearing this, the already infuriated judge immediately ordered that Socrates be put to death by administering poison. As soon as the sentence was pronounced, he was chained and imprisoned. Barring a few of his disciples and well-wishers, everyone hailed the verdict and in a jubilant mood, broke into a celebration.

But, a pall of gloom had descended over Socrates' disciples. They felt that they needed to raise Socrates' spirits and soon began visiting him regularly in prison. But Socrates remained unruffled by the death sentence. On the contrary, he consoled everyone, saying, "Foolish fellows! Why are you so sad? It is up to them to administer poison, but to die or not is entirely up to me! So, do not worry. I will not die even when they administer the poison!"

Socrates' words failed to reassure his disciples, but they knew that arguing with their master would be a futile exercise. Besides, Socrates' cheerful attitude, despite the death sentence, compelled them to believe in the possibility of his survival. Several days passed by in this ambiguous manner, and they realised that the day of Socrates' execution had arrived. Many of his disciples gathered close to him in his final hour, some weeping copiously. But in stark contrast to all of them, Socrates was brimming with exuberance; there was no trace of fear or anxiety either on his face or in his behaviour. On the contrary, he was eagerly waiting for the poison to be administered to him. It was his firm belief, and he was confident that the poison would have no effect on him! Meanwhile, even the man concocting the hemlock, a poisonous drink, was stunned on seeing Socrates' cheerful demeanour. He was clearly upset that his poison would put such a cheerful man to death. He knew that he could not save Socrates, but yes, he could at least delay his death as much as possible. So, the man took time to prepare the hemlock. Clearly, his intention was to let Socrates live a little longer. But Socrates was astute; he had gauged the intention of the man concocting the poison. Waiting eagerly to drink it, Socrates soon became impatient and told the man, "Why are you wasting time? And why are you looking so despondent? You are not administering the poison to me; it is the blind followers of tradition who are doing so. You are merely discharging your duty. Hence, perform your duty with utmost sincerity and quickly administer the poison to me."

With a heavy heart, the man prepared the poison and quickly administered it to Socrates. The poison rapidly spread inside Socrates' body and its effect could be clearly seen by one and all. As soon as it reached his feet, they became numb, but that hardly bothered Socrates. Instead, he told his disciples in his inimitable style, "My feet have become numb, but I am still alive!" Meanwhile, the hemlock had spread to his arms and abdomen. Socrates spoke once again, describing his condition to the disciples, "The poison has now consumed seventy per cent of my body... but I am still alive." Finally, the hemlock spread to his brain and heart, but Socrates continued speaking, and in a soft whisper, murmured, "Listen, O people of the world! The poison has almost destroyed my entire body! But I am still alive. This means, there is no greater falsehood than death." With these words on his lips, he breathed his last, but became immortal in the history of mankind.

MORAL: The problem with a human being is that he perceives himself and his life as existing on a physical level. But in reality, both he and his life exist on a mental level. It is true, that every single body is mortal, but physical death occurs only once and is insignificant. The person himself does not have to experience death; it lasts only a moment. So, you must understand clearly, that the life of a human being exists entirely on a mental plane, and it is people's mindset, which distinguishes them from each other. Generally, most people die a thousand deaths at the mental level, while there are people like Socrates who willingly embrace death and become immortal. So, a person's status or his possessions have no connection with his life. The quality of one's life is determined by whether one has lived life with zest or whether one has been compelled to 'die' a thousand deaths every single day as a result of one's actions.

72 A 'Quiet' Message

Lao Tzu was an ancient Chinese philosopher and writer, born in 604 BC, in the Henan province in China.

A learned and wise man, Lao Tzu led a strict and disciplined life. Every day, following his routine, he would go for an early morning walk with his friend. One day, a friend of his friend happened to join them along the way. Since he was meeting Lao Tzu for the first time, he courteously greeted him. Lao Tzu, however, did not respond to the friend's greeting. Thinking that perhaps Lao Tzu had not heard him, the friend once again looked at him and greeted him with a smile. To his surprise, Lao Tzu did not respond this time either. Obstinately, the friend repeated his greeting several times, but every time it was met with silence.

Upset with Lao Tzu's behaviour, the friend told him, "My friend is greeting you, Lao Tzu!"

Lao Tzu replied tersely, "I heard him."

Everyone, including the friend, was stunned to hear this reply. Out of curiosity, the friend asked Lao Tzu, "Then why did you not respond to him?"

With a gentle smile, Lao Tzu replied, "I would have, if the reply to his greeting had come from within."

MORAL: Lao Tzu was absolutely right. The response to a greeting should stem from one's heart, but since childhood, you are taught that it is good manners to be courteous to everyone. That is why you are quick to greet each other with inane greetings like 'Hello', 'How are you?' 'What is going on?' Similarly, the people you greet, reply with equally inane answers — 'I am good', 'Thank you', 'God is kind' – which are spoken in a mechanical manner without the ring of sincerity or truth in them.

Do you know the sole reason behind unhappiness and failure in the world? It is the human habit of lying! In fact, whenever a person resorts to lying in the external world, he also ends up lying to himself. And the greatest form of lying is saying or doing something that does not come from your heart. What needs to be learned from this story is that wise, happy and successful people do not even greet a person if the greeting does not stem from their heart. All their actions and expressions invariably and spontaneously spring forth from the depths of their heart. As for us, well, even when we pray to God, we do it half-heartedly or with a selfish motive of gaining something.

73 Helen Keller, The Angel of Fortitude

Helen Keller was born on June 27, 1880 in Alabama, USA. As a child, she was very beautiful and vivacious, and her family believed that a bright and promising future lay ahead of her. However, life had a different story written for her. When she was one and a half years old, Helen suddenly fell ill, and the fever was so intense that she lost her ability to see, hear and speak forever. This was undoubtedly an unexpected blow that life had delivered to the little girl. But the ability to endure such hardships and emerge victorious is the essence of the human spirit. Allowing the misfortunes of life to push you into despondency and despair, or getting alarmed by these tribulations and seeking refuge or assurances is definitely not the sign of a genuine human being.

So, rather than recede into her cocoon or plunge headlong into gloom, Helen marshalled her inner strength and remained resilient in the face of a storm. Despite losing her sense of sight, speech and hearing, she made efforts to lead a normal life. With her mother's help, she learnt to perceive and understand the world around her and even started learning sign language. Using these newly acquired skills and understanding, she gradually began to communicate with everyone around her. For instance, if she shook her head from side to side, it meant 'No'. And if she bobbed her head up and down, it meant 'Yes'. By the time she turned four, Helen also began helping her mother with household chores; folding clothes became her favourite task. She soon developed a sharp acumen and could easily identify her clothes from the heap of clothes belonging to the entire family!

It was during this time that she became good friends with Martha, who was the daughter of the cook, and Martha's pet dog. In the company of her new friends, Helen's life took on a new meaning and with their assistance, she began strolling in the gardens and exploring cowsheds. For Helen, this was a far more blissful experience than the promise of an imaginary paradise in heaven. To be able to communicate better with each other, Helen and Martha began devising and practising new gestures. For instance, whenever Helen wanted to eat ice cream, she would act as if she was shivering with cold and Martha would immediately fetch her an ice cream. Slowly, but surely, Helen began discovering the little joys that life had to offer, making her life easier.

When Helen was seven years old, her mother, noticing her daughter's talent, decided that Helen should acquire formal education. Always eager to experience new things and progress in life, Helen was thrilled and looked forward to embark on this new journey in her life. Soon, a twenty-year-old teacher named Anne was hired to teach Helen at home. Anne's priority was to ensure that Helen recognised objects by name. To achieve this objective, she would place the object in one of Helen's palms and on her other palm, she would spell out letters of the words with her fingers. But was it possible for Helen who could not hear, see or even speak to understand all this? Indeed, it was, for, Helen was blessed with extraordinarily unique qualities and quickly understood Anne's method of teaching. One day, while she was playing with water from a hand pump, Anne quickly ran to her, grabbed her hand and wrote the word, 'water' repeatedly on her palm. Helen finally understood that this cool liquid falling on her hand was water.

Thereafter, there was no stopping her! Learning by running her fingers across words embossed on a cardboard, Helen steadily progressed in her studies. It was due to her zeal and inborn talent that she quickly learnt innumerable words. The magic of the written words continued to weave their spell on her and within no time, she even began reading books with the help of words embossed on boards. Seeing her rapid progress in academics, her family and friends were not surprised when she successfully passed high school, enrolled in a university and even completed her graduation.

Helen's indefatigable spirit and talent did not go unnoticed, and the entire world acknowledged and saluted her. Almost overnight, she had become the most-talked-about young woman in the world. But now that she had overcome her disabilities, the desire to spread her wings and soar higher to achieve greater heights consumed her. So, Helen learnt to use the typewriter. Once she had mastered the skill of using a typewriter, she never looked back. Helen became possessed by a desire to express her thoughts and ideas, and using her typewriter, commenced on her journey as a writer. Her proficiency with the written word and her passion to give wings to her thoughts were reflected in the twelve books she authored during her lifetime. A girl who could not see, hear, or speak had succeeded in communicating her thoughts and emotions to the world through words. Clearly, this feat was nothing short of a miracle! But Helen was not one to rest on her laurels. Now that she had begun to easily communicate with the world, she soon learnt of the deplorable condition of millions of people like her, who had lost their sensory faculties. She made it her life's mission to help such people overcome their disabilities. In order to achieve her goal, she put her heart and soul into learning how to express words by miming.

At the age of sixty-six, Helen added another feather to her cap and the feisty, dynamic woman travelled all over the world. In the next eleven years, she travelled to as many as thirty-five countries. Now, that was certainly a whirlwind world tour for Helen! Wherever Helen went, she was not only felicitated by the presidents and prime ministers of those countries, but even eminent personalities made a beeline to meet her. A beacon of light and hope for those with similar challenges, Helen continued to be a source of inspiration to the world. She worked with zeal and fervour upto the age of eighty-eight, when she finally bid adieu to the world, leaving behind a trail of achievements that will be written in letters of gold in the annals of human history.

MORAL: During Helen Keller's lifetime and till her last breath, she had accomplished her life's mission. She has left an indelible mark on the world through her indefatigable spirit and work. Her exemplary life is a shining example of what a human spirit can achieve with resilience and determination. Indeed, life throws many curveballs in our path. But then, isn't this what life is all about? Being daunted by challenges and meekly accepting defeat does not befit a human being. Seeking refuge in mosques, temples and churches for solace to overcome these difficulties are all futile attempts that lead man nowhere. A human being becomes the master of his life when he overcomes adversities with his invincible spirit and proactive attitude.

But a human being is easily daunted by the most inconsequential challenges that life throws at him. Even negligible losses in business, minor illnesses and petty squabbles with loved ones are enough to take us spiralling down into a vortex of gloom and despair. We then rush to mosques and temples and grovel at the feet of the *maulvis* and the priests asking them to redress our problems and alleviate our sufferings. From coloured threads to amulets, we wear them with intense devotion, without the realisation that we have become bound to them, and blindly follow their dictates as if they are the words of God.

Helen, however, did not resort to such 'solutions'! Neither did she become depressed and despondent, nor did she complain to God. Moreover, she did not curse her destiny, nor did she seek reassurances from priests. She forged ahead with the indomitable strength of the human spirit that God has bestowed upon every human being.

Let us all acknowledge and accept Helen Keller as an 'Angel of Fortitude', and make a promise to ourselves that whenever we encounter adversity in life, we will remember Helen's difficulties and her indomitable spirit to surmount them. No matter what kind of difficulty or setback rears its ugly head in life, it can never be worse than losing the ability to see, speak and hear. So, let us consider our difficulties as minor setbacks and with the strength of our spirit, overcome them. Every human being should make this pledge. Otherwise, the untiring efforts of this 'Angel of Fortitude' would go to waste.

74 Dayanand Saraswati's Moment of Truth

The legendary Dayanand Saraswati is highly revered not only as one of the greatest saints of India, but is also known as the one who laid the foundation of modern India. He had established a sect called the Arya Samaj, the Hindu reformist movement that took the country by storm in the late nineteenth century. Known for his strong opposition to idol worship, Dayanand vociferously spoke against rituals. In his opinion, it is a useless and redundant practice in the attainment of spiritual growth. Let me recount an interesting incident from his childhood that will shed light on the event that preceded his radical change of mind and his stance against the worship of idols in temples.

Dayanand's father was an ardent devotee of Lord Shiva. One day, he took young Dayanand to a Shiva temple with him. In keeping with age-old traditions, the temple also had an idol of Lord Ganesha along with that of Lord Shiva. Now, in India, there is an ancient custom among Hindus to offer *laddoos* (sweet balls made from chickpea flour or wheat flour) to Ganesha. In accordance with this ritual, several devotees were offering *laddoos* to the Lord. Watching them intently, Dayanand suddenly noticed a few mice nibbling at the *laddoos* that had been offered to Lord Ganesha. Seeing this, a surprised Dayanand asked his father a pertinent question, "Father, who were these *laddoos* offered to?"

"To Lord Ganesha, of course!" replied his father.

Hearing the reply, Dayanand said, "Well, the mice are stealing the *laddoos* that rightfully belong to him! Now, Lord Ganesha will certainly get angry and punish them!"

"No, nothing of the sort is going to happen," said Dayanand's father, smiling at his son's innocent remark.

"Why not, father? Is Lord Ganesha not powerful enough to punish the mice?" asked Dayanand.

Taken aback by this unexpected question, his father could not think of an apt reply to satiate his son's query. Dayanand immediately realised that the idols inside the temple were lifeless stones. Thereafter, he not only refused to visit a temple and perform idol worship, but also emphatically denounced such practices for the rest of his life. It was his opposition to idol worship which laid the foundation of 'Arya Samaj', a movement that has entrenched its roots in the minds of millions of followers of Hinduism across India, who abstain from idol worship.

MORAL: The intelligence of a human being cannot be gauged by the acquisition of formal degrees, style or theoretical knowledge, but by one's ability to change oneself. Life is a continuous process of learning and adapting oneself to changing times. It is in the best interest of a human being to be able to change himself for the better and lead an enlightened life. This is known as 'grasping power', and its intensity is the greatest among all forms of knowledge.

75 Turning the Tables!

One day, Tom, who was in desperate need of money, confided in his close friend James, the reason behind his sudden requirement. Tom requested James to lend him one hundred and fifty thousand rupees and promised to return the amount after three months. Since James was wealthy, he could spare the money. Besides, he knew that Tom was honest and sincere in his dealings. So, without hesitation, James loaned the amount to Tom for three months.

However, at the end of three months, Tom was unable to repay the loan as promised. So, he requested James to give him another month's time to arrange for the money. But before Tom could realise it, another month had elapsed and he was still unable to arrange the money to repay the loan. When he requested James for more time, not only did James refuse, but also demanded that Tom repay the amount without further delay. In order to recover his money, James would frequently call Tom and harass him. In fact, James went a step further and began embarrassing Tom in public, angrily demanding his money in the presence of others. Distressed by James' behaviour, Tom found it difficult to bear the humiliation he had to face in public. But, finding himself in a helpless situation, Tom was left with no choice but to swallow his pride and endure the humiliation. As days passed by, James' taunts became even more acerbic. Though Tom genuinely wanted to repay the loan, he was unable to arrange the money. And because of this, Tom's reputation had taken a beating and was considerably tarnished.

Finally, one day, Tom decided that he had suffered enough humiliation and insults. He thought to himself, 'I will just have to find a solution to this problem. Otherwise, my reputation in the city will be totally tarnished.' The moment he became resolute and made this firm decision, he came up with a plan. The same evening, he rushed to James' house and sincerely apologised for his inability to repay the loan on time. Tom also profusely expressed his gratitude to James for his generosity and in a grave tone, added, "You know me well. I am not the kind of person who would cheat anyone. It is just that I am going through tough times and am unable to repay you. But now, I have finally managed to arrange it. Actually, in about a month from now, I shall get the five hundred thousand rupees due to me. Now, since you have been so kind and generous until now, please loan me another fifty thousand rupees for a month. I will repay the entire amount of two hundred thousand rupees to you by next month."

Now, James had plenty of money to spare. Besides, the manner in which his friend had requested him for the extra money made it difficult for him to refuse Tom. So, he promised Tom that he would lend him another fifty thousand rupees in a few days. Relieved, Tom left James' house in a happy state of mind. However, James found himself in a quandary. He did not want to take the risk of lending another fifty thousand rupees to his friend. So, even though he had promised to help his friend, he decided against giving him any more money. On the other hand, Tom had astutely turned the tables on James. Every time they met, Tom would not give him the opportunity to demand his money. Instead, he would ask James in a demanding tone, "Hey, when are you giving me the fifty thousand rupees you had promised?" Soon, he even began demanding the money from James in the presence of others. Now, it was James' turn to feel embarrassed. Whenever Tom demanded the money, he would hastily reply, "I'll give it soon," and make a quick exit.

Happy that his ruse had worked, Tom left no opportunity to pester James for the money. James, on the other hand, was flummoxed, unable to comprehend the sudden change in the situation. He was being humiliated by his friend who owed him money! Finally, one day, when he could not think of a way out of this embarrassing situation, James went to Tom's house early one morning and said, "Look, I am irritated by the manner in which you keep demanding fifty thousand rupees whenever we meet."

Tom immediately replied, "But am I doing something wrong? You had promised to lend me fifty thousand rupees!"

At this, James said, "Actually, I had said it without meaning to honour it. I have no intentions of lending you an additional fifty thousand rupees. But let us arrive at a compromise today. You can return the one hundred and fifty thousand rupees whenever you manage to arrange it. I will not demand it, but please, stop asking me for fifty thousand rupees in public." Smiling triumphantly, on hearing James' words, Tom heaved a huge sigh, relieved at the success of his tactic.

MORAL: This is the real game of life. If your motive is good and your intentions are pure, you must learn to find these little solutions in order to survive. But bear in mind, this should be done only if your intentions are pure! Using this tactic with mala fide intentions will have an adverse effect. A wrong deed will remain so under all circumstances.

76 It's All a Matter of Time

Lord Shiva is an extremely popular deity in the Hindu religion. His guilelessness, anger and exuberance have attracted devotees from all over the world since centuries.

According to mythology, Shiva and his wife Parvati resided in the snow-capped mountains of the Himalayas. In all the stories pertaining to that era, Hindu gods have been portrayed as majestic beings, dwelling in ornate palaces, living a luxurious lifestyle surrounded by servants. But Lord Shiva's lifestyle was starkly different from the other gods. And it was this difference which one day attracted the attention of Narada, the itinerant saint who had a penchant for triggering quarrels between people.

Narada appeared at Shiva's abode in the Himalayas. He met Parvati, and in his characteristic style, the saint began instigating her. "Why don't you ask Shiva to build a beautiful palace for you? Why are you leading a life of hardship, residing in these freezing caves? When all other gods live in magnificent palaces and lead an opulent lifestyle surrounded by servants and beautiful maids, then why should you be the sole exception and live such a difficult life?" he said. Taken in by Narada's glib talk, Parvati immediately went to Shiva and requested him to have a palace built for her.

Shiva said, "I have no objection, but actually, it is 'Time' that decides where a person should stay and under what circumstances. And in accordance with 'Time', we are at the right place. It is not wise to be influenced by one's ego and go against the will of 'Time'."

Parvati replied, "You are God! The entire world worships you and bows to your supremacy! 'Time' cannot be greater than you." Smiling benignly, Shiva replied, "No, dear, you are mistaken. God is actually the highest state of mind a person can reach. But ultimately, he is just a human being. And whether it is a human being, or the moon and stars, or anything else for that matter, ultimately, all are governed by 'Time'."

But Parvati was in no mood to relent. She insisted, "I am not interested in all this talk about 'Time', I need a palace, that's all! All I know is that, if you decide to do something, 'Time' cannot create obstacles in your path."

Unable to convince Parvati, Shiva acquiesced to her wish, and on his orders, the construction of a magnificent palace commenced. Parvati was elated. In due course of time, the palace was almost ready. Workers were now giving a final touch to the palace, after which Shiva and Parvati would soon reside in their palatial home. But, 'Time' apparently had other plans. For some unknown reasons, the exquisitely carved pillars of the palace began crumbling, and the beautifully decorated walls came crashing down, along with the intricately designed ceiling. Within no time, the palace had collapsed into a mass of rubble. Shiva was aware of the impending tragedy, so he remained unperturbed by the devastation of the palace. Parvati, however, was deeply shocked by this incident.

Parvati stubbornly refused to believe that 'Time' was the sole reason behind the collapse of the palace. She was upset by the fact that construction work had commenced without taking into account the *mahurat* (a point or a period of time considered astrologically favourable). Parvati had, in her haste to build a palace of her own, failed to realise that a *mahurat* too, was just another form of 'Time'. But how could Shiva convince Parvati? When it was not the right 'Time' to build the palace, how could there be an 'auspicious hour' to begin its construction? Despite being aware of this profound truth, Shiva decided to keep his own counsel. On Parvati's instructions, an auspicious hour was chosen and once again, construction work of the palace commenced. Finally, the day arrived when the palace was completed and ready to be occupied. Parvati was overjoyed, but this time, she did not want to take any risks. She called a *pundit* to perform the *puja* (a house warming ceremony). With the *puja* solemnised, it was time for the *dakshina* (a fee or gift given to Brahmins for their services). According to customs, a Brahmin could demand anything as his *dakshina,* and could not be refused. So, when Parvati asked the Brahmin what he would want as his *dakshina,* he kept quiet for some time and then spoke, leaving everyone dumbstruck. He said, "I love this palace. This is what I would like as my *dakshina!*" Parvati was flabbergasted and could not believe what she had just heard. The plate of sweets she held in her hands slipped and crashed to the floor. In those days, it was unusual for a Brahmin to demand ostentatious gifts for his services, let alone an entire palace! But this Brahmin was obviously different! Parvati felt hurt and dejected. Turning on her heels, she immediately left the palace in a huff, leaving Shiva to fulfil the Brahmin's demand.

Shiva, though aware of this eventuality, could not bear to see his beloved wife looking distraught and unhappy. He attempted to reason with her and said in an affectionate tone, "I had already told you that everything is governed by 'Time'. No one gains anything by going against it. So, let us stop dreaming of staying in a palace and resume our blissful life in these wonderful caves."

Parvati obstinately refused to let go of her dreams. Instead, she said, "If 'Time' is truly responsible for these incidents, then why don't you go and tell 'Time' to change its stride? After all, who can ever disobey you?"

Attempting to convince Parvati once again, Shiva explained, "Time determines its stride according to its own reasons and arithmetic. It has never changed its stride in deference to someone's command or to favour anyone. So, it is futile to harbour such expectations."

However, Parvati was adamant and refused to see reason. Acquiescing to her demand of a palatial home, Shiva had to once again give in to her wish. It was decided that once the palace was ready, Shiva would go to 'Time' with an earnest request to change its stride in his favour so that he and Parvati could live in a palace without further mishaps.

Once again, construction of the new palace began in full swing and soon it was ready to be occupied. As decided, it was now time for Shiva to visit 'Time' and request it to alter its stride. Before leaving, he looked at Parvati lovingly and said, "My dear! As you had wished, I am now going to visit 'Time' with our request. But bear in mind, if 'Time' does not accede to our request, then we will set fire to the palace, for, I do not want your dream to be shattered once again. So, if 'Time' does not accede to my request, I will perform the *Tandava Nritya* (dance of destruction). When you see me dance, take it as a sign that 'Time' has refused my request, and set fire to the palace."

Parvati quietly nodded her head in agreement. Early the next morning, Shiva paid a visit to 'Time'. He apprised 'Time' of Parvati's desire to live in a palace and earnestly requested it to change its stride so that his wife could fulfil her dream. After listening to him in rapt attention, 'Time' replied, "How can I ever turn down your request, my Lord? I have just one condition, though. If you perform your famous *Tandava Nritya* for me, I will change my stride." Now, what could Shiva do? He at once started performing his *Tandava Nritya*. When Parvati heard the beat of the *Nritya,* she thought that 'Time' had refused their request. With a heavy heart, she set the newly constructed palace on fire. So, even though 'Time' had consented to change its stride, the event that ultimately occurred was precisely what was meant to occur, in accordance with the stride of 'Time'.

MORAL: There is no greater knowledge in human life than that of recognising the importance of 'Time'. If a person begins to understand it, he can lead a life full of happiness and success. A person must understand that there is a right time for everything. And anyone who knows precisely when to forge ahead, step back, halt, move faster, work harder or get some rest, achieves phenomenal success. A person's desires – and even his relentless efforts – that go against 'Time' do not lead to positive outcomes. Great people have experienced phenomenal success in their life only by flowing with the tide of 'Time'. Therefore, if you too want to achieve greatness in life, gain the knowledge of 'Time'.

77 When Bhima Mocked Yudhishthira

This is an anecdote from the life of the five brothers, the Pandavas, from the ancient epic, the Mahabharata.

The Pandavas had lost the last round of gambling against their cousin, the Kaurava prince, Duryodhana. According to terms insisted upon by Duryodhana, they were condemned to thirteen years of exile in the forest. The Pandava princes were now leading a difficult and austere life in the dense and dangerous forests, far away from the comforts and lavish indulgences of the palace.

One day, an ascetic arrived at their hut, and saw a young man of noble lineage standing at the door. It was the eldest Pandava Prince, Yudhishthira. When the ascetic asked him for alms, Yudhishthira looked at him in silence, unable to say anything. According to Indian traditions, anyone who asked for alms could never be sent off empty-handed, especially if he was an ascetic. But the five brothers were leading a frugal existence, and thus, had nothing to give as alms to the ascetic. Feeling extremely embarrassed at the predicament he was faced with, Yudhishthira also known as *Dharmaraja*, the King of Justice and Propriety, felt that upholding tradition was his duty. The harsh reality, however, was that they had absolutely nothing to give to the ascetic. Feeling guilty and deeply troubled at the prospect of sending the ascetic away empty-handed, Yudhishthira folded his hands and in a humble tone told the ascetic, "Forgive me, but I have nothing to offer you as alms. But please come tomorrow. I promise, I will not send you without feeding you to your heart's content." Hearing this, the ascetic, agreeing to return the next day, departed.

Meanwhile, Yudhishthira's brother, Bhima, who was chatting with their wife, Draupadi and the rest of the brothers inside the hut, overheard the conversation between Yudhishthira and the ascetic. He got up quickly and picked up a drum lying in a corner of their hut, and stepping out of the hut with the drum around his neck, began playing it loudly. Surprised by Bhima's strange behaviour, the rest of the family members stepped outside to see what he was doing. When Bhima saw that he had the attention of his family, he began playing the drum even louder and with greater fervour than before. Meanwhile, by sheer coincidence, the beloved friend and cousin of the Pandavas, Krishna, happened to arrive at the hut to enquire after them. The four brothers and Draupadi stepped forward to greet Krishna. But Bhima continued to play the drum even more loudly, as if in a trance. Puzzled at the spectacle, Krishna asked the reason behind Bhima's boisterous playing of the drum. Replying in unison, both Yudhishthira and Arjuna said, "It appears that our gluttonous brother, Bhima has gone insane because of hunger." But Krishna was aware of Bhima's innate wisdom and held him in high esteem. So, instead of forming a biased opinion, he thought it prudent to ask Bhima in order to understand the crux of the matter.

Eagerly waiting for someone to ask him this question, Bhima instantly replied with great enthusiasm, "Krishna! Something incredible has happened today! My elder brother, Yudhishthira has conquered 'Time'! A little while ago, he not only requested an ascetic to come for alms tomorrow, but has also promised to feed him to his heart's content. Can you believe it? He has gained immense knowledge of the future! He is highly confident that, both he and the ascetic will be alive tomorrow. He is also confident that the ascetic will visit our hut with a desire to eat, and he too will continue to harbour the desire to feed the ascetic! Moreover, he is also certain that tomorrow there will be plenty of food in our hut to feed the ascetic. So, you see, Krishna, my brother is absolutely certain about the occurrence of an event which itself is dependent on numerous other factors! Now, when my elder brother has attained such profound knowledge, shouldn't I celebrate?" On hearing this, Krishna couldn't control his mirth and guffawed, while

Yudhishthira's face turned red with embarrassment as he glared at Bhima for making him the butt of his joke!

MORAL: Human life exists only in the present moment. The future is always uncertain. Bhima was right when he pointed out that even the smallest of events which is yet to occur in the future, depends on several other causes. A person can lead a life full of joy only when he learns to live in the present moment and thinks sparingly about the future. The sole purpose of human life is to live happily, free of all worries. Yudhishthira had promised to feed the ascetic the next day. But even that small promise by him was enough for Bhima to mock and tease his elder brother. You can imagine what Bhima would have done on hearing our elaborate plans of the future, or on hearing our religious leaders preach about heaven and hell! This is the reason why those who know the true psychology of religion consider Bhima as one among the few knowledgeable beings after Krishna from the era of the Mahabharata.

78 What a Waste of Time and Energy!

Ramakrishna Paramahansa is among the most revered sages of India. One of the places where he stayed during his long and eventful spiritual journey was an *ashram* by the banks of a river. Early in the morning, every day, Ramakrishna would conduct intense spiritual discussions with his disciples at the *ashram*.

One fine day, a stubborn ascetic arrived unannounced at the *ashram*. He was a local resident and spoke against Ramakrishna at every given opportunity. Ramakrishna, however, remained unperturbed by his behaviour and maintained a stoical silence. When the ascetic stormed into the *ashram*, Ramakrishna looked at him calmly, expecting him to spew venom once again. But this time, the ascetic appeared to be in a different mood. For the past several years, he had been secretly learning the art of walking on water. And now, he had mastered the skill and was adept at it. He had meticulously planned his visit and course of action before arriving at the *ashram*, to flaunt his skill and denigrate Ramakrishna. Assuming an air of arrogance, he addressed Ramakrishna and asked him, "You pretend to be a knowledgeable saint, but do you know how to walk on water?"

In all humility, Ramakrishna replied, "No, brother. I do not know how to walk on water, but this inability is not a hindrance to me at all. Yes, I certainly know how to walk on land though, and it proves very useful in my daily routine."

At this, the ascetic puffed his chest out a little more and spoke disdainfully, "Do not try to hide your weakness behind a veil of great words. Now, listen to me! I know the art of walking on water!"

Hearing this, Ramakrishna's disciples present in the *ashram* looked at him in amazement. The look on Ramakrishna's face was clearly evident of what he thought of the ascetic's boastful talk, but, in a calm tone he addressed the ascetic, "If you really know how to walk on water, please do give us a demonstration, for, even we would like to enjoy watching this feat."

The ascetic smiled victoriously and walking arrogantly, took Ramakrishna and his disciples to the riverbank. Everyone stood in anticipation, with their mouth wide open, gaping in utter surprise, as the ascetic stepped on the water and effortlessly began walking on it, even as Ramakrishna's disciples rubbed their eyes in disbelief. Meanwhile, the ascetic walked on the water to the opposite bank of the river and returned. The disciples standing there watched the ascetic's feat in awe. However, Ramakrishna, stood absolutely calm and unaffected by the ascetic's antics. He merely smiled, looked deep into the ascetic's eyes and remained silent. The ascetic was puzzled at such a tepid reaction from the great sage. Contrary to expectation, there was not a word of praise from Ramakrishna, nor was there any sign of surprise or admiration in his expression. "Why are you smiling like this?" the ascetic asked in an irritated tone. Ramakrishna did not reply. Instead, he beckoned a boatman and asked him, "Brother, will you take me on a boat ride to the other side of the river and back?"

The boatman was only too happy to comply. So, he helped Ramakrishna board his boat, and after settling him down comfortably, set off with the sage on a leisurely ride to the other side of the river. The ascetic and the disciples were mute spectators, wondering what

Ramakrishna intended doing, too stunned to even utter a word. They had absolutely no clue why the sage had suddenly decided to take a boat ride. All they could do was curiously watch, as Ramakrishna enjoyed the ride and returned to the riverbank where they were standing. The disciples now waited eagerly to see what their guru had up his sleeve.

Once they reached the bank, Ramakrishna alighted from the boat and asked the boatman the price of the ride. "Two paise," the boatman replied. Paying the money to the boatman, Ramakrishna turned around, placed his hand on the ascetic's shoulder and calmly asked him, "Tell me, my brother, how many years did it take you to learn this art?"

The ascetic instantly replied, "Twenty years."

Ramakrishna laughed and said, "You mean you spent twenty years of your life learning an art that is worth only two paise!" At a loss of words, the ascetic fumbled for a response, but could not find his voice. Embarrassed at his own stupidity, the ascetic, without looking back, beat a hasty retreat and fled from the spot.

MORAL: Human life revolves entirely around 'Time' and 'Energy'. Every person should bear in mind that in a life span of 80 years, he spends 25 years sleeping, and the rest is spent in attaining education and attending to routine activities and responsibilities. Now, if he spends the remainder of his 'Time' and 'Energy' in futile pursuits or activities, when will the person work towards achieving happiness and success? So, bear in mind that everything you attain here is by expending your precious 'Time' and 'Energy'. Therefore, before endeavouring to achieve anything, you must carefully calculate the amount of Time and Energy you will be investing in it. And venture into it only if the 'deal' seems favourable to you. Believe me, this is the best, foolproof method to attain happiness and success.

The Fickle-minded Youngster

A young man was sitting with his father at home, watching the beautiful sunset. It was around seven in the evening. They had been chatting for a long time, and the day had almost come to an end. Thinking of the next day, the young man had begun planning his schedule. He thought he would begin his day with some exercise. So, he told his father, "Please wake me up at five in the morning. I will go for a walk." However, as soon as he uttered these words, his second mind objected, 'Why did you ask your father to wake you up at five? Don't you know you have a practical exam in college tomorrow? If you wake up so early, won't you fall asleep during your exam?' Just then, his third mind interjected, 'Oh, what nonsense! You should certainly wake up early. In fact, if you wake up early and study, you will get better grades in your practical exam.'

Later, in the evening, after a sumptuous meal, the young man felt lethargic. In an instant, his fourth mind intervened, 'I don't want to get up early in the morning.' The youth obeyed this command and asked his father not to wake him up early the next morning. But, the fickle-minded youngster's foolishness did not end there. By the time he went to bed after watching TV, his lethargy had disappeared, and his fifth mind manifested itself with a stern warning, 'You have to wake up in the morning, if you want good grades, else you may not fare well.' So, the youth went to his father and once again requested him to wake him up in the morning.

The next morning, when the clock struck five, his father woke him up. By then, the youngster's sixth mind immediately shot back in anger, "Is this the time to wake someone up? Do you want me to get up now and sleep through my exam?" he shouted at his father and went back to sleep.

The father was flabbergasted at his son's impetuous outburst. "You were the one who had asked me to wake you up, and now you are screaming at me for waking you! What a silly fellow you are!" he said. But his son had gone back to sleep, blissfully unaware of his father's angry retort. When he finally woke up, refreshed himself and sat down for breakfast, he regretted his decision of not waking up early. Reprimanding his father, he said, "Even if I had refused to wake up, you should have shaken me out of my slumber! You know I have a practical exam today, and you also know how important it is for me to wake up early in the morning and prepare for it!"

What could the poor father say? Speechless, the father looked incredulously at his son, and silently walked away from the dining table, shaking his head in exasperation!

MORAL: The human mind is an instrument that changes rapidly. It never remains stable, because a human being possesses not one but several minds. Until a person becomes aware of the depths of all his minds, he should not decide anything about the future course of his life. Until then, it would be better if he just remains in sync with the flow of his mind.

80 Be the Light unto Yourself

I am Buddha. You may find this hard to believe, but I am addressing you at present, because I think it is important for you to know what my thoughts were during the final moments of my life. I feel, perhaps, this narration could help you improve your life in some way.

I remember clearly, I had fallen severely ill and was also fully aware that they were the final moments of my life. At that time, my disciple, Ananda, who had been with me for twenty-five years, was by my side. Seeing my health deteriorating by the moment, he was naturally grief-stricken. But for me, his despondency was an unpleasant surprise. I wondered with remorse, 'If the thought of my impending demise has distressed him, then what has he learnt during the years he had spent with me? If my disciple has been unable to free himself from sorrow in spite of having spent twenty-five long years with me, then what have other people learnt from me?'

Even before I could come to terms with his plight and overcome my surprise, Ananda astounded me once again with his request, "Please reveal a truth to me that will liberate me forever." So, what did he think I had been preaching all my life? Was it not the truth? Did Ananda think that I had held back a great truth to myself so that I could reveal it to him in my final hour? Besides, who was I to reveal the truth to anyone? I could only show the path, which I did, but each person has to attain the truth himself by treading on the right path. A person does not give anything to anyone, nor does he snatch anything from anyone. So, I told Ananda, "*Appo Deepo Bhava* (Be the light unto yourself)."

This is what I had said to the world when I was alive. And today, after two thousand five hundred years, I am once again repeating these words for you. *Appo Deepo Bhava!* Be the light unto yourself! Actually, these words encapsulate the essence of whatever I have said and done in my lifetime. I can assure you that, if you abide by these words and understand the profound wisdom behind them, you will instantly begin to walk on the path to progress. I have shown you the path before leaving for my heavenly abode. Now, it is up to you to walk on that path and attain the truth. I can only help you up to a certain limit, but you have to complete the rest of the journey towards attaining enlightenment on your own.

Think deeply, I could do nothing for you even when I was alive; so, how will my idols help you? And how will you benefit by donning an attire similar to mine? So, steer clear of this charade, and stop deluding yourself. Just follow the path that I have shown you and start seeking the truth. It is only through your own efforts that you can ensure progress. Rest assured, there is no other way. You have to become your own 'light' and shine in life with your own efforts.

81 The Midnight Hymn

It is said that children are the purest form of God's creation. They are a reflection of the Supreme Soul. Guileless and unabashed in their behaviour, how would social etiquette and norms concern them in any way?

For their parents, however, they can cause acute embarrassment when attending a social function. A common nightmare and ordeal that most parents face at such times is when their child comes to them and loudly announces that it wants to "go for a pee". Now, although attending to Nature's call is normal, some parents feel embarrassed when their child says this in the presence of guests.

Today, I am going to narrate the story of one such self-conscious mother who devised a smart solution to this problem. Well, at least she thought it a clever idea. Taking her two-and-a-half-year-old child into confidence, she said, "Whenever you want to go for a pee, just say you want to sing a hymn. I will immediately understand and take you to the washroom. You must never say 'pee,' or 'piss' in front of guests. It is bad manners. Okay?"

The child nodded his head vigorously in agreement. After all, how does it matter to children what terms you use for certain activities. They are only concerned about getting their work done. What's in a name as long as one's purpose is served?

Now, this type of an arrangement between the mother and child worked fine for a few days, but one day, the parents had to travel urgently to another city, leaving their child in his grandfather's care. Since the parents were away, the child slept with his grandfather. At around midnight, the child suddenly woke up with an urge to use the restroom. He woke his grandfather from sleep and said in an urgent tone, "Grandpa, I want to sing a hymn." The grandfather was already irritated at having been woken up in the middle of the night, and the child's absurd desire to sing a hymn annoyed him even more! In a grumpy tone, he told the child, "Be quiet and go back to sleep! This is not the time to pray!"

Startled at his grandpa's response, the child implored, "But Grandpa, how can there be a specific time to sing a hymn? When the urge strikes, you just have to sing!"

Exasperated at the child's demand, the grandfather snapped, "I told you, you can't sing right now! And 'No' means no!"

Desperate and helpless, the poor child once again pleaded with him, "That is impossible, grandpa! I just have to sing, otherwise there will be a dirty mess." Irritated and troubled, the grandfather wondered what to do. He could feel anger rising within him against the child's parents. But since the child was adamant, he had no choice but to give in to his wishes. Angrily, he told the child, "Alright then, without making much noise, just pray in my ear, so that no one else gets disturbed."

At his wits' end, and desperate now, as he could no longer control his bladder, the child shot a jet of warm 'prayer' right into his grandfather's ear!

MORAL: This is exactly what all of you do in life. You keep praying in the wrong manner at the wrong places! Excessive importance is given to words assuming that they are everything. You do not understand that it is alright to use impressive words to name visible things, but when we talk about the invisible, meaning psychology, it is imperative to use correct words. Whether it is your happiness or sorrow, friend or foe, religion, God, prosperity or business, sin or virtue, right or wrong, all these words are empty. And until you arrive at your own definitions of these words, you tend to use them vacuously. It is akin to assuming that 'visiting the bathroom' means 'praying'! This is a dangerous habit, and you indulge in it every minute, playing a reckless game only to impress people by using high-sounding words. When you are consumed by this desire to impress, how can any of your actions lead to a positive outcome in life? Have you ever analysed the reason why your friends, family, religion and God are deceiving you, and professional success is eluding you? It is because you are using words defined by others. But once you ascribe your own definitions to all the psychological words that are used in life, they will lead you closer towards happiness and prosperity every time you use them. Until then, you will continue to sing 'hymns' and find yourself in all kinds of trouble.

82 The Joy of Living

In a small town in India, a trader had a well-established business, built painstakingly by him over the years. He led a happy and prosperous life with his family. His business was running smoothly, so he worked for only six hours a day, which left him with plenty of time to pursue his hobbies as well as spend quality time with his family and friends. Moreover, not only did he enjoy a well-balanced diet and maintain an exercise regimen, but also had enough time to listen to music and read books.

The trader had a brother-in-law living in the city, who was a professional software engineer working for a gigantic multinational company. Ambitious and competitive by nature, the brother-in-law, in a career spanning a decade, had switched four to five jobs to ensure rapid vertical progress in the corporate world. He was always on tenterhooks, waiting expectantly to 'hit the jackpot'.

One day, the trader and his brother-in-law were chatting idly, enjoying a drink. The trader casually asked his brother-in-law, "I have often wondered about it, but just cannot understand what exactly you want to do in life."

The brother-in-law smirked and smugly replied, "Once I set up my own business, establish it and begin to earn well from it, then my life will be a bed of roses. It is as simple as that. What is so difficult to understand?"

Startled, the trader thought for a while and said, "But, even if everything goes well, according to your plan, by the time you achieve your goal, you will be at least sixty years old. What will you do after that?"

The brother-in-law instantly replied, "What do you mean? After that, I will live in peace and happiness."

Hearing this, the trader laughed aloud and remarked, "But you can live in peace and happiness even today if you stick to one job! Why do you need to wait for another thirty years and take risks?"

Stumped, the brother-in-law fell silent, unable to give an answer to this simple query. And, I am sure, neither can you. If you are intelligent enough, then read between the lines and mend your ways. But if you fail to understand my message, well... there are many 'brilliant' people with futile ambitions who are sitting idle, twiddling their thumbs!

MORAL: Contentment is considered to be supreme wealth because a person who is content, revels in the present moment, rather than constantly hankering after something which is uncertain. If you spend your entire life in a frenzy of gaining and losing things, or wallowing in sorrow, how will you ever experience light-heartedness or peace of mind? Talking of success, it can never be achieved by someone who unnecessarily gets affected by the vicissitudes of life. You must clearly understand the psychological truth that only a person with a contented state of mind can scale the pinnacle of happiness and success. It is only because people are unaware of their own natural psychology, that they consider teachings that encourage contentment to be hindrances in the path to success; whereas the truth is that this very psychological ignorance is primarily responsible for all the failures of humankind. Contentment is not the enemy of success, but is, in fact, a friend to success. Therefore, be content. You will not only attain instant peace, but your state of contentment will also open the doors of success to you. Remember, only a person who is stable can discern opportunities when they arrive, and he alone has the energy to take advantage of those opportunities. The one who is not content, ends up being enervated, frightened and exhausted because of the relentless knocks of life and the endless running around.

83 The 'Stiff' Measure

Since time immemorial, the biggest destroyer of happiness has been the consumption of alcohol. Alcoholism has wreaked havoc in the lives of millions of people, destroying relationships and careers across the world. Despite being aware of its potency to destroy, people continue to fall prey to this habit.

This is the story of a young, married man who lived in the busy, overcrowded city of Mumbai. He was fond of drinking and could not do without his mandatory three pegs of whiskey every day. Fortunately, he never drank beyond his capacity and never misbehaved under the influence of alcohol. His wife, however, did not take too kindly to this habit and would glower at him every time he stepped out for a drink with his friends. She wanted him to be rid of this addiction at any cost. She often tried to reason with him by pointing out the health hazards of drinking, but failed in her attempts to convince him.

One day, a friend advised the wife to take her husband to a psychiatrist. She instantly warmed up to the idea. However, she knew that taking her husband to a psychiatrist would be an uphill task. He would refuse to accompany her outright if she told him where they were going. But being a smart woman, she devised a plan to ensure that he accompanied her without a fuss. Taking the psychiatrist into confidence, she apprised him of her husband's addiction and the objective of her visit. She told him that she would bring her husband to see him on the pretext that she needed to see a psychiatrist for her problem. It would then be the psychiatrist's responsibility to broach the subject of addiction and get her husband to quit his habit of drinking.

The psychiatrist readily accepted the challenge. As per the plan, the wife took her husband to the psychiatrist. For some time, he discussed the wife's problem, pretending to treat her. Then suddenly, the psychiatrist broached the subject of alcohol. He discussed it in such a manner that even an incorrigible alcoholic would have acceded and quit drinking. This man, however, was a tough nut to crack. The discussion with the psychiatrist had certainly reduced his desire to drink to an extent, but ensuring his complete abstinence from alcohol seemed to be an impossible task at that point of time. The psychiatrist too was not one to be daunted so easily. He was determined to cure the man of his addiction. He continued with his persuasive tactics and finally managed to convince the man to quit drinking. Seizing this opportunity, it was now the wife's turn to inveigle her husband into promising her that he would abstain from alcohol. The poor husband, caught between his wife's entreaties and the psychiatrist's advice, had to finally relent, and giving in to pressure, promised to quit drinking forever.

After the meeting with the psychiatrist, the wife returned home and the husband went back to work. Everything was running smoothly until evening approached. It was only when he was returning home that the man was caught in a dilemma between his desire to drink and his promise to his wife. It had been a daily routine with him to stop at a bar and enjoy a few pegs of whiskey with his friends before heading home. Today too, due to sheer force of habit, his feet were automatically leading him towards the bar. But when he remembered the psychiatrist's solemn advice and the promise to his wife to quit drinking, he stopped in his tracks. Standing outside the bar, the man stood in deep thought, scratching his head. True, he had buckled under the pressure of his wife and the psychiatrist, and had promised to quit drinking. But then, a promise made by the 'Brain' can never influence the 'Mind'. Woefully, he cursed himself for acquiescing to his wife's request. He also tried to control his mind and soliloquised, 'How can I bring myself to break a promise that I had made only this morning? There is something called 'willpower', isn't it? And a man must exercise it... sometimes, at least.' It seemed a Herculean task to conquer his vacillating mind, but he succeeded in doing so, and started walking towards his house. However, after walking a few furlongs from the bar, he felt his resolve weakening. Firmly reminding himself that a promise was, after all, a promise, he continued walking resolutely towards his home, constantly vacillating between the dictates of his brain and mind. He had barely walked twenty steps from the bar when he suddenly halted. His eyes widened with elation as he realised something. Patting his shoulder in appreciation, he told himself, 'Wow! I passed by the bar, but did not step inside for a drink. I have succeeded in keeping my promise! This certainly calls for a celebration!' He retraced his steps back to the bar and ordered his drink. Holding the glass in his hand and raising it high, he said loudly, 'Here's to my commitment and determination!' And gulped down two pegs in one large swig. Eventually, in keeping with his habit, he went home only after having had his three pegs!

MORAL: If a person has a weak inner personality, he can never rely on external influences and pressures to transform himself. Even if he behaves superficially, the change that he has thrust upon himself because of external influences and pressures can never reach the mind. Unless there is a transformation of the 'Mind', everything else is futile. So, if you wish this transition to happen from the deep recesses of your mind, and if you want this transformation to be permanent, then you must never attempt to change yourself superficially at the physical level. Change your mindset first in order to transform your life completely.

84 The Jain Monk and His Muslim Disciple

Everyone is aware that the very tenets of Jainism propagate the principles of non-violence. Needless to say, discourses by Jain monks eulogise the benefits of strictly adhering to these tenets.

One day, a Muslim youth decided to attend a discourse of a Jain monk. When the monk began his sermon by propounding the harmful effects of animal slaughter, the Muslim youth suddenly jumped to his feet and shouted loudly, "My name is Sajid Khan. This is the first time I am attending a Jain monk's discourse. Truly, I am very impressed by your pronouncements on cruelty to animals. They have really touched my heart. I wish to share my thoughts on this as I have realised through my experience that animals are extremely useful to us humans. In fact, I was once saved by a fish!" Hearing the Muslim youth agree to their tenets, a ripple of excitement ran through the entire congregation. The monk's followers were highly impressed by their guru and looked at him in awe. After all, he had achieved the impossible! He had, through his power of oratory, influenced a Muslim youth, which was definitely an impossible feat. As for the monk, he was basking in the glory of his achievement, and his ego soared to the skies.

No sooner had the Jain monk finished his discourse, than he called the Muslim youth over and beguiled him into becoming his disciple by offering him wealth and gifts in return for his services. The youth was assigned a simple task. He had to accompany the monk wherever he went for a discourse. And when the monk was halfway through it, the youth had to suddenly stand up and introduce himself, passionately declaring before the congregation that he had once been saved by a fish. Their little ploy worked like magic. The Muslim youth's presence began attracting hordes of people to the Jain monk's discourse. Overnight, the monk's stature was elevated, and he gained respect accorded to those belonging to the upper echelons of Jain monks. The discourses continued in this manner for a year, when suddenly, one evening, the monk realised that he had never asked the Muslim youth how he had been saved by a fish. Beckoning him to his chamber, he asked the youth to explain in detail how he had been saved by a fish.

Excitedly, Khan began to narrate his story. "I had once gone trekking in the forest with a few friends. Unfortunately, I was separated from them and lost my way. Hungry and thirsty, I wandered alone in the forest for two days, but neither could I find my friends, nor a way out of the forest. Finally, on the morning of the third day, I stumbled upon a small pond in which I saw a shoal of fish. I was starving, so the moment I saw the fish, I caught a big one, roasted it and ate to my heart's content. Hence, the fish turned out to be a saviour in my most difficult hour!"

By the end of Khan's narration, fear and anxiety gripped the monk's heart. Worry lines creased his brows, and in dismay, he looked at the youth, appalled at what he had just heard. But the monk was smart. Recovering quickly from the shock, he gathered his wits, and assuming a solemn expression, said, "You will continue to attend my sermons and enact your part as you have been doing so far, but mind you, do not ever tell anyone how a fish saved your life, or else you will lose this job."

Khan was smart and practical; he knew that he stood to gain by maintaining silence. He had no intention of jeopardising his job, especially when he was being paid a huge sum of money to utter two sentences. Sealing this pact, the duo thus continued to play upon the religious sentiments of gullible people for years to come. And with the passage of time, the monk's stature grew by leaps and bounds, and people revered him for having initiated a Muslim youth into his fold!

MORAL: No matter which religion they belong to, leaders of religious groups and their followers share a similar relationship. They use impressive words and propound lofty ideals to beguile the world. Their main aim, however, is to prove the importance of their own religion. They are not concerned with the true essence of religious tenets. In fact, the only objective of most religious leaders and their disciples is to indulge in hypocritical practices to satiate their ego. No one is interested in elevating himself to a higher state of mind. Instead of propounding lofty ideals, those who live in sync with the reality of their mind are far better off than these so-called religious leaders whose lives are nothing but a charade.

85 The 'Leap' of Faith

One day, when a city-based executive returned home from work in the evening, he was delighted to see his four-year-old child playing with toys in the living room. So, he quickly freshened up and joined the child. After all, who would not want to spend time with a playful child? He had hardly spent ten minutes with the child when the man, suddenly lifted him up and placed the child on top of a seven-foot-high cupboard. The poor child began to quiver with fear and beseeched his father to lift him down. Naturally, for a four-year-old child looking down from a height of a seven-foot cupboard was akin to staring down into a deep chasm. He was extremely frightened, but the father turned a deaf ear to the child's entreaties. Instead, he began persuading the child to jump, saying, "Don't worry, I will catch you!" But the child hesitated. How could he jump? What if his father failed to catch him? He would end up breaking his bones! All he wanted was to be simply lifted down. Unfortunately for him, his father was in no mood to relent. He even blackmailed the child emotionally, saying, "My dear, if there was even a remote possibility of not catching you, would I ask you to jump? In fact, I fret even when you get a minor scratch. Don't you trust your own father? If you don't, then you can stay up there all night. I will not lift you down, and will also make sure that no one else does."

Helpless, the poor child was left with no other option. He had tried his best to plead with his father. There was nothing more he could do. He did not want to spend the night alone on top of the cupboard. His father, in no mood to relent, obstinately continued to insist that the child must jump. The only option left before him was to trust the open arms of his father and jump! So, the child shut his eyes, mustered courage and leapt from the cupboard. Unfortunately for the child, it was at that very moment that his father moved away. The child fell down on the floor with a loud thud and suffered injuries. Wailing loudly, he lay sprawled on the floor. The father, however, was in a strange mood today. Instead of pacifying the child, he shouted back angrily and said in a menacing tone, "Stop crying right now! You have only been slightly hurt! Listen to me and learn a lesson from this! If you want to progress in life then do not trust anyone, not even your own father!"

MORAL: If you take a closer look around you as well as your own family, you will find that these lessons are being imparted to children on a daily basis. Trust, which is the foundation of a healthy relationship, has taken a backseat. Instead, children are being taught not to trust their own father! Our entire life revolves around trust. Whether you are studying or buying an insurance policy, you do it only on the basis of trust. You trust in the belief that the sun will continue to rise for the next fifty to hundred years and you will continue to receive oxygen from the air. So, whether it is Nature or your own life, they both function on the basis of trust. By imparting these warped lessons to children with the aim of making them resilient to face the vicissitudes of life, we sincerely need to address an important question: "Are we really moulding them to be good individuals or paving the way for them to turn into evil, corrupt and unsuccessful individuals?"

86 When Galileo Faced the Gallows

You are aware that Galileo Galilei was the first polymath to state that the Earth revolves around the Sun. However, instead of triggering a scientific debate, his statement had raised the hackles of many people in medieval society, including, of course, the all-powerful clergy. As a consequence, he faced grave risk to his life. Do you want to know the reason? Well, here is the answer. According to the Bible, the sun revolves around the Earth (Old Testament, Ecclesiastical 1-5). In fact, there are more than fifty other gospels in the Bible that are based on this assumption. Galileo's statement, however, was in stark contrast to what the Bible declared. Not only that, his statement also implied that all the other gospels based on the Bible's assumption were false. The priests were outraged. How could Galileo utter such blasphemous statements? The clergy were baying for Galileo's blood and raised their voice in protest. The matter reached the court; the judge who presided over the proceedings, was a staunch follower of the Bible. The priests were adamant in their demand that Galileo must retract his statement and apologise or face the gallows. A huge crowd had gathered inside and outside the court, with most people vociferously protesting against Galileo.

Meanwhile, Galileo was brought to the court, handcuffed like a criminal. The proceedings began, and the judge admonished Galileo in a severe tone, "Withdraw your statement and apologise, or else I will sentence you to death." Hearing the judge's warning, Galileo glanced at the people present. The entire court was filled to capacity with members of the clergy and fanatics, including the judge, ready to proclaim the death sentence if Galileo did not retract his statement and concede to their demand.

Galileo was intelligent and gauged the mood of those present in the court, and the unbridled animosity which simmered within them. He immediately understood that if he did not listen to the judge and apologise to the court, he would certainly be sentenced to death. So, in deference, he pleaded to the judge, "Your honour! I apologise and withdraw my statement that the Earth revolves around the Sun. I accept the Bible's claim that the Sun revolves around the Earth." As soon as Galileo finished speaking, everyone shouted in jubilation, and began singing praises of the Bible in unison. Galileo was set free. However, as soon as he stepped out of the court, he boldly declared, "I have certainly retracted my statement. But that does not mean that the Sun will start revolving around the Earth. I still stand by the truth that it is the Earth which revolves around the Sun."

MORAL: Many lessons can be learned from this incident. First of all, a person must surrender to the demands of 'Time'. When fools become hostile towards you, it is pointless to display wisdom, because under such circumstances, your priority should be to save your life! If Galileo had lost his life due to his obstinacy or ego, the world would have lost a great man of vision. Science has now proved that it is the Earth that revolves around the sun. But to date, zealots and fanatics have not apologised for the treatment meted out to Galileo. And it is futile to expect them to apologise, because the foundation of religious fanatism is based on inflated egos. Surprisingly, even though the statement in the Bible has been proved wrong, it has not affected its popularity or the people's belief in its authenticity. And it is this 'wonderful' quality of a human being which barred Galileo from being included in the list of intelligent beings.

87 Light Up Your Life!

The electric bulb is one of the most path-breaking inventions in the history of the human race. To appreciate its value, all we need to do is to imagine modern life without it. The very thought of spending an evening in darkness suffocates us and makes us restless. We are all aware, it was the legendary Thomas Edison who invented the electric bulb, an invention which permanently changed the lives of human beings on Earth. However, only a few of us know that the story behind this indispensable invention is no less inspiring.

Inventing the light bulb was a dream Edison had harboured for a long time. After he had managed to convince a group of other accomplished scientists to join him on his mission, he finally entered the laboratory one day, with his team. As soon as he set foot inside his laboratory, he was consumed by passion and the determination to fulfil his dream. Everything else around him had ceased to exist. All that remained was his laboratory, his team of scientists and the equipment required for the invention of the bulb.

They began experimenting with numerous filaments in earnest, but their efforts came to naught as the bulb did not light up. Without losing hope, Edison and his team laboured ceaselessly, experimenting with various filaments, but with each failure, the morale of the team sank. As days passed by, the young scientists in Edison's team were losing patience, and their enthusiasm had dipped to an all-time low. Edison's passion, on the other hand, and the hope he nurtured in his heart to discover the correct filament, remained intact. Applying his mental prowess, Edison laboured on, with single-minded devotion. He had to accomplish his mission at any cost. However, even after twenty days of relentless experiments, success eluded Edison. The team had already experimented with over 4000 filaments, but to no avail. Dejected and demoralised, his colleagues finally lost patience and hope. A few of them even advised Edison to quit the search, because finding the right filament to light up the bulb seemed a Herculean task. "We have already tried out umpteen filaments without success; we have to admit that we have failed," one of them spoke morosely.

Edison did not lose heart, and instead of agreeing with them and deciding to quit, he stunned his team with his response. "We have not failed, but are rapidly progressing towards success. We have already discovered thousands of different filaments that will not work. This means we are now about to discover the filament that will light up the bulb. Believe me, we are knocking right on the door of success!" he said with a smile and a twinkle in his tired eyes.

Finally, after two years of relentless experiments, during which they tested and discarded more than 6000 filaments, Edison and his team discovered the carbon filament that lit up the bulb, dispelling darkness from the world forever.

MORAL: For two years, Thomas Edison relentlessly worked, drinking, eating and sleeping in his laboratory. Despite initial failures, Edison did not allow them to dampen his spirit. Instead, brimming with exceptional enthusiasm, he moved ahead with conviction. Indeed, the world should salute the indefatigable spirit of Edison for inventing the electric bulb and permanently transforming human life on Earth.

Everyone must imbibe these outstanding qualities of Edison. Progress in life comes to those who live their lives with enthusiasm, confidence, concentration and far-sightedness. Success is not achieved with empty words or academic degrees, or with someone's blessings and assurances. Success depends on how much fire you have in your belly to accomplish the impossible. So, today, let us make a pledge to develop the qualities of Edison in our own children and strive to raise an Edison in every household.

88 False Valour

On a dark, moonless night, a bus packed with passengers was winding its way through a forest. Among the passengers, there was a retired soldier carrying a licensed gun with him. On the way, some people stopped the bus and informed the passengers to be cautious as they had seen some dacoits lurking in the darkness.

The driver, conductor and the passengers were frightened out of their wits on hearing this. They decided to halt for the night and resume their journey in the morning. The decision of his co-passengers, however, pricked the pride of the retired soldier. His ego was hurt. He thought, 'How could the passengers feel afraid, when he, a soldier, was here to protect them from the dacoits?' Narrating a few anecdotes of his heroic feats in a boastful manner, he advised them to continue the journey. He assured them that he would take care of the dacoits in case they attacked. He even fired a couple of shots in the air to drive home his point. The soldier's words and his gunfire were enough to convince some of the passengers and they felt assured of their safety. Besides, they were in a hurry to reach home. Agreeing unanimously, the passengers decided to continue with their journey, placing their trust explicitly in the retired soldier. The fear of the dacoits, though, was palpable; all the passengers anxiously sent out a silent prayer to God to protect them. The soldier had certainly made them feel secure, but the possibility of an attack by the dacoits had unnerved them. To assuage their fear, the retired soldier repeatedly assured them, "I am here to protect you; why do you worry?"

Steering his way cautiously forward, the driver kept a sharp lookout for any movement as the bus had just entered a particularly dense area of the forest. Suddenly, a group of dacoits emerged from the shadows and ambushed the bus. Scared stiff, the passengers cowered, trembling with fear. Reassuring them once again, the retired soldier spoke calmly, "Why are you worried? I am right here! The dacoits have only stopped the bus. Let them dare climb aboard, and then I will show them!"

In the meantime, the dacoits climbed onto the bus. Seeing this, two-three passengers panicked and called out to the retired soldier nervously, "Sir! The dacoits have boarded the bus!"

However, the retired soldier just smirked and spoke reassuringly, "So what? Don't you worry! They have only boarded the bus. If they dare to loot any of the passengers, I will show them my mettle. They will scamper away like scared mice!"

In the meantime, the dacoits started pillaging the passengers. Panic-stricken, the passengers hollered at the retired soldier this time. "Sir, they have even started robbing us!"

The retired soldier once again reassured them and said, "Don't worry, let them have their fun, what will they accomplish by merely stealing the luggage? If they dare take the loot with them, then I will not spare them!"

The soldier continued to reassure them with empty words, while the dacoits escaped into the forest with all their belongings. Seething with rage, the passengers pounced on the retired soldier and furiously shouted at him, "The dacoits escaped with all our belongings and all you did was give false assurances!"

The soldier's face fell on hearing this as he said dolefully, "You are right, the dacoits really crossed all limits of decency. They did not have respect even for a retired soldier. But never mind. At least, we will reach home on time!"

Slapping their foreheads in exasperation, the passengers could only curse themselves for having placed their trust in the foolish soldier.

MORAL: The so-called caretakers of religion around the world are doing exactly what the soldier did in the bus. Claiming to be in direct contact with God, they keep doling out false assurances, fooling gullible people with glib talk. But when our problems remain unsolved, and we find that the perversions of our mind have not been removed, then we go and ask them, "O, holy Father, we did all that you asked us to do, but to no avail. We placed our faith in your assurances and squandered our precious time and wealth, but our hard-earned wealth is still being pilfered. Why is this so?" Without batting an eyelid, they reply, "Ah! Yes, even we can see that. Really, such unfortunate things are happening in spite of our presence! This is the limit!"

Remember, you will continue to face troubles, till the time you do not take the reins of your life in your own hands. Until you, yourself establish direct contact with God, you will continue to be besieged by problems. Why don't you understand this simple truth? How can you live your life relying on the hopes and assurances given by people who themselves live off your charity and offerings? The path that every person's life takes, is determined by whether he has understood this truth or not.

89 Appearances Are Deceptive

A villager named Gopal travelled to the city for the first time. An absolute misfit, Gopal looked around in wonderment, soaking in the sights and sounds of the vast city. For a country bumpkin like him, the city was an enigma. However, to his misfortune, no sooner did he set foot in the city, than he was robbed of all his money and belongings. With neither money to return to his village, nor a friend or relative in the city, he felt helpless and nervous. Wandering aimlessly without food or water for three days, he looked bedraggled and dirty.

Feeling miserable, Gopal thought, 'If I narrate the story of my misery to some benevolent people, perhaps they will be kind enough to lend me money for food and the fare to return to my village.' With no idea where to begin or whom to approach for help, he thought that compassionate and charitable people could only be found in temples, mosques and churches. So, he hastened his steps towards a temple. Standing at the entrance, he stopped every visitor coming out of the temple and apprised them of his terrible experiences in the city which had turned him into a beggar overnight. But no one spared a minute to hear him out. As the evening wore off and night quietly slipped in, Gopal stood outside the temple, a forlorn figure, nestling a faint hope in his heart that someone would stop by and help him. But not a soul took pity on his condition.

Frustrated and despondent, Gopal aimlessly loitered around the streets near the temple. He was passing by a street corner when two drunkards coming out of a bar noticed Gopal. His deplorable and dishevelled state clearly indicated that he was in great trouble. The two men, although in an inebriated condition, took pity on him. Out of curiosity they enquired what the matter was. Overwhelmed by the concern shown by the two strangers, Gopal instantly broke down and narrated his woeful misadventures in the city to them. Moved by his story, they took him inside the bar and fed him to his heart's content. Soon, his heart-wrenching experiences in the big, bad city spread around the bar and tugged at the heartstrings of everyone who heard it. In no time, everyone present there had collected five hundred rupees for him. Unable to believe his eyes, Gopal soliloquised, 'God, you are truly great! The place where you actually live and the one where you send people to for worship, are poles apart!'

90 Ghalib, The King of Poetry

The legendary Urdu poet, Ghalib lived in northern India during the Mughal era. Ghalib was a prolific writer and tremendously passionate about poetry. Words seemed to flow out seamlessly from his pen as if emerging from deep within his soul, thereby giving them a mystical, ethereal tone.

But, along with poetry, Ghalib possessed an incredible zest for life and was also fond of wining, dining and gambling. But, all the wealth that Ghalib possessed was a treasure trove of poetry from which he could barely earn enough. For Ghalib, however, these were trivial matters, not worth worrying about. But the ways of the world are different, and Ghalib could not sustain his lavish lifestyle on his passion alone. His debts started mounting and the situation worsened to such an extent that debtors began harassing him and making life difficult for him. This not only hampered the pursuit of his passion and lifestyle, but as a result, he had to endure great mental stress.

It was during this time that he received good tidings of some ancestral property he had inherited in Kolkata. Selling the property would free him of the burden of debt. This windfall was just what he needed, so he immediately set off for Kolkata from Delhi. But Ghalib was so obsessed with poetry that, throughout his journey, he recited his *nazms* (Urdu poetry that is normally written in rhymed verse and also in modern prose style poems) to anyone willing to lend him an ear and reached Kolkata only after a year.

Now, this is called passion! He was penniless and his debtors were incessantly hounding him. The inheritance would not only alleviate all his sufferings and free him of debt, but he could also pass the rest of his life in relative comfort. But what did Ghalib do? Consumed by his love for poetry, Ghalib could not forsake it for all the riches in the world!

MORAL: A person whose passion remains undiminished even in the face of crisis and need, can create immortal works of art. The creativity that surges forth from within a person with such untamed ardour makes the creator attain greatness in the world. Whether it is Krishna's Gita, Edison's inventions, Mozart's compositions or Picasso's paintings, they are the wondrous outcomes of such zeal and vigour. A life devoid of passion is a life wasted.

91 The Witness and You

There was once a great Indian saint named Ram who lived in a small picturesque village nestled in the foothills of the Himalayas. Famous for his teachings, he had many followers spread across the world. One day, the disciples decided that the saint should take a trip to the USA. Reluctant at first, Ram finally acceded to his disciples' insistence and undertook the journey.

Now, the peculiar attire that saints wore would attract the attention of people even in India, where people are quite accustomed to seeing saints in strange outfits. So, one can imagine the kind of attention it must have drawn in a foreign land. He received a warm welcome from his disciples as he walked out of the airport. But a group of Americans, standing nearby, found the strangely dressed man amusing and began to mock him. Soon, more people joined the group, sneering and passing lewd comments which offended the saint's disciples. Unable to hold back his anger, one of the disciples told the saint, "What disgusting behaviour! These people are unaware of your achievements and are shamelessly laughing at you because of your clothes."

In a calm, quiet tone, the saint replied, "Well, perhaps even Saint Ram dislikes it, but honestly, I am really enjoying this situation. Look at Saint Ram's condition! He thinks he is wise, but is ignorant of the kind of clothes one should wear while travelling to a foreign land!"

The disciples were surprised by the saint's words. He had spoken about 'Saint Ram' as if he was a third person, while using the word 'I' for himself. The disciples wondered, 'Was the saint imagining that there were two people within him – Saint Ram and himself?' Some of them felt that the saint had probably been seriously affected by the ridicule heaped on him by these Americans.

MORAL: How can someone who loses his mental equilibrium be a saint? Well, the disciples may not have understood the meaning of the saint's words, but it is extremely important for you to understand the difference between the 'Saint Ram' and the 'I.' Both these personalities always reside within you as well. One bears a name, while the other, who functions at a much deeper level, is nameless. The one with the name performs various deeds in this world under the spell of its ego and its sense of doer-ship. And it also faces the consequent reactions of others which are in accordance with their own ego, desire and understanding. This interaction continues till the last breath, but you are not this personality that bears the name. Actually, you are just a witness who watches this game being played by the ego.

Think of yourself as the screen on which movies are projected. The movies keep changing and various scenes are played out on the screen. They could be good, bad, happy or sad, but they do not affect the screen in any way. So, you too must consider yourself as the screen on which the film of your life is being projected. Then, no matter what the scenes of your film contain–respect or disrespect, success or failure, happiness or sorrow–you will remain unaffected. You are only the witness, and all you have to do is analyse why that personality bearing your name has had to face certain situations and how that personality is dealing with them.

One day, you must be able to laugh and say, "See, he thought he was very smart. But he made such a stupid mistake and now he is in deep trouble. Serves him right! This is so much fun!" The day you are able to say this, and enjoy the game that your ego plays, you can be certain that you have reached the zenith of awareness. You will no longer need to visit a temple, mosque or church, or remain a slave to a religious text.

92 Only Time Will Tell

Prophet Muhammad was the medium through whom the sacred religious text, the Quran was gifted to the world. Now since he had enunciated the Quran, he obviously had a thorough understanding of 'Time'.

Let me narrate an incident to prove my point. It is said that once Muhammad was passing through a forest on horseback with a few soldiers. Hiding under the cover of the thick foliage, his enemies suddenly emerged and began to chase him. The soldiers accompanying him were frightened, but Muhammad showed no trace of fear. The soldiers were amazed at Muhammad's calm demeanour in spite of the fact that death was chasing him.

As they rode on, they suddenly noticed a cave on the right and everyone quietly sought refuge in it. Frightened, the soldiers sat together, hunched in a corner, afraid to even breathe. Muhammad, however, sat quietly, leaning against the wall of the cave and watched the play of emotions flitting on the face of the soldiers. Finally, one of the soldiers could not control himself any longer and anxiously asked Muhammad, "What is going to happen now?"

With a smile on his lips, Muhammad replied; "Only 'Time' will tell. But yes, it is certain that nothing bad is going to happen. If our work on Earth is complete, then the enemy will search and find us here too, and if our work is incomplete, then there is no way they can find us in this lifetime. It is only 'Time' that can decide whether we have finished our work on Earth or not. We cannot decide that."

MORAL: Great people, whom we consider to be prophets, saints and gods, are blessed with a special quality; they are able to surrender themselves completely to the demands of 'Time'. Submitting oneself unconditionally to the demands of 'Time' means synchronising oneself to be in tune with its working, which will ultimately lead to the greater common good of mankind. The desires of all these enlightened personalities are driven by the desire of 'Time'. And as for their personal desires, well, they have already overpowered them and become their master.

93 When Christ Appeared on Facebook

Sitting on a fluffy white cloud on a calm blue sky in heaven one day, some angels informed Jesus Christ that even 2000 years after His departure from Earth, there were billions of people across the world who loved him very much.

Deeply touched by what the angels had told Him, Christ decided to establish direct contact with His followers to check their progress in life. He was aware that technology had advanced by leaps and bounds, and people could connect with each other from any corner of the Earth within the comfort of their homes. 'Then why should I not utilise this technology to connect with my beloved ones?' thought Christ. He decided to appear on Facebook. Now, this was a momentous event, the biggest 'breaking news' of all time. Within a span of a few seconds, the entire world knew that Christ was on Facebook. Overnight, more than 500 million people became His followers!

Writing his first post, Christ affectionately asked His followers how they were faring in life. No sooner had He posted this, than He began to receive millions of replies. Almost all of them read, "We go to church regularly, read the Bible, celebrate Christmas and pray on Good Friday every year. Despite following all these rituals, neither have we become free from sorrow and pain, nor have we achieved the level of success we expected we would. On the contrary, our anger and frustration are increasing day by day."

Christ was aghast on reading these messages. He immediately shot back a reply, "Who has asked you to follow all these rituals?" Millions of people replied instantly, and the gist of all their messages was that the priests had asked them to follow these rituals.

Can there be anyone wiser than Christ? He instantly understood the game that was being played by priests in His name. Posting another message, he asked everyone a simple question, "During my lifetime, did I ever ask anyone to build a church, visit it and pray to me or to celebrate Christmas and perform rituals on Good Friday? Please read and understand my entire life, and you will realise that I had never asked you to perform rituals. I am aware that all these activities are futile. In fact, my earthly existence was spent in protest against these rituals. But it appears that you have been trapped once again. The synagogues have gone, only to be replaced by churches; the Cohens (Hebrew priest) by Fathers, and the Jews have been replaced by Christians. What I cannot understand is, where did all these Christians come from? I had loved everyone equally and had affectionately said, "Whoever wishes to, can come into my fold!" Then why have you given a separate identity to the people who love me? How is it possible for a compassionate soul like me to love only Christians or ensure that they alone benefit from my blessings? There can be nothing more humiliating than this! This is a trick by priests to create a rift amongst you and continue to expand their business as usual."

Christ's simple message was clear and understood by all. But they now found themselves at a deep end, unable to break free from the centuries-old shackles that bound them. They requested Christ to once again descend on Earth and rescue them from the churches, Fathers and Christianity, just as He had earlier rescued them from Jews, synagogues and Cohens, so that they could live together in harmony as human beings.

Hearing their plea, Christ felt hurt and dejected. In a clear, but stern tone, He told them, "Do you think I have nothing else to do but to descend on Earth time and again and rescue you, despite being warned not to fall into such traps? I have explained the truth to all of you once again. You now live in a scientific age, so use your willpower and break free from this trap."

Reflecting deeply on Christ's reply for some time, His followers pleaded, "Dear Lord, we shall free ourselves from this trap for sure, but what should we do after that? How will we attain happiness and success? Please show us a simple, straightforward path that can lead us to success and happiness."

Conceding to their request, Christ posted an elaborate reply on Facebook. "I have outlined the path to achieve happiness and success, not once but a thousand times over in the past. But it seems that under the influence of the church and the priests, you have ignored my teachings, so, read what I have said and contemplate; then you will remember everything.

"Once more, for the last time I shall repeat it. I had always said: 'Whatever you share and give, will come back to you manifold.' I had also said that, 'Whatever is shared, will be replenished, and if someone tries to hoard something for himself, it will be snatched away from him.' This is the underlying principle of success, which applies not only to you or Christians or the people who love me, but to everyone. In fact, this principle of success will remain true as long as there is life on Earth. To follow this principle, you do not need me, the priests or the Church, or even Christianity. Observe your life carefully and you will realise that your actions and deeds are in contrast to what you want to attain. You want to receive love, but you spread hatred. The laws are not going to change according to your whims. So, when you spread hatred, it comes back to you a thousand-fold. Similarly, although you desire happiness for yourself, you give grief to others; you desire success, but create hindrances in the path to other people's success; you want people to trust you, but in return you do not trust anyone. You continue to live your life in this manner. These are not rare instances. All your actions are the results of how you think.

"Take a look at the history of humankind. Buddha Imparted knowledge and received far greater knowledge in return from Nature. Krishna spread love and in return, he received the love of hundreds of *gopis*. Remember the adage: 'As you sow, so shall you reap'. What you give the world, the world will give back to you. So, the first thing to do, is to decide what you want to attain in life, and then start disseminating them to your fellow human beings. Do not feel proud of giving things which are redundant to you; things which you want to discard from your life. This is the simple truth which I want to convey to you. If your life is not progressing on the path you have chosen, then halt in your tracks and reflect. Maybe, what you crave, is in complete contrast to what you are giving out to the world. And, now I am going to delete my Facebook account. I have seen your plight, and have also discovered the reason behind your pitiable state. I have also shown you how you can free yourself from this miserable condition. The power to carve your life the way you wish to, and move ahead, rests entirely with you. Every human being is free to lead his own life."

94 Kabir, God's Own Man

The 15th-century Indian mystic, poet and saint, Kabir, was much loved and revered by all. He was considered to be a divine, simple soul, akin to God. He was not an entrepreneur, but a simple weaver who wove rugs to earn a livelihood. After laboriously toiling away for weeks, he would manage to weave a few rugs. And in his largesse, he would end up giving these rugs free of cost to people.

Unhappy with this habit, Kabir's wife and son Kamaal would often attempt to make him understand that they would all die of starvation if he continued to give away rugs for free. Kabir knew that what they said was true and promised them that he would not repeat his mistake again. He would also make a mental note as a reminder to abstain from this habit of giving away the rugs for free. But once a rug was ready, he would forget all about his resolution, and his generous spirit would once again compel him to give the rug away, free of cost. Often, the buyer would ask him the price of a rug, but Kabir would say, "What price are you talking about, brother? The thread belongs to God, it is God who has woven it and it is God who will use it. So, tell me, how can God ask God to pay a price for God?"

Needless to say, Kabir's family lived constantly on the verge of starvation. His wife and son despaired at this habit of his and did not know how to deal with Kabir. In his heart, Kabir was aware that if he did not charge money for the rugs, it would become difficult to survive. But he was blessed with such a tender heart; what could he possibly do? All that he saw around him was God. So how could one blame this divine soul for his generosity?

MORAL: Kabir's perception of the world around him and his sentiments are the true essence of God. There is no God in Nature greater than a human being's purest sentiments. So, instead of frenetically running around in search of God, focus on your sentiments and purify them. Then you will soon connect with Him, truly and directly.

95 The Double-edged Sword

The Greek philosopher Socrates was one of the pivotal figures in the history of Greek philosophy. Blessed with a unique style of communication laced with subtle humour, none could surpass his oratorical skills. He could impress his thoughts on a person simply on the strength of his convictions.

One day, Socrates was sauntering around the marketplace when he happened to bump into a friend, who was lost in deep thought, contemplating a vexed issue. When Socrates enquired about it, the friend replied in a grave tone, "I have received a marriage proposal, but I am in a dilemma; I cannot decide whether to marry or not."

Breaking into hearty laughter, Socrates said, "Why are you confused? Of course, you should get married. Look, if the wife turns out to be quarrelsome and insolent, you will turn into Socrates. And if she turns out to be a loving and caring person, then your life with her will be peaceful. Do you understand what I am saying? Marry by all means. These opportunities do not present themselves often!"

MORAL: There is simply no possibility of losing in the game of life. If your actions lead to a favourable outcome, enjoy them wholeheartedly. But if they do not, then just experience the futility of your actions. Do not grieve for things you have lost, because of your miscalculations. Instead, move on, with a positive frame of mind. The traveller who keeps forging ahead, can never fail in life.

96 More to it than 'Meats' the Eye

Gautam Buddha was a firm believer of non-violence. In keeping with his principles of abstaining from violence in any form, he staunchly propounded the benefits of following a vegetarian diet. A strong advocate against the consumption of meat of animals, he also spoke vociferously against non-acceptance.

According to him, all suffering stems from a human being's non-acceptance of reality. It is precisely this non-acceptance of things around him that has besieged human life with sorrow, and has become the root cause of man mired in a whirlpool of negativity throughout his life. Therefore, Buddha had issued strict instructions to his disciples to accept with a smile and gratitude whatever they received as alms, and eat only what is put in their begging bowls. They were strictly warned not to reject anything they received as alms.

One day, an incident occurred that put one of Buddha's disciples in a great dilemma. A vulture flying high in the sky inadvertently dropped a piece of meat from its beak, and it fell into the begging bowl of a disciple. Now, Buddha had always preached abstinence from meat, so the disciple could not eat the piece of meat. But, at the same time, Buddha disliked any form of non-acceptance. This was, indeed, a delicate matter which had to be dealt with prudence. What a vexed situation this was! To extricate himself from this dilemma, the disciple finally decided to approach Buddha and seek his advice. In a perplexed state of mind, he rushed to Buddha with his bowl and narrated the entire incident to him. When Buddha heard this, he, too was stunned. Indeed, it was a unique incident. Meanwhile, the other disciples too, were waiting with bated breath to see how their teacher would resolve this intricate problem. They even began discussing among themselves whether Buddha would allow the disciple to accept the piece of meat or reject it.

After hearing the disciple's dilemma, Buddha had slipped into deep contemplation. He knew that if he asked the disciple to accept the piece of meat, everyone else would take it as his consent and immediately begin consuming meat. But if he instructed the disciple not to accept the meat, then the others would also start rejecting whatever they did not like as alms. So, no matter what he said, the disciples would find an excuse to ignore at least one of his instructions.

Finally, Buddha made up his mind, and thought to himself, 'How often do vultures drop pieces of meat? Moreover, vultures do not actually kill animals; they merely feed on animals that are already dead. So, if I say it is alright to accept the meat of animals which are already dead, then it will curtail this desire in the disciples to eat meat and nip this problem in the bud. But if I tell them not to accept the piece of meat, then everyone will start treading on the path of non-acceptance.

This will be a far more dangerous situation, because it is precisely this non-acceptance of things around that has besieged human life with sorrow.' After much contemplation, Buddha announced his decision to the disciples, "There is nothing wrong in accepting the meat of an already dead animal."

Buddha had tried his best to inculcate the right teachings, but little did he realise that man would misconstrue his words. So, although they follow Buddhism, people from China and Japan, to Korea and Tibet, consume the meat of dead animals. Indeed, it is man only, who possesses this most 'wonderful' quality of misinterpreting knowledge to suit his interest.

MORAL: No one is stopping you from doing whatever you want to. But do not veil your desires behind Buddha's teachings. If you cannot comprehend the sentiments behind the messages of great people, then let them be. But do not degrade their messages and teachings to suit your selfish conveniences. You may choose not to follow what Buddha, Muhammad, Krishna, Christ or Kabir have said. Refusing to follow them will not create problems for you. But misinterpreting their messages, according to your own convenience, can cause you a lot of trouble. Resorting to this malpractice will not only hinder your growth and self-improvement, but will also prevent you from understanding the true meaning of their teachings. You will then always be under the illusion that you are following their teachings; so, you do not need to work on self-improvement, and there is no need to transform yourself. And because of your erroneous assumption that you already understand their teachings, you will not feel the need to try and understand the profundity of their messages. Unfortunately, all the religions, their custodians and followers today exist under this illusion. People have buried the core essence of the teachings of these great people a long time ago. Now, all that they do, is accord their own meanings to the teachings of great people and fulfill their own desires, and proudly proclaim themselves to be true devotees of God.

97 From Sinner to Saint

In the jungles of ancient India, there was a notorious dacoit called Ratnakar, who lived with his family of four. One day, he crossed paths with the itinerant sage, Narada. Ratnakar immediately accosted him, and brandishing a huge sword, threatened the sage to part with all his valuables... He was armed to the teeth and his voice was as fierce as the expression on his face, enough to scare the wits out of any man. But how could Narada be frightened by anyone? For the very mark of sainthood is to be free from these latent emotions of fear and death. So, without batting an eyelid, Narada looked straight into Ratnakar's bloodshot eyes and asked, "Why don't you give up this path of sin and violence?"

Ratnakar replied gruffly, "If I stop stealing, how will I feed my family?"

Narada replied calmly, "You are not aware of it, but you are digging your own grave with your actions, while the other members of your family are living off your earnings, enjoying themselves without a worry. Heed my advice, it is you, who will pay the price for committing the sin of stealing, not they. Listen to me. Before you steal from someone else, you should first ask your family members if they are willing to be partners in crime and share the burden of your sins with you or not. After all, you are taking the trouble to do all this only for them, aren't you?"

Ratnakar immediately retorted confidently, "Why won't they stand by me? After all, I am doing all this for them." Narada laughed and said, "Don't just assume it, my friend. Go and ask them and everything will be clear to you."

Ratnakar thought to himself, 'Why not prove the sage wrong. There was no harm in asking my family and clear this niggling doubt that the sage has put into my head.' He rushed to his family and asked them if they would, on the day of judgement, bear his sins with him. To his utter astonishment, all of them refused to do so. The family's response was like a bolt from the blue, and it instantly brought Ratnakar to his senses. At that very instant, he ran back to Narada, and falling at his feet, made a solemn promise that he would immediately stop stealing. It was because of this inner transformation and awakening that his life took a new turn. And the former belligerent dacoit became a highly renowned and much revered ascetic, whom the world today knows as Valmiki, the author of a popular epic of India, the *Ramayana*.

MORAL: All those people who are willing to cross any limit to provide happiness, peace and prosperity for their family, or are sacrificing their lives for the sake of their loved ones need to ask themselves this question: 'Does my family approve of the means I have adopted to provide for them? Will they stand by me in times of trouble?' As a matter of fact, can a person really do something for another person on a permanent basis, even if he wants to? In Nature's scheme of things, it is a lonely ride from the womb to the tomb. It is you, yourself who has to bear the repercussions of your actions alone. So, before putting your life at stake, it would be advisable to contemplate on these questions.

98 A Heart of Gold

It was a cold winter evening and the temperature had dipped drastically. An old, homeless man was lying on the pavement opposite a famous shrine, quivering like a dry leaf in the freezing cold. The devotees who came to the shrine to pay obeisance, paid scant attention to the old man.

It was customary for people to offer a shawl at the shrine as a token of reverence to the saint. A long serpentine queue of people stood outside the shrine with exquisitely designed shawls, awaiting their turn to offer them to the dead saint. The old man looked at the shawls, hoping that some benign soul would take pity on him and give him a shawl, for, it would definitely protect him from this freezing cold and ward off certain death. Even if one of them walked across the street and offered him a shawl, his life could be saved. But why would anyone give the old man a shawl? What would they get in return? Their shawl was meant for the tomb of the saint, so that they could then bargain for a bright future for themselves.

A little while later, a labourer passed by and noticed the old man shivering from cold. The labourer realised that the man would certainly die if he spent the night out in the open. He walked towards the old man, and helping him up on his feet, asked him to come home with him. The old man was taken aback by this unsolicited help. He had also noticed that the labourer was the only man who had not visited the shrine. The old man asked the labourer, "Brother, don't you want to visit the shrine and ask God for anything?"

"Yes, I do. However, I am not sure if He will grant my wish. But if I work hard, I am certain that I will reap the benefits of my labour. Well, let us leave all that aside and head home," replied the labourer. Since the old man was in dire need of shelter, he went along with him. The labourer was a kind man, and after feeding the old man, also shared his blanket with him. The next morning, the old man woke up feeling much better than he had felt the previous day. Deeply touched by the heart-warming generosity of the labourer, the old man looked up at the sky and said, "You are truly great, Allah! You let people go to ornately carved magnificent shrines searching for you, but you reside in the hearts of the merciful poor!"

99 When Porus Lost the Battle but Won the War

Around 326 BC, Alexander III of Macedonia invaded India and defeated Porus, the King of the Pauravas. According to a custom prevalent during that era, the defeated king had to receive the victor the next day and hand over his kingdom. A lavish welcome ceremony had to be organised along with a grand banquet by the vanquished king in honour of the victorious emperor.

After Alexander was given a warm and ceremonial welcome, Porus led him to the royal banquet hall. Seated at the place of honour, Alexander waited to be served. However, while everyone was being served delicious food, Alexander was served precious gems and jewels. Seeing this, a surprised Alexander looked questioningly at Porus.

Astounding all those present, Porus answered with a theatrical flourish, "Excellency, you have travelled such a vast distance only to acquire these jewels and precious gems, haven't you? So, I was under the impression that you have them for your meals too!"

Speechless for a moment, but recovering his composure quickly, Alexander embraced Porus and commending his courage, said, "I really must admit, Porus, though you have been conquered, you remain undefeated!"

MORAL: Victories and defeats that we experience in life are at the mental level. People with a defeatist attitude towards life, lose even before they have been really defeated. Porus had lost the battle and it was his last day at the palace. But in spite of this, he did not give up. He was not a broken man; in fact, he courageously stood up to Alexander as an equal. It was extremely dangerous for a vanquished king to behave in this manner. Porus could have been imprisoned for his audacity, or could have been put to death too. Nevertheless, he fearlessly stood his ground. People who refuse to be defeated psychologically, often tend to turn the tables on their opponents.

100 Alms with a Difference

One day, Buddha stood outside the door of a house and begged for alms. When he knocked on the door, it was opened by a woman. Surprised to see a mendicant standing at her doorstep seeking alms early in the morning, she scolded Buddha and slammed the door angrily in his face. A neighbour, who was standing outside his house and watching the entire scene, felt elated on seeing Buddha being humiliated, for, he harboured a great dislike for Buddha.

The next day, Buddha again knocked on the door of the same house asking for alms. This time, the woman became furious as soon as she saw Buddha, and threw garbage on him. Coincidentally, that day too, the same neighbour witnessed the scene, and was overjoyed at the insult meted out to Buddha. Unable to hold himself back, the neighbour, rubbed his hands with glee. The next day, Buddha walked towards the same house for the third time to seek alms. This time, the neighbour looked at Buddha with a shocked expression on his face, astonished to see him walking towards the belligerent woman's house, even after being repeatedly humiliated by her. Before Buddha could proceed further, the neighbour stopped him on his way and said, "I am a Brahmin and a bitter opponent of your teachings. I vehemently disapprove of your views against Hindu scriptures. So far, I was very happy to see you being humiliated by that woman. However, today, I am a little surprised on seeing you. I fail to understand why you have returned to the woman's doorstep seeking alms even after being insulted."

Buddha simply smiled and replied, "There is nothing surprising about this. You are shocked because you have no experience of human psychology. Insulting someone, or even hurling garbage at them, is also an act of 'giving'. Repulsion is also a form of attraction. If the woman gave me garbage yesterday, then one day, she will give me food as well."

Unconvinced by Buddha's words, instead of replying to him, the neighbour decided to quietly watch the drama. He thought gleefully, 'Let us see what happens when he knocks on the door. Let the woman hurl burning embers of coal on Buddha, then I will have this discussion with him again.' Buddha continued on his way and reached the woman's house. He knocked on the door, and when the woman saw him at her door for the third time, she became livid with rage. Leaving the door ajar, she rushed inside the house and returned with a broom to beat Buddha. The woman had decided to end this matter once and for all. She lifted the broom to strike him, but when her eyes fell on Buddha's face, the broom slipped out of her hand. His calm and smiling countenance shook her to the very core of her being. Although the urge to hit Buddha was strong, she could not bring herself to strike him. She was so captivated by the gentle ripple of a lotus-like smile playing on his lips that she stood transfixed. Gathering her wits, she quietly went inside the house and returned with two *rotis* (Indian bread) and put them into Buddha's bowl. Expressing gratitude to her for the *bhiksha* (alms), Buddha turned to go. But the woman could no longer contain her emotions and fell at Buddha's feet, seeking forgiveness for her previous behaviour. Buddha gently placated and calmed her. Watching from a distance, the neighbour was stunned to see this sudden turn of events. Moved to tears by Buddha's compassion, he came running across the road and fell at Buddha's feet, pleading with Buddha to initiate him into his fold. Embracing the man, Buddha told him with a smile, "I have never received alms from any household that were greater than what I have received today. Along with food, I have received a disciple too."

MORAL: You must always remember this law of the 'Mind' – bias is the root cause of all human suffering. The 'Mind' does not differentiate between hate and love, or between a worldly person and an ascetic. At the level of the Mind, it does not take long for hate to change into love; and neither does it take time for a worldly person to turn into an ascetic. A person can attain stability at the mental level when he has transcended all sorts of give and take.

101 They Beg to Differ

The great Jain saint, Mahavira would always advise his disciples not to ask for anything when they went begging for alms or were invited for a meal at someone's house. He would always advise them that they should accept whatever the host served, irrespective of the quantity, considering it to be *prasad* (a devotional offering made to God) received from the Supreme Soul. Asking the host for something is not only considered to be bad manners, it was not wise either, for, it could put the host in an embarrassing situation, in case he is unable to comply with the monk's wishes.

Mahavira's advice was simple and straightforward, with no scope for misinterpretation. But how can someone's pure sentiment ever bind a *Muni* (Jain monk)? So, most of the Jain monks never utter a word whenever they visit someone's house for a meal. After all, they have been specifically instructed by Mahavira not to ask for anything. They gesture with their fingers, and the person serving them understands what the *Muni* wants.

Now, understand the intention and import behind Mahavira's message, and see how his instructions were misconstrued later by his followers! The question to ask is, do these psychological teachings of the highest order pertain to sentiments or actions? Most certainly, it is the sentiment that is important! However, since harbouring pure sentiments is difficult and requires deep understanding, not only Jain monks but even pundits, *maulvis* and priests resort to cheating the masses. And the psychological truth is, that a fraudster is more dangerous than a genuine non-believer!